Ten Years on Paper

Complete Collection

Poetry

Written by
Chris Sapp

This book like all the others before and after is dedicated to my wife, family, friends, teachers, and other people in my life that have had a profound impact on me, leaving me with feelings I was able to put into words in the passages. This book has a lot to do with all I have learned from loving and losing and it is particularly dedicated to my experiences with others that made me understand life.

ISBN#: 978-0-6151-6604-9
Copyright: 2007

Tuesday September 11, 2001

No soft spoken words will do justice to those lost today
And no angry words can express the need for retaliation
No cheerful words can mend the wounds in families all over
No words at all seems the best thing I can do now
I don't want to turn on a television
Because I already understand enough
This is going to be in the news for the rest of my life
Why would I need anymore punishment today
I don't want to turn on a radio
Because right in the middle of song; Interruption!
Takes over and begins repeating
What may be the most repetitious torture for some
Hearing over and over and over again
About how thousands of people are dead
And we don't even get a day off of school
This is as big as the Challenger explosion
Someone mentioned something to me to the effect
That we were warned 3 days ago by a terrorist
With all this fancy equipment we can't even protect
Ourselves from planes on our own soil?
Everyone in the rest of the world is probably cheering
Laughing at our misfortune and the sad truth
That even as the most powerful nation in the world
We are as vulnerable as a newborn baby
I have not prayed in a while, especially not for real
But now I am praying to whatever is out there
Please let this incident stop today
And not be the start of something worse
I would rather live my life knowing just this
And no other reference to war on our soil again
Except in books and memories and words
Which I don't have to describe at all

A Bum

Laying on the front yard
In my high-rent no class house
Gazing up at the heavens

Pinholes of light in the black night
I think to myself
What is all of this for?
Later, further in the ghetto
I see a man risking his uniqueness
For a couple of laughs
And a bit of money from the coke he sells
Getting angry about the life
He has made for himself
Does he ever notice the beauty
Of the world around him
The pinholes in the sky
The light shining down from above
Or the voices in his head
Telling him this is wrong
No, the money has got him
And later a bullet will
Bleeding in the emergency room
His ignorance runs out
He realizes the truth
And dies

A Friend's Advice

Hell is other people and their problems
It is seeing yourself in their shoes
While making different decisions
Hell is from wishing you could change them
Hell is the inner dialogue going on while you listen
Especially the ones you know well
Where you are akin to the situation
And you have shared with the person your opinion
Especially if it's been going on for months
Especially when the two of you have nothing in common
Occasionally for a good listener Heaven appears
Or better yet Divinity starts when you only listen
And they make the choice on their own
Occasionally either direction is a nice break
Occasionally Divinity becomes constant when the crowd is right
To truly be a righteous and impartial person

One would have to never take the shoes of others
Just empathize instead of sympathize
To avoid trying to compare it to anything else
To honestly know that the two situations are different
What are people with problems that talk asking for
Asking for solutions or your opinion are two wrong answers
A real listener is there to be silent and echo back
What the person is saying out loud, maybe for the first time
What in their opinion may be the center of the known universe
Being a good enough listener without analyzing
That you are actually keeping track constantly
Maintaining eye contact if necessary to catch every word
Being if they get lost or off subject you can help then
Being as you were listening and have a short term memory
Life is absolutely 100% what you make of it
There are no strings attached to you or your mind
You have the inert ability to succeed at anything if you try
Life is making decisions whether good or bad and going on
Life is not regretting but learning in an ever-going quest of knowledge

A Ring

A ring that I once had is lost
I miss it
I miss what it represents
A constant reminder
That someone loves me
In this place away from everything
Where I have no friends
And I constantly need to know
That I am loved
I can't remember where I put it
I don't know where I saw it last
I have checked everywhere
And it seems to have just disappeared
I need that ring back I tell myself
Without it I might forget

A Spell

I wish I could cast a spell
To actually meet someone
My high expectations met
Without all the bullshit
Telling the truth is key
A smiling face is nice
Laughing with me at times
Not afraid to cry
With a strong sense of self
And opinions all their own
Willing to argue for fun
But acceptance of all
Not perfect, but with faults
Which make them more real
Able to forgive mistakes
Looking over accidents
Present and Future focused
Unchangeable past a teacher
Lessons and Experience
To guide and remember
Spontaneous with surprises
Maybe flowers or a trip
UN-judging without Rumor
All up front from day one
No book to guide them forward
With man's ideas of God
But self-motivated in spirit
Never quitting until done
Walking away only for air
To think and try again
For words to make it simple
So I can comprehend
Personnel left personnel
Friends left as friends
Our private paradise
Through the turns and bends

A Decent Weekend

Keri has completed her visit
Everything went perfectly
Meaning I was very good
And she was herself
We had a good weekend
I will remember it smiling
And she even bought my lunch
And snacks for me while leaving
She actually stole a bag of chips
But it was a complete accident
Because Subway® wasn't watching
And she forgot about the cookies
I saw Liz for a moment Sunday
It was warming just like the letter
An e-mail from the day before
Telling me she wanted to see me
It feels so good having just a touch
Of reciprocation and appreciation
Right now I feel less walked on
Than I can remember for years
I am actually in control mostly
At least of myself, and watching
Every decision I make important
Because it is unchangeable in time
Got to go to class before break
After Yoga Tues morning I'm gone
Turn in my slack paper knowing
The weekend was well worth it
My family now needs my support
And I hope I can be there
At least to be present and listen
Because his days are numbered
Dad I really miss you right now
And you're alive just 160 miles away
I need you to keep trying for me now
Because I'll be home for good soon

Again

So I'm in love again
Another woman has attempted
To fill the void my first love
Left in my barely existent heart
Each one comes less closely
To filling the ever-growing hole
Remaining as each takes another piece
As they move away from me
Some more than others
But each takes part of me
And leaves it in a recycling bin
As they leave my life

Ambitious Dreams

I just want money
It may be the root of all evil
But to me
It's the answer to all problems
I like to impress
Myself and others
I like to buy my friends
I like to buy my happiness
The question is
How do I get money?
A rock star, a movie star
Win a million dollars sitting in a bar
Try my luck at the slots
Build some new robots
Make a million web pages
Save up my monthly wages
I just can't think of a way
To make money grow on trees
Cause this lazy bastard
Ain't gonna work for it

Amputated

I can't say that I like being amputated
So why do I continuously attach myself
Thrown away and forgotten or worse
To be left as a decoration on your shelf

I can't say that I ever ask permission
To fall in love with so many fakes
Use me until I am drip-drop dry
What can I say, everyone makes mistakes

If emotions were as easy as these words
Maybe someday I would learn to differentiate
Between the one who will someday love me
And all those who just contaminate

The faith that there was one perfect person for me
Died long ago without a second thought
The theory of right time and right place
Is soon to be completely overwrought

Forget me not always becomes forgot
It seems like years since I was one sought
Yet each one has their glamour snapshot
Which ties my heart up in this knot

When I look at the test of the inkblot
Like being blinded from a sunspot
Always I find the female hot
Never to see the obvious cheap shot

Another Hello

Just outside the door
As I approached
It opened up with him
And you said hello
I replied politely only
Because of surprise

7

And his presence
Kept me nice
The words I would say
Hurt you back now
Like you have done me
Listen for me once
Just take it to heart
Every soft word
And choke on it
For fucking me over
Fuck your sister too
Fuck the both of you
Because I felt for you
Indescribable disillusionment
Left here thinking
About your brain fucks
Each time we conversate
For more than thirty seconds
Sometimes I think
You will just disappear
For a few days you do
But then you're back
Fuel for my brain
To write and to rhyme
I'm sure that I'm done
Awasting your time

Another Lecture

His words don't reach me
This tall man down front
Standing at the podium
Making all the commotion

I should just sleep
But out of respect I don't
I just sit motionless
Waiting for this to end

Almost as if the waves

Of sound change languages
Before reaching my ears
Where I hear only noise

The overheads make no sense
And the sound clips are too loud
The movies are too long
And the lights are too bright

I'm shaking in my seat
Trying to resist the urge
I have to glance at my watch
It's only 11:01

I still have an hour?
This can't be right
I will go crazy
If it's a second longer

I'm so drenched in sweat
As I sit up in the bed
Only a nightmare
What a scare it was

Never again will I study
By sleeping on my book
I think this osmosis thing
Has a bit to it

Another Spell

To meet you
For things to work
Stimulating conversations
Long outdoor walks, sailing
Traveling to the corners
To experience it all together

Just one person
Not perfect at all

9

Attractive in some way
Enjoys my poetry, music
Sacrifice as I for her
She meets me in the middle

I hear as a Pisces
I have this certain way
To predict future events
To some degree of certainty
By willing them to happen
So I wish of this spell

Find me a good soul
A true companion
In it for a long long haul
And please make her as sweet
As the many souls I've touched
Along the ride there

Back Home With Sister

Right now my blood is boiling
Just because you left on a light
It might seem kind of trivial
But it makes me want to fight
I know it was an accident
Which makes it all the worse
Even though if you knew it bothered me
You would cast on me a curse
So many times you find the thing
That makes me lose my cool
And then continue doing it
While laughing till you drool
This time it's me who's crazy
And needs to just let go
But I have no will power
When it comes to you my foe
You've played me like a game
And you're as selfish as a cat
You only speak for self-betterment
I wish you to be hit with a bat
Maybe then you would pay attention

To just a few things of you I ask
Let me have my peace and quiet
Leave me in the dark to bask
I am obviously sick as hell
To think up such a dirty thought
But I have no medical insurance
And no remedy can be bought
Can't you just hear me the first time
Or maybe by my lucky number thirteen
Get the point when I tell you
Don't repeat the offense so mean
The monotony of you kills me
Never once thinking to say hi
But you always remember
To piss me off till I cry
I want to have a new sister
Because your model is outdated
Or I'm just malfunctioning
You left me god-damn jaded
Others shoes will be foreign
Until your eyes open up to see
There is more than one point of view
And one of them is me

Bad Dream

Dream of me with gun in hand
Bloody fingers drip in the sand
Red footprints show trail of dead
Shooting frenzy ends in bed
What triggered with awful thought
And worse no worry of being caught
In dream I realized all was fake
Without rules reality would make
Just laughter and bullets in my mind
Pressing me forward not to decline
The horrendous tragedy that I cause
Like an angel of death I did not pause

Bad Karma

Call up someone you love
Tell me you love someone
Other than the someone
You initially called

Could develop a tad
Of bad karma in you
Making winds blow harder
Against you the next day

Pity is for the birds
And self-pity is worst
Nothing preordained here
But balance must remain

A beacon I will not be
The light of hope for good
An example ample
Of truth for all to see

I got what I deserved
Reality reacted
To my initial touch
And gave retribution

As master of myself
Responsibility kept
Weighing down my conscience
Like a ton of concrete

20 Roses and a Beer

I gave you 20 roses
For your 20th birthday
You put them all in vases
To get them out of the way

You told me you felt happy

No one had done this before
Then you took off all your clothes
And we closed the bedroom door

I won't describe the actions
That took place that very night
But we did not sleep enough
And we almost had a fight

I was looking for friendship
And she got the wrong idea
Where I'm from roses for my friends
And to get laid, bring a beer

Beliefs

How can I believe in God
I can't see him
How can I believe in Science
I can't understand it
How can I be Satanic or Wiccan
Gypsy, Buddhist, anything but what I am
I understand a few things
Love, me, school, friends
And only a limited view on these
I also understand brainwashing
The reason everyone thinks they are
Firm in their beliefs

Best Friend

Someone to cheer me up and make me smile
Someone whose phone number I can always dial
When I spend time with them its a perfect day
I will do it again in the future not far away
Someone who is always there when I need them
Someone who is willing to go out on a limb
Someone who has common interests with mine
Someone who knows how to give me a sign

Someone who is always easy to talk to
Someone who likes things that are new
When I see them they wave and hug me goodbye
And occasionally a hug when we say hi
Someone who understands the way I feel
Someone who makes my problems seem less severe
Someone who is warm like a teddy bear
Someone whose feelings about I do care
Someone who can keep secrets and never tell
Someone who would pick me up if I fell
Someone I can care about and dearly love
Someone sent to me from heaven above
My best friend

Betrayed

Ever so often in your life
A special person comes along
Promises are made, Secrets are told
Maybe you fall in love

Trust is something that is hard to find
So you cherish it deeply
And when that trust is lost or broken
It hurts life a knife stabbing in your heart

So once again you're searching
Trying to find that one special person
And this time you're really sure you're in love
So you get married

Then your trust is lost
Affairs and family distress begin
No doctor can help you work this out
Once again you have been betrayed

Big Change

Why do people have to change so much

It's like they wear a different face every day
What ever happened to being yourself
Seems like a concept long thrown away

One day they seem angry and the next fine
Maybe they need a doctor like I see
To keep the ups and downs within bounds
While still making your choices all free

Mood swings that make PMS look invisible
But not instantaneous, rather weekly or so
Reminds me of a child much too immature
To understand when to stop and when to go

I really always try to be myself
And at least that's an effort that I make
It makes life so much easier in so many ways
When you can be straight and not fake

Why do people have to change so much
It's like they wear a different face every day
What ever happened to being yourself
Seems like a concept long thrown away

Birth of a Leader

Maybe I could forgive G Bush Jr....if he wasn't a governor first

Smoky before the screen
Can't you see what I mean
Distance unknown time zone
Maybe this is too late

Writing to find anyone
Who feels like I'm worthwhile
Who will exchange places
In the penalty of death

I am an innocent
But I want to change round

I want to preach and help God
So if you are a follower

Give up your life for me

This is what God would do
As Jesus did on the cross
Paying for all the sins of man forever
Use him as an example

I'm here in Texas USA which means
Smoking a joint can be lethal
My lungs seem to feel Okay
But my ass is in prison

Undemocratic as I can imagine
United we stand - states fall alone
Should have let them go years ago
Texas separate with 49 united states

Then maybe we would still have
Twin towers in New York
Maybe I would have done excellent
That depressing last term

Bleach

Bleach
Taking away my colors
Draining away the last
Of my old self
Slowly I feel it
Burning, Cooling, Itching
All that was is gone
The new is here
Erase Me
What was me
I need to stop
But I can't
Do I like this?

I can't remember anything
Anything about the real me
Only others' expectations
Do I look Cool
That question I am always asking
Asking everyone but myself
Is this me
Was that me
I wonder
Will I ever know
The bleach will decide that
Taking away my color
Bleach

Blind

No one sees things quite the way I do
There are other equal perspectives
But none that I can yet understand
And to others mine is also strange

My stubborn and reckless point of view
Buried under concrete foundations
Which much be chiseled away bit by bit
Before one can make sense of the mess

But upon making it to the next plateau
Finding only more and more fences
And walls and combinations locks
Covered in barb wire and land mines

Fuck it, exactly, you will never know
Anything about what I'm thinking
And I will never know for you
So just give up and start listening

My voice and words have a hint
Since they come from inside me
Stop this senseless analyzing
Of that which you will never get

Real me so simple in some ways
Never all but quite enough
To decide whether to pursue
Or just give up

Blue

Dreaming again for the first time in years
Sometimes I remember the pain or the tears
Like my unconscious is open to free me from fears
And myself is returning, removing shell with shears
Able to say yes or no and stick with it
Confident in my decision to stand or to sit
Overlooking easily all the others' bullshit
Judge only yourself, let them have their fit
Without any protection at all in this world
I feel safer just knowing that I'm in control
No longer turning to the pill or the bowl
Just me and myself in this little black hole
Confidence rising up so high so don't fall
Need to be proud and to always stand tall
Forget the voices and all of their call
Imperfect individual curled into a ball
Exercise can help, and so can meditation
But it all boils down to self preservation
I have to keep up this propelling motivation
Finish what is started without agitation
Thoughts are for thinking inside my head
Not for public scrutinization by those in my bed
Or those who waiting likes hawks to attack
Would strike at me weak when turned was my back
Keep living, keep dreaming, keep hope alive
Things will work out and I will survive
Everyday to be cherished just the way it is meant
An unchangeable moment, gone soon as it's sent
Keep up my hard work and maybe someday
I'll end up where I'm meant to after my decay
But wasting more tears for just one helpless soul
Is not very useful, to work toward and toll

If they have given up already, nothing I can do
Will bring them back or change them from blue

Both

I enjoy stating the obvious
In a very obtrusive way
I love being sarcastic
At least fifty times a day
Hurting people's feelings
Comes naturally for me
Insulting each person that approaches
So that people flee
Unfortunately being nice
Is the same way too
Speaking many ridiculous compliments
Is something I must do
Maybe helping lift people up
To let them soar with birds
Is actually to make them lower their shields
So I can hit them with harsh words
I really don't know which I like
Helping or hurting them
Both give me extreme pleasure
And hurt me deep within

Break Away from Life

Smoking instead of swimming
How many more times will this happen
Getting high instead of anything
Happened already too much

Too numerous the number
Of classes missed and days thrown away
Just being stoned and forgetting it
Whatever it may have been

Too unfair the thought of those

Who inadvertently I hurt
Just because they were too close for truth
My whole life was a huge lie

Now I'm back under control
From that bagged leafy green substance
That I need to use every moment
It doesn't matter too much

I failed my own test so now
It's time to stop having fun and work
I need to remember all of it
The things important have been

Hiding from me illusions
In my false reality from smoke
So get to school and study all day
My life no longer huge lie

But pothead for a week
Then for a month too
And I think I'll be this way
Far past twenty-two

Candy

Treachery and pain I have been through this day
Waiting for your voice which never came
I have nothing and yet I have found love
In an unlikely place from which it does not return
Betrayed by mother and sister
You, you are the one for whom I grieve
But yet, I am also in pain
A pain that still seems invisible to you
You make me worry with tales of eternal slumber
And I cannot ignore even a chance that it could be true
Yet in a promise you once gave me
Death for you will be coming naturally
Conscience is making a vile person of me
For I cannot let go of what I once held

To your hand I once professed my love
The rest is emptiness

Cellular

This cell phone kills me
But should I be surprised
My initial bill low with low minutes
And the bill is 13 pages

Where did I go wrong this time
I didn't use it that much
And the rates can't really be changed
What a sucky situation

And this will remain my main line
Until next March when I begin car payments
And continue paying off the credit
For all the mistakes I have wasted money on

I don't regret anything
But I would like to declare bankruptcy
Move to a different country
And wait 7-10 years for memories to pass

Then back again to scam again
Because they are all scamming me
Work enough to get the good credit
Only to retreat back to my new country for 7-10 more years

There should be no credit system
It explains my problem as well as America's
Don't lend anyone anything at all
True value is learned from the process

Spending every hard earned cent
On luxuries you don't need
And gifts for people who don't matter
So yourself is left empty, poor, and wasted

Chameleon

O chameleon
So much like myself
Making camouflage by changing
To avoid some and protect thyself
Much as I
In costume and mask
Appear to be one of the pieces
Of a puzzle I don't belong to
Colors flowing too bright
As thy mate approaches
To gather attention
And be seen by all
Much as I
Become loud and sweet
When she is visible
Or when her sweet voice
Still echoes in my head
Words worth more to me than gold
And time standing slowly still
With each embrace
Never change back
Always striving for brightness
Then she is gone
I grow gray and weak
And camouflage again

Changes

Changes must be made
New roads need to be laid
This depressing rewinding tape has to stop
And the time is beginning to fade

Equality is not only a dream
It is a possibility
Too bad the congress gets paid off
And nothing seems to change their humility

"We are the best country in the world"
I've heard it enough to make my ears bleed
Let's make some progress instead of regress
Plenty already have, many more in need

A leader, president, or spokesman
Has to be for the people, and by the people
Not the money, the sex, drugs, or chaos that reigns
Not for the church or its steeple

So many easy answers to the problems
That we overlook them and make things complex
Fuck capitalism and the American way
What works on paper can only decay

Overthrow this bullshit and give us a chance
Rich, poor, and middle all in a dance
For a gram of hope, I'd trade a pound of gold
Because this old system is starting to mold

Lets get over the past and on with the new
Radical, liberal, whatever you do
Just make it fair, like it should have been
And someday, somehow, we will all win

Enough with this verse and my tired words
Like drums beats slowing they become only blurs
I just had to say it for once and for all
Someday I hope this whole system falls

Chaos

It only took one solitary night away
How can this much happen in a day
One day things appear so great
I was so blind again to impending fate

Why do I just keep on setting myself up
To be dropped from the 13th floor down
Crashing hard like a falling coffee cup

Being used as an ashtray like just a noun

A person, place, thing, or idea only shed
After offering me a place in her bed
To understand this chaos cannot be
Just left here lonely but at least free

Free to think about her every moment
Whether or not she even talks to me again
The memory fades when I decide confident
That she is safe and loved but new begin

This chaos cannot continue forever
And I will end my quest never
To find the love that treats me fair
And offers endless hugs like teddy bear

Childhood

Walking under weeping willows
Reminds me of my young childhood
Having competitions with pillows
Playing games we never understood

So unfortunate life only gets harder
And experience only adds more perspectives
If this trip had been backwards
I would be smart when I was a boy that cared

Society could slowly take hold of me
Instead of just letting completely go
Following trends without thinking
Letting society rule me as it would

Now all this glass false reflections
I am always just like a confused mouse
Lost in a maze that contains shockers
When I don't find the cheese fast

Physically I have always been ready

But mentally I fear I may never be
It seems whatever comes my way
I accept without questions naturally

Choices

I feel like I can't do the right thing
Every choice will hurt someone
Making a selfish decision
Seems so unfair

Thinking and Praying
Talking and Laughing
Nothing seems to make it easy
To decide who gets hurt

The faster I decide
It will all be over
Never able to take back
The pain I hand out

Why in these awkward situations
Do I always find myself trapped
Trying to figure out
A perfect solution

Maybe someday I will understand
How I get into these things
And how to get out
Without feeling like shit

Cigs

With each exhale
The pale gray smoke
Brings back another echo
From a past I tried to forget
A depressed me
That everyone liked on the outside

But was no better off
Than an inmate on death row
My insides tearing me apart
Wanting to say what I thought
Not the appropriate bullshit
That I learned in some classroom
Each puff of smoke
Is like looking at the cloud
And finding a picture
That is so clear and real
And never once the same
That cloud was for me
And then its gone
With a gust of wind
Every taste of tar
Reminds me of the reasons
Why I never wanted to smoke
Back when it all happened
Memories at full force
Like an ocean wave
Knocking me down
And drowning me out

C

Long Blond Hair
Smile Shines
Endless black hole in eye
Long legs
Firm hug
Pleasure to escort
Pleasant laugh
Easy to entertain
Innocent to an extent
80's movies
In search of prey and victory
This seems so 5th grade-ish
I do bad things
With two 2-liters
What a short crush

Clearly Fate

It's a clear night sky full of stars
And I am not slightly tired
Her square lips have me entranced
The soothing touch of soft skin
Hands make magic all over
Tears of guilt create closeness
Tonight a trip round the world
Without leaving her blanket
Wonderful infinity
Time stands still for us two
Like a rainbow's pot of gold
Warm and fuzzy inside me
All are perfect as they are
Each soul somehow different
Passing through me like water
She creates ripples and waves
Eternity would not be
Long enough to spend with her
But each second passing by
A gift from the God itself
Dream of angels and flowers
A reflection of your self
Honesty flows forming lakes
And oceans blue as pictures
I melt from her awesome heat
Coming to terms with future
I'm falling with no bottom
In love

Confused

Too confused
To make up my mind
To see the truth
From all the lies
Everything has a mask
And I don't know
Who lives underneath

Any of them
Getting to know you
Could be a mistake
Taking another piece of my heart
With mysterious smiles
And empty "I love you"s
Draining me from being whole
Being an individual
Is it possible
For nothing to be left of you
Because it has all been taken away
Never to be returned

Confusion

Laying on the front yard
In my high-rent no class house
Gazing up at the heavens
Pinholes of light in the black night
I think to myself
What is all of this for?
Later, further in the ghetto
I see a man risking his uniqueness
For a couple of laughs
And a bit of money from the coke he sells
Getting angry about the life
I see all around me
Why its so often thrown away
Without even thoughts of recycling
Or lost somewhere quiet
Where it is never found
I want to enjoy it all
Every moment and emotion
And to keep a memory
That is why I'm here
Not to mope around
Complaining and bitching
Leaving things worse
Than how I find them
Everyone around here

Is not clear or alive
But system sedated
Rarely can they wake

Cori 1

I am not happy anymore
I don't feel like smiling
You're not funny, you whore
There will be no reconciling

Back and forth your feelings go
So often I am getting sick
Why must I suffer this woe
Finalize your feelings and pick

Why is this so hard for you
It's either him or I
I can't see from your point of view
And I can't hear you cry

If this is goodbye
Then just let me be
I am not going to die
I'll carry on soullessly

Cori 2

Today you kissed someone else
Are you really my love at all
You come at me with feathered angel wings
That are sharp and cut my heart to pieces
Always melting me from ice to water
Only to evaporate me into nothing
Clouds that quickly darken the sky
To rain on your parade with surprising accuracy
Underestimating me like this as a fool would
Almost as if you need someone or something
To keep you in check

All those words you say lost their meaning
When your behaviors show me the true you
Never satisfied, always searching
Trying to find a solution to your problem
A fix to make your smile last longer
And to take away the heat in between your legs

Cori 3

You seemed to have misplaced the key
To the chains you keep me in
So I have been left locked up
Unable to think a solitary second
Without your face overwhelming my head
making me a prisoner
Inside this mound of flesh
We like to call a person
My wrists are growing tired
Of these shackles rubbing
Beginning to think I'd rather be dead
Than look into your eyes again
Next time you visit me
Will be the last time
I am overcoming your chains
With my will power
You will never be
More important than me
Keep that in mind
And see what you find
Don't look for me again

Cori 4

We can hardly be lovers
Together our hands on one another
But apart our hands not idle
Trust is a foreign concept
While infidelity and cheating are not
If we stay friends more than a few days

I might be overcome by surprise
But I am not because I know you
Next time we meet-we will repeat
All the same mistakes that got us here
Regretting the decisions we made
And wishing things had begun differently
Right person, wrong time...no
I think just wrong person
I cannot be anything but what I am

Cori 5

How can one be so right
That each night my head fills
With her image
And my thoughts never wonder
Is it all just a dream
Torturing me everyday
These feelings so perfect
I cry tears of happiness
Each day I awake
Smiling with the knowledge
That it is all real
My Cori lives

Cori 6

You occupy my thoughts day and night
Even my dreams are not safe
And yet somehow I still feel alone
Almost as if I have become invisible

I would rather be invincible
Making harsh words disappear
Before they can reach my core
And inflict their intended damage

Using these glasses does not help me to see
How quick you are

Running around so fast as light beams
Hiding your cruel intentions

The smile of deceit is your only sin
Leaving me wandering in search
Of something that will never be mine
And never be shared with me

Handkerchiefs are still damp
From your multitude of tears

Cori 7

Time is slowing to a standstill
While you are away from me
Butterflies fill my chest
Wings fluttering like whispers
My body won't stop shaking
It seems like winter again
The warmth you share is absent
During my long month at home
Smiles are a relieving commonplace
Knowing you're happy wherever you are
And the longer I wait for you
The closer you are to reaching me

Cori 8

The rose you left in my room
Died the day you packed
I lost your picture in a drawer
Another fool with feelings you attract
Sometimes I wish I never met you
But I have really changed
I learned a lot more about me
My life seems rearranged
All you represent seems circular
Able to make 180 degree turns
Your icy lips are cold without feeling

And your claws scratch and burn
Constant jokes trying to take back
The pain unleashed by your every movement
Each illogical and selfish thought
Leads you further from improvement
Why do you have to be so beautiful
Like a tree of forbidden fruit
A chance to learn so much
But I don't wear a bulletproof suit
Your words and actions hurt
They twist and beat at my core
And make me realize my naiveté
For letting you through my door
So you can ignore an apology
And just continue back into your cycle of sad blue
Running in phone booths to change your mask
So no one sees the true you

Cori 9

Maybe now it's finally over
Or at least it seems that way
Memory is beginning to fade
We have nothing left to say

It's scary how your face haunts my mind
Or did till we called it quits
Replaced me so fast my brain still spins
Recalling the pieces and bits

That incredible smile and your gaze
Played tricks on my heart and head
The fog you left dissipates slowly
Each night alone in my bed

I guess I should thank you for something
But words are failing me now
You helped me prepare for the next one
Why don't you take a deep bow

Impossible quests to forget you
No chance to succeed this time
Just perfect, I think not my angel
You committed the harsh crime

Needed you to be in love with me
And not play this pointless game
So I turned you off and pulled the plug
Because you're the one I blame

Cricket

There is a cricket on my shoulder
I assume it was crawling in my clothes
Nothing fell on me but there it was
Looking me in the eyes there is a cricket
Delayed in my reaction I flicked it
Upon the floor undisguised was a roach
Disgusted I began to trap it
Crushing it slowly delayed in my reaction
A sad smudge on my floor
That was previously an uninvited guest
Roaches have no place in this house
Sick of the annoying pest

Dark

I like the dark
I can always close my eyes
But without light they can be open
And still see nothing
In the dark my friends can comfort me
And it is all so real
With my eyes open
In the dark
I can go on a journey
Without moving an inch
And later realize I haven't moved
When my imagination makes me flinch

In the dark I can't remember
Whether I'm asleep or awake
Dreaming or imagining
Letting nightmares come true
The light just smothers me
It showers me with bright reality
The sudden rush of colors wipes me out
And pushes me back to a dark place
Where I can relax again

Destiny

I wish someone could convince me
That everything I do
Is really just my destiny
And not just a long path of mistakes

I wish that when I looked at memories
That I could just relax
And stop remembering everything wrong
That happens on a regular rotation

I wish that I could save each tear
To show you that I do hurt
So you could realize that I love you
And maybe give me a chance

I wish your smile was forever
Locked in my mind's eye
Always ready to calm me
When I am drowning

Don't Dig

Listen and remember
Try to be a perfect ear
Never try to change her
Your words make you queer

Don't ask questions
Don't dig like a worm
Leave out suggestions
So she wont squirm

Understand what you can
Without overstepping the bound
Turn on the fan
And cool yourself down

No need to get deeper
Wipe away facade and see
She is not a keeper
Who could feel you with glee

Walk away soft like
And don't make a sound
If followed on bike
Throw her to the ground

Get away from me bitch
You scream and you shout
After discovering the witch
She is without a doubt

Just stop when you're told
And don't dig yourself deep
Because if I may be so bold
Someday you might need some sleep

Dreams

Every night
When I sleep
I dream a dream
That I am swimming deep

I am swimming under
All of the fish
I am further under

36

That any man could wish

In the dream
I wear no mask
The further I go
The lesser the task

I don't have to breathe
There are no bubbles
There are no sharks
There are no troubles

When I awake
I think about
How real it seemed
There was no doubt

It was all real
It was not fake
What powerful things
Your mind can make

Note: This was my first poem in 8th grade (1992)

Dusk

Blowing leaf is caught
In heated smoke from chimney
Black ashes falling
Creating a smoke
Darkening air and blue sky
Speeding up the dusk
Monochrome
Only various grays
Tiny atoms separate
Dirt and Dust
Air and Water
In Everything
In us
Blowing leaf is caught

Emily

Dear Emily
I wrote you a poem to say
That I am really thinking
About you all hours of the day
I wonder what you're doing
I wonder if you'll call
Are you really OK?
Hope you did not fall
Please keep me informed
I enjoy all the secrets
I am only a person
That is caught up in your nets
I hope that you know
That I am here because I want to be
I really want you better
I want you to be free
Listen to what I say
And what you say too
Soon you'll learn to love again
And you can start something new
Until then I am here
Waiting for you to cry
I will treat you like a sister
Until we say goodbye

Fall Curse

What makes me so enticing
That for just one week
You want to be with me
Then I'm flushed away

Maybe my weak expectations
Leave me open to suffering
And I deserve it all knowing
That I could be a hard ass

I could protect myself with armor

I could wield a sword in battle
I could respond when words were said
I could breathe without you here

All this I've done before you
But it seems harder than when
Your ears caused arousal
I haven't seen in years

Your kiss so romantic
And your voice such a joy
Your innocence so pure
I would feel like a rapist

But what we had was romantic
Everything I imagined and more
Something new always opens
After you shut one door

Theme less and wordless I write
No theory or theme behind me
Just alone without you writing
To this screen which listens

Take a few days to adjust
And wait for the phone call
God Damn it for my curse
Which happens every fall

Father

Trying to understand him
Is so difficult
He is so primitive
He is such a stereotypical male
Words reflect off him
Conversations are one sided
Even when he seldom focuses
His mind is still wondering
Maybe it's guilt showing him

All the wrong things he has done
So constantly that reality
Has ceased to exist
I wish it was
But I think not
He is just empty
A shell
Regrets are foreign to him
And if I'm wrong
I wonder how he can hurt us
And not see it
I don't understand him
Because he acts without thinking
And ceases to think afterwards
Leaving us thinking

Feelings about M

You must really not know where I am coming from
The feeling of being used entirely
I spend every cent with you
Presents and anything to make you happy
All spare time that can possibly be with you is
Yet you have no appreciation
How would you feel with a deadly hopeless crush
I feel much worse than that
Because I don't know that it's hopeless
I actually still think I have a chance
That makes me hurt that much more
I will love you that much more and become more attached
You are already my essence of life
The more time you lead me on
The worse it gets
So please
Make up your mind
Yes or no... it's simple
Do you like me or not?
Do you love me or not?
Do you think we should continue dating
I know your life is confusing

Maybe you need time to sort things out
But time alone...not time leaving me hanging
That is not fair to anyone
If you decide no then see other people
If you decide yes then we can love each other
If you are not sure fix yourself
Take the time alone...
I cant bear to see you trying to make up your mind with me
And dating other people
Can't you see how easy an answer seems to me
It is probably just different for you
I had built up so many walls to protect myself from this happening again
But your glance broke them down
I need an answer
I never lied to you
Or purposely did anything to hurt you
So please make it quick and less painful

Fucking Evil

In this world of dirt and stone
I raise my voice for all to hear
In all directions I go out
To destroy the weak, my message clear

Think about the golden rule
When has it ever helped you
I don't see any great God
You stupid Christians belong in a zoo

Church of Satan is coming to town
Going to burn you up and spit you out
Fire is the only truth
So Christians better begin to pout

Finally

I have been thinking
About all the reasons to live

Only there are none
To be found

I am like a pet cooped up in a cage
I only do what I am told
My own opinion is gone
Just like my conscience

I think more and more
About how I will make it end
I lie and cheat
And I feel good doing it

Friends are just temporary
Like everything else
Families die, love ends
But death, it is eternal

I want to be free
But what is left to have
Freedom is nothing because
After life is emptiness

I am alone now
As I have always been
I cannot save myself
And I don't want anyone to save me

I cant think
I cant talk
I cant love
I cant live

First free day

Today was a pretty good fucking day
Talked in classes and passed a quiz
Friday night and I smoked some dank
Didn't run into them so nothing to say
No one came to pay me a vis- (it)

But still my paper isn't blank
Even without running into the three
They came up in my mind too much
Wish I could just forget the week
I feel trapped here even though I am free
Because I can be lured by touch
Any random time she choose seek
Me out in this room where I sit thinking
Becomes all emotion at her
Trespass into my breathing space
Only soon to go next door from drinking
Leaving me teased, an alone blur
Shaken from her use and her pace
At bringing me to complete waste
Useless to resist this feeler
Hurting me only with smiles and blinking
In court this girl would have no case
Against leading me on with purr
But I will stay afloat, keep from sinking
Because I am not someone weak
Slamming my foot hard on the clutch
Smashing what was us into a big tree
I am not nearly to my peak
I refuse to be lured by such
Never again will you come and hurt me
Nothing here is easily sank
Time to take control of this dizz (yness)
No lame brain ideas like tell them I'm gay
Get someone else to turn your crank
I have got to go take a wiz
Hope I don't have to tell you go away

First Love

After one's first love
How do you avoid a rebound
Is it even possible
To not just love someone
Because they love you
I really hope so

I never know
Why I fall in love
Only that it hurts
Worse than any torture
And longer than any eternity
When it ends
And while it's alive
It feels better than any heaven
And no present
Could equal its worth

First Sighting

Been three days waiting for it to occur
First eye contact with you seems a blur
Maybe saying hello was a bad idear (southern drawl)
I could see his eyes were not too clear

This jumbled mess we're in together
Changes instantaneously just like weather
Never knowing how to act or speak
Wondering when he'll reach the peak

Of tolerance for me he can endure
Before he taunts me in attempt to lure
An engagement I'm avoiding still
I just sit back writing with my pill

This medication keeps me straight
So I don't try to obliterate
Everything you have I've learned to hate
Against him I do discriminate

Needless to say this will happen more
This sightings with him I can't ignore
My friendship tossed without a thought
So in the abuse you can stay caught

Like you're addicted to him without escape
I have to close my window drape

So I don't see you two walking by
Holding hands and watching deep blue sky

Just please don't come back to me for console
When it inevitably ends leaving you charcoal
My hand outreached has been reclaimed
Leaving you and him to share the shame

First Visit

Mass confusion would be the theme
From the knock on my door to the end it would seem
Out of sleep I arose to talk
With the girl who three days past took me for a walk

She asked if I knew where he was
"What do you think," I responded noticing her buzz
She asked if my room had air flow
Inviting her in I prepared for final blow

Sister was angry about mail
Miscommunication my fault so here I fail
And once again we sit silent
Both recognize the potential for me violent

Never laid a hand on female
But as far as the other someone I would nail
Just provoke me only one time
And both will be bloody hurt from committing crime

Touching me softly with her feet
She flirts without response and continues to cheat
I think its time for you to leave
Holding back hardest yet from her I do believe

Don't keep this up just walk away
Each time you make me believe you want to stay
The game has ended so just leave
Don't ever look back to me from shoulder or sleeve

Flaw

What can you mean by a character flaw
It's just something about me you dislike
Sometimes I could just hit you in the jaw
You're approaching the critical third strike

No opinion is a universal law
Each of us is independent and self-determinate
Don't expect me to step back in awe
Nothing is concrete, nothing is permanent

I see no perfect example to live by
Especially not standing before these eyes
Re-examine yourself and the mistakes try
To adjust and correct the wrongs before one dies

When others begin assuming things I only sigh
Keep your mouth shut if you have nothing nice to say
There is not enough time to put up with a lie
Later on we each shall have a judgment day

Flaws are the part of us which is unique
Stop seeing the future as dismal and bleak
We are all people strong and weak
Time to learn to turn the other cheek

For Someone You Hate

I'm up for hire
I write hateful letters
It is my specialty
You need a letter?
Well you're in luck then
We cater to the
Following list of common
To uncommon customer interests:
Heartless, Black or Dark,
Void or Empty, Dead,
Break ups, Friendships, Weddings

Family, Business or other
I guarantee my product
And best of all
It is completely free
Just come and bitch
Complain like a baby
And I will write
So you can express
What you only repress
Maybe things getting better
Could end up worse
But at least not hiding
Surrounded by your hate
Let go of it
Not worth your time
Could have been worthless
Take the next step
Now we can hang
And talk about them
All the ones gone
To increase our safety
Maybe if we don't
It would even be
Cooler don't you think
If we are males
Inconsistent rules suck bad
So let me write
A letter for pain
You've felt this night

Free to think

I think I can honestly say
That it feels good to be free
Now that I have found a way
Not to fight or flee

Overcome now for time being my worst ail
And how wonderful life is without it
Seems like some lost fairy tale

Back when I was buried knee high in shit

On occasion I stumble back
To remind myself of why I quit
Then again I get on track
Because it just doesn't fit

My life too good to toss to trash
Just to get some buzz for an hour
And after I tap out that ash
The money gone and no power

Need motivation to keep me up
While it tries to keep me down
Smoking pot like eating ketchup
Is sure to only make me frown

Laugh a while with friends
While funds drain to non-existent
For some high that comes like trends
And leaves me so inconsistent

Front Yard

Crucified myself this time
Just hanging here for the crime
Of falling in love much too quick
So I can be labeled as another dick

According to chaos something will change
But when, where, and what I need a range
So I can just give up looking hard
For something that isn't in the yard

It's out there somewhere I can't see
Far far beyond the horizon of me
Sick of being hung out to dry
Without fabric softeners I am too shy

Travel someone far away

Where reinvented I can stay
For at least a brief sum of time
To figure out this accursed rhyme

Once I have my life complete
I'm sure the right girl I will meet
But getting there is so damn hard
When she isn't in the front yard

Philosophy on Life

Sexual physicality need not be emotional
And emotional bonds need not be tied to sex
Love between friends can develop slowly
Into a fantastic all incorporating explosion
Or to just an honest and mutually respectful place

If it worked out immediately it would be too easy
One must crawl before they learn to walk
Taking chances is always an enormous risk
But with each occasion there are new lessons
Drawing from them good and bad as experience

Then there is the problem with subjectivity
Things may be skewed because you are the viewer
Try not to compare apples with oranges
Every person a unique autonomous individual
Without exception circumstance new at the time

Let go of past and future, ideal and expectation
Destiny is only what one makes of oneself
All is incomplete by nature and by nurture
Explanations are not always the most important
Just the understanding and acceptance of what is

Ever changing is the nature of our whole being
From atomic sub-levels to our conscious thought
True prediction is an impossibility
Living involves some forgiving and some slippage
Of information under the layer of unconscious

Gabby

Perplexed
Cunning
Wild Fire
Gabriel
Endless surprises
Always listening
Suggestions galore
Punk rock indie-chick girl
Fun on top of fun in cases
Ready for someone's new ideas
Opinions easily attained
Forever friend to never end
Always herself
Down to earth
No aliens present
Realistic dreams
Excitement
Wonderful
Passionate
Gabriel
What do you see?
A painting on the wall
Many colors bright and dull
People gather and stare
What is it, do you care?
A person walking down the road
Singing a song about flowers
You see her from your window
What are the words that make her go
Your mother is crying in her room
Tears falling like a rainstorm
You wait at the closed door and listen
Wonder what she did not win
A friend calls you on the phone
Talking fast and rambling on
A gun shot rings through your ear
Your body shakes up with fear
Not me

God

What is God Anyway
A belief, a person, a myth
He's just a standard
A good example to live by
How is someone going to be greater than man
We rule over the earth
Not Him
The Bible does not stop evil
It is just another thing to go against
God- Yeah right!
I could worship shit the same way
What is the big deal
He doesn't help me
My prayers are not answered
I don't get questions answered
Just more questions
Who made God anyway
Nothing is there

Graduation

Well today I got a senior survey
I diligently filled in the number
For strongly agree, disagree,
And don't know hardly thinking

Wish those forms were as good
As the teacher evaluation forms
Oh yes that one bad teacher
And all those wonderful ones

I loved the long blank backs
Where I could really express
Maybe an example or something
Of how much the teacher taught

And how much we all grew
Or some of the amazing things

I learned about myself inside
New wisdom and improvement

Smiling often in the class
Of pure joy from new ideas
That I had not yet thought of
And was amazing all alone

But it happened so often
Just pure happiness concentrate
When the rhythm was right
And the people were present

Even days when I couldn't speak
Because of some stupid reason
They all inspired my thought
And helped me gradually become

What I am now and forever
An ever-changing person
Adapting to a specific environment
Over time and eternity

Great Family

The one you love loves another
This you can understand
But her choice is your brother
Too much for you to stand
Time and love you put in
And all you get out is lies
First a girl and now your brother
In one day you say two good-byes
Giving up is so hard to do
But it is the only choice you see
Someone once told you love is forever
And forever is a bond you cannot break
Then you realize you loved her
And that is also forever
Now you think of all the pain

And know it too will last forever
So you life's conquest begins
To get back the one you love
You pray that not many get hurt
But you know that is a lie

Ha Ha

Religion
What a joke
How can one not sin
What good is forgiveness
When you know you're just gonna do it again
If you mean it, does that mean you don't repeat it
Bullshit
You're just gonna run out and fuck everyone over
Like the selfish bastard that you are
Dreams crushed, hearts broken, feelings hurt, promises turned to lies
Just a repeating cycle of shit
Is any of this important
What is the point of praising someone
Or something that does not interact until you're dead
As many ordinary people have said
"If there is a God, then let him stick me with lightning now"
Hell, I would settle for a headache or broken nail
Just a sign to prove an unreal existence
A book written by men proves nothing
And nothing is exactly what religion is to me
What a joke

College Haiku

Beautiful Erin
You are very ticklish dear
Even on your head

Her kiss was so soft
I wished it would never end
But we went to sleep

Very strong feelings
I do not know what to think
But I am happy

To be this confused
Makes my head spin in circles
Will it ever stop

I close my eyes now
And all I can see is you
My eyes stay shut tight

Every time I laugh
Erin asks me why I did
But I never know

When I hold your hand
The smile never leaves my face
Until I let go

Your hair is so soft
I have to touch it some more
Will I mess it up

Perfect short blond hair
My fingers glide though the waves
Smells like fresh flowers

She is cute asleep
Breathing in and out slowly
Crest rises and falls

Almost got engaged
To a person named Adam
Glad I get a shot

Thanksgiving is here
Four whole days without her near
I will be OK

Really need to cry
But the tears are not coming
So I sit and think

Back in love again
With the same one as before
Better luck next time

Carrie is my friend
She has beautiful red hair
Waitress at Damons

Thomas is a boy
That Carrie has a crush on
It is confusing

Misty is funny
She smokes a lot of reefer
With her friend Summer

Misty hates big heads
Therefore she hates Dezendorf
Gigantic heads suck

Laughing in lecture
What a pathetic haiku
Oh well I don't care

Summer ex-boyfriend
Was way too old to fuck her
Statutory Rape

Misty and her rum
She will get drunk off her ass
We will laugh at her

Summer is crazy
She has a bowl named Bowltar
It is a guitar

Cori my sweetie

Why must I keep testing you
Be good by yourself

A haiku for you
Seven short syllables long
As simple as that

Falling down so fast
Reaching out to grab her hand
Almost missed her sleeve

Pulling her up now
Feet are almost to the ledge
Let go watch her fall

Hitting the ground hard
Not even twitching muscles
Walk away smiling

Demented I am
Too bad for her sorry ass
She should have been nice

Hell and Back

Trying to think of the right words
The best method, a perfect moment (time)
Things can be almost impossible
So I revert back to simplicity
I   Love   You
There... I said it
Now I just need a reaction
And each second I spend interpreting it
Is being stuck between heaven and hell
In a black hole where time stands still
Hanging on by a mere string
Praying for the response I need
You tell me an answer
"I'm sorry I don't love you"
Into hell once again

Until someone else draws me back into limbo
Where I can go for another ride

Her

Starting off as only a glance
Another could be the romance
Attempt to be a knight with lance
Again truthful words start the chance

Response surprise but also smile
I feel that I could fly a mile
Her honest eyes lock mine meanwhile
Innocent ways long out of style

Open up with nothing to lose
Many decisions we could choose
Upon her return there will be news
Pulling me from my deepest blues

Heart races fast at just her name
Pray this isn't some sort of game
Different from the rest all same
Locked lips in love without the shame

Dreams far in distance that could be
Growing inside me like a tree
Sometimes thoughts I wish I could see
But that would end surprise for me

Her 2

Now two months past since sight
A lot has gone down and we are cool
Only friends but why not, I need a few
And John, Lea, and her make a few
more than two

I am very confused about one thing

Although I am trying to help her
To get over what was the one four years
I can't get over the girl who left me
Only two days past

If I only had one wish right now
It would be to lose responsibility
To lose all guilt and feeling
Like Michael Myers wreak a little havoc
Revenge is OK

Then I could just get institutionalized
I'll be out as soon as I want
I am a psychology major
It's what I know-how to be sick
Isn't that sick?

Her voice cheers me up with conversations
That we must go back to having regularly
I miss all she does for me by just listening
And she usually has something to tell me
Dualistic Usage

How perfect is that, sucking each other dry
So nothing leaks out into our reality
Can't have a mess unless it's private
Those are the rules in this democracy
Freedom my ass

High

As I lay back onto the dirty floor I forget myself
All my problems seem to have evaporated into thin air
Just staring up at the sky seems interesting
And the world is moving in slow motion
Each step I dizzily take echoes in my head
And my limbs go numb one at a time
I wish I was not alone in this state
Where rainbows can erupt without rain or sun
Then sleep comes upon me

A tiredness I have often felt
Being drained from sensory overload
I must sit down and rest for a second
Then it's over
I wake up and life is once again ordinary
Un-satisfying, boring, plain...

Hypocrite

How can I be
Such a hypocrite
Being what they want me to be
Changing for each one
Lying back and forth
Uncountable times
To hide the truth
From being discovered
Words I don't mean
Said to them all
Kisses drawing the life
Out of each of them
So that I can use them
And abuse them
Leaving them stranded
And all alone
Each one proves
That love is not real
From such an empty soul
Like mine

Holy

Walking through the woods
The trail is very clear
A cool breeze blows me softly
There is nothing to fear
I make my way to a stream
And approach its shore
To listen to the trickle

Of water I adore
The rocks have gathered moss
By getting in its way
Tiny rapids of God's water
Reflecting a perfect day
Coincidence I think not
That I approached this creek
The purifying water
Has a message it must speak
Forgive me of my sins
After each one I say
I baptize myself with Jesus
God enters my heart today
I will never again be alone
From this day forth I see
That every step I take
God will take it with me

Hot

Heat upon Heat
Sweat Gathering
Forehead Soaking
Wet Droplets Fall

Fans blow air waves
Trying to cool
Useless Moping
Waiting for call

It will not ring
Impossible
Who is joking
High Chair too tall

Blue surrounds me
In this darkness
Self Created
My little box

Oven maybe
Baking me dry
Not sedated
Safe from the tox-

Ins working in
I am not here
Just frustrated
In my white socks

To feel her once
Would be a dream
Laminated
The perfect fox

<u>I am one</u>

I keep asking
Is this okay
Are you fine
What do you want
Do I really care
About your feelings
Doubt it
I just like the feeling
You know, from helping someone
I can only get it from others
They buy into my illusions of happiness
It is not real
Make-believe, if even that
I do nothing for anyone
But me, and sometimes not even for me
Everyday I need you more and more
And you never really needed me to start with
God, where are you now
I feel like shit and it is getting worse
Please God help me
From this sin
I can't do it
With or without you

Damn fucking asshole
Me, I am one

I Don't Know

I wish I had the patience
I wish I had the time
I wish I had the guts
To do what's in my mind
All these ideas in my head
Overflowing in my bed
All the dreams while I'm asleep
Promises that I will never keep
Giving up is so hard to do
When you haven't yet begun
I don't know what I can't
And I don't know what I can
No one here to help me
No voice that makes it clear
No batteries for the flashlight
In the cave of life I'm in
So many ways to turn
I am so lost and blind
Life is such torture without choices
But I can't make up my mind
Giving up is so hard to do
When you have not yet begun
I don't know what I can't
And I don't know what I can

I Had it

You were the best
That I am ever going to get
And I treated you so badly
Now I must settle for less

All that survives is memories
That force me to judge them

These new people who come
And try to take your place

But if you came back
I would not be worthy
Just a wasted kid
Dreaming of stars I can't reach

Close my eyes and remember
All the love that we had
Until I turned my back
Always looking for something better

The veil just got lifted
And I can see leaving
Was walking off a sky scraper
And falling past the ground

From hell things look different
And believe me I have regrets
I don't pray to anything for more
Because nothing believes in me

It all went to my head
Just like you always said
And now I have to pay
For the false happiness I feel

I will keep on pretending
Until the end of my life
But I know you were the best
And you're out of reach

Ignorance

All the pain
That you ignore
I don't know
If I can take it anymore

63

An act of being happy
Leaves no room for a frown
And the play ends
You never knew I was down

Everywhere you go
You hold back and save your breath
You're not gonna need it
Until you face your death

Maybe in My Head

Why do I feel so rotten
Each girl brings new problems
Which really are not new
Just new people
The problems grabbed hold of me as a boy
And they hide most of the time
Maybe in my head
Emerging every time someone gets close
Drawing me away or making me hurt
Until they are gone
Then they go back to wherever
They hide
Maybe my head
And I return to reality
Alone

Indian Giver

When you can't have something
It is always more appealing
But if you ever get it
The fascination fades in days
And you're wondering
What it was that you saw to begin with
But if you give it up
The fascination returns
When you see the joy

If the eyes of a new recipient
Taking the enjoyment you once had
From the one you once enjoyed

ING poem

75% water alive able to think
More miracles I see with every blink
Sometimes a smile or a wink
Can keep me floating from the sink
Ing feeling something's amiss
Maybe simply I am pissed
Looking for some perfect bliss
I keep writing on this list
Ing whatever comes to mind
Eyes close tight leaving me blind
To the forces from behind
Pushing me forward in the line
Ing up like dominoes
Try to stay off others' toes
Hope I have more friends than foes
To keep me from the lowest show
Ing all I have to give
In this life I have to live
Hope I'm not too talkative
If I am oh please forgive
Ing what I should not say
Waiting for another day
Wish there was some other way
To end this game I like to play

Instant Message

I missed a phone call
I figure about a month
Passed Since no message
Or word from Heather

Tonight I saw her online
She did forget to say goodbye
She is pregnant now
And back with the guy

No one seemed to like him
Although Heather I trust
To pick the correct one
She knows herself well

They are keeping the baby
And I gave her my happiness
A scrap I had left for one day
When a simple word can change everything

I at several points dated her
And wished so bad for it to work
But it didn't ever really work
So giving up we returned to friends

Slowly that faded with school
I never saw her around much
And visits were very different
Knowing she was involved

Asking for a hug seems unfair
Even knowing it is a last goodbye
But she did not know that at all
Just my fortune telling again

No anger only happiness here
So maybe just a little bit of that energy
Can go out and reach Heather
To make things right and have a family

Intentions

I tend to think that everyone
Has intentions behind actions

66

Later realized after all done
Each was only automatic

Never really felt anything
It's all just some big endless dream
That I will never wake up from
Until I wake up from your spell

Damn the power of some people
To just take me over like a remote
I don't like having buttons pushed
I don't work for anyone but me

Now you've gone and made me angry
Which means your remote is useless
And so is mine-RUNRUNRUN girl
Cause this one is gonna sting like scorpions

Isn't it Pitiful

Just sitting here without any motivation
Each second slowly creeps by
Waiting here for something to happen
Never knowing what it will be
I walk in circles, eat all day
Trying to make time begin to run
But then it begins to crawl
Even slower the time passes as I wait for nothing
No music appeals to me right now
No activity can hold my interest
There is plenty to do
But no one to do it for me
Just here and not there
Out the window even everything is normal
Just here in this room, in this head
All things are distorted
Why I can't just stop hearing the voices I don't know
But the picture is forming
It is a picture of me
My head hurts just looking at it

What is wrong with me
Why Can't I get anything right
AWHHHHHHHHHHHHHHHhhh

It hurts

Cut out my heart with a spoon
Or maybe you can think of something worse
Replace it with one from a baboon
So I can keep living tortured with your curse

Leave me sitting here and waiting
With strings attached to every limb
Ready to come back anticipating
When you call me at want and whim

Wish I were a female Wicken
Believing you will get it back times three
But you're not even worth a chicken
So why do I care when we never agree

Just go turn back around
And stay out of my glass room
Break things here you are bound
Make sure you take your gloom

It never ends

Today I saw her again
Like a trace memory
Calm and peaceful message
Denial of the last act

I'm not sure if I believe her
But it doesn't really matter
The circle has rotated
She is no longer in the loop

After the book she was to disappear
But painfully enough she survives
Like a ghost of past reminding me
That I am not always Mr. Happy

Damn me for having this reaction
Although I don't know what else
Just words quickly jotted down
So maybe I can forget her again

Like an angel she mystifies me
Maybe I never forgot at all
Just escaped from my reality
With my old and usual habit

Be nice to have a fast forward
So I could see how things will work out
And not have to wait here making choices
Without knowing any of the outcomes

No second chances for me here
And no rewind button to go back
Guess my only option is to deal
Just like it always has been

Jackie

Threats I should not have to make
If only my advice you would take
Empty promises I will not forget
Retribution will come while you sit
Unknowing maybe to this day
Threat carried out, nothing else to say
Permanently removed except in dream
Almost an illusion it would seem
Without regret no chances remain
Of a friendship we could not sustain
A chapter closes in this book
Some part missing that you took
UN-whole continuing on this quest

A life I try to live my best
Lessons learned remind me still
Broken glass will never heal

<u>J</u>

I wish she would look me in the eyes
Just a simple locking interaction
Maybe she would sense my fear
Maybe she could see right through me
What color are her perfect eyes?
Reflecting herself in mine I'd know
I wonder if she knows how beautiful she is
Miss Julie pales in comparison to
This southern angel with a slight accent
She showed me her room and frog collection
Kept up a good conversation, so much hospitality
We sat down and watched the TV
Inventing the Abbots is a strange movie
Like an anonymous note left on a windshield
I am captivated by your mystery
I remember brushing your foot with my finger
Under the blanket we shared on the sofa
I should have kissed you with fresh lip gloss
But still one soft kiss goodnight won me over
Smells of sweet perfumes surround you
Our embrace genuine and warm
My smile seems to be permanent
I feel like a bright yellow sunrise exploding
And it only gets sweeter everyday just thinking
Especially the days without hangovers
I'm sure I will ask how work went that day
But I know you will catch up on sleep
The memory of our first night together remains
For us to use as we choose
I am somewhat lifted looking back
And it was only yesterday

Jewish Girl

It's funny how as my memory fades
I can only remember the good things
Although you physical presence is missed
I long for your personality during conversation
I continue to lose romantic notions
While enjoying the thought of friendship
But even without hearing your voice
My love for you will not fade
Only inflating to levels beyond me
Engulfing my being and guiding me
To new understanding of myself
Not purposely, but because of the intensity of it all
The hours seem to form mountains to climb
While waiting for your arrival
And as I slowly reach the peak each day
The infinite hills ahead seem somehow reachable
Sad love songs put me in tears nightly
Before I lie down alone again to sleep
Your face in the emptiness of my shut eyes
And your laughter echoing in my ear
Although the form may gradually change
My love for you has become a constant
Through you my heart has reached the next plateau
You have become my basis of comparison
I will meet others and I may love again
But never again will there be another you
One who touched my heart so tenderly
And left trace fingerprints behind

Just Verses

As our love started its foundation
I was amazed how fast it grew
What looked to be a flawless house
As vulnerable as a spider web to the wind

Telling someone they are wonderful, fantastic, and great
After every sexual encounter and repeatedly

Reaffirming how things only get better and how strong
The bond of love between us is growing to be

Then with the rise of the dawn the love vanished
Leaving a jet trail of exhaust fumes leading me
Over to Europe where you could just relax
While my broken heart and I suffered alone here

Every time I think that our friendship will renew
I realize that would involve your finding another eventually
And each time that thought enters my mind pain from
The weakly sown stitches tearing my heart again

Would the person hear the same things I heard
Will the person end up being the one because
No vacation or distance conflict got in the way
Would the person suffer as I did if it ended

Each day I wake up with your picture
Burned into the back of my head as my eyes open
And each night I kiss the picture beside my bed
And pray that someday we will be together again

Kerri

The memory of our first kiss is not fading
Like a story etched in stone in my mind
Each second passing by me like I'm frozen
I only feel your soft lips, then rewind

Two weeks passed and I don't remember
Who you are or why I wrote this
Was it just a dream I had about you
Because I usually don't forget such a kiss

Or a name completely as I have yours
Just more information for me to observe
About myself and how callous I can be
Apparently myself is all I preserve

Still not coming up with anything
God does this mean I'm one of those pricks
Who has a one night stand and stops
Calling back or keeping touch like a brick

I doubt its really as bad as it sounds
Because I know myself too well
Probably more like a desire I had
That faded when real life got swell

K

I remember the first kiss
As well as the last
Your soft lips touching mine
And that lingering silence
Every bit of my body relaxed
Just hoping it would never end
I remember all the smiles
Glimmering out at me
Reminding me of a happiness
We share together
Each and every rose
Never one as perfect as you
I remember your touch
Soft as a pillow
Slowly breaking all barriers
All my defenses dropped
Your heart merged with mine
And locked into place forever
I remember the words
Softly spoken I love you's
That made my temperature rise
And my heart race
Each one adding
To a never ending love for you

K 2

Too bad you took that love
And threw it away
You saw our hearts merged
And took a shovel to them
So many pieces you broke
That my heart is deformed
It looks like some ball of pus
You left me in shambles
My life will never be the same
Our friendship cannot even last
Through this brutal feud
It has ended and
You won

K 3

Today I am a little bit sad
I just found out she has a man
Which should not mean anything
But it does, to me

We dated for almost two years
And I thought there was still a chance
I should have known this would happen
I have already done it to her

I told her I had dates
I told her about each hook-up
She did not tell me about anyone
And now some guy has taken her away

What am I talking about
I never had her to begin with
But it felt so good to know someone loved me
And now it is lost forever

I want her to be happy
Although I don't anticipate anything developing

Because she is a little brat
That must have everything her own way

One day maybe she will change
But I think instead
Some sucker will put up with her
And she will stick to him forever

K 4

So pretty
That long blond hair
It shielded me from
The person underneath
The bitter sarcasm
And rude remarks
Somehow missed me
Most of the time
I was blind
To the truth
To the person
Who I loved
A love so innocent
And so pure
That nothing could be wrong
Except that it was an illusion
In a mirror
Reflected inside out and backwards
Of the truth

Kind of Similar

By no means perfect or exact
Tonight is kinda like another
One where I was waiting on
A call from the sweet girl
I really have no clue once again
But as always I'm optimistic

It's up in the air forever
As far as most things go
Getting to know her better
Sometimes too much sleep
Sometimes not enough class
But just subjective opinions
No need to change anything
She is so wonderful to me
As long as I get remembered
Sparse visits better than none
I don't foresee anything here
But that is the best thing yet
Because I'm on my two feet
Holding hands beside her
Don't think she will be reading
This poem in two hours today
Bet she doesn't call me back
And I sit here waiting for her
Break will be nice for me
I need to see my family and
Gather up strength to finish
Strong and ahead in classes
My dad will inspire me likely
With a heart to heart convo
Or just a few words here and there
While we laugh, eat, and watch
The television will be back
You just called and spoiled it
I'm wrong again about you
Surprises are so nice

Katastophe

I cant believe you blame me when you break the news
Maybe you should lay off all the boo's
I feel like your Hitler and I'm one of the Jews
In this situation my choice is lose or lose

All these things in you I so quickly confide
And now I feel like I've only been lied

To believing we had something over which I'd have cried
But at least I can say that I really have tried

I thought a lot about your point of view
I really don't understand, I think you're askew
Being pushed in all directions from all around
In just one day you were sent homeward bound

To the one who is probably the cause
Back to the one who broke all the laws
He clutches and holds you with his claws
And slowly devours you into his jaws

You seem lost like you're someone new
Maybe if I just gave you one mountain dew
You'd wake up and realize there are only a few
Who will be able to accept who you are as just you

I think the manipulation is going too far
I think you've been brainwashed and they left a scar
So much drinking but not able to go to a bar
Alcohol mixed with meds makes you feel like a star
When you're actually like a fairy caught in his jar
The last night I remember we spoke in my car

You'll lie to protect anyone else
But you'll tell the truth when it hurts everyone else
It doesn't make sense
It doesn't add up
You're just taking the easy way out

That Lake

Sitting on the grassy bank
I stare at the sparkling lake
Watching boats slowly coast by
Skipping stones across their wake

Ripples shake the waters calm
Distorting the reflection

Of mountains covered with trees
Coming from each direction

Mutli-colored leaves falling
Form a blanket for the earth
She needs it in the dark night
For warmth is needed for birth

As the sun lowers slowly
And the moon begins to rise
All my troubles creep away
I feel I'm in paradise
Let Truth Be Told

Not really such a bad guy
Walking right up to me for a talk
I could tell he wasn't shy
He started to spell it out with chalk

Not too high an opinion now
For the girl he dated for a full year
Cheating on him like some cow
Probably because she had too much beer

Manipulate this, you bitch
Your act won't work on us anymore
Hope the next guy feels an itch
Cause you're acting like some fucking whore

Don't ever return my phone call
The point of which was to remind you that
We are through and it was no ball
You are never my proletariat
Letting it out

This paper is for expressing myself
It is making thoughts concrete and visible
And creating a living record
That they actually occurred in my mind

Sometimes I am in a good mood
Maybe everything is hunky dory
And during those times I'm content
Usually don't turn to the monitor for thinking

Sometimes I am in sad mood
Usually it involves a girl
Also the superstructure
And I get to express myself in poetry

Sometimes I am very angry
It too usually involves a girl
And also the superstructure
And I get to express myself in poetry

Because the happy times are not concrete
And I don't use words to articulate
The fuzzy feeling inside well
I am less likely to remember them

I will look back at all the poems
And see how much abuse I've received
And how much I wanted to give
To many of those around me even today

But tomorrow is a new day
So will be the one when this is read again
Each day could be wonderful from now on
Just trust in yourself that you will make it

Don't forget all those happy times
And the sad and angry times too
Because each one teaches you new lessons
To help you make it through

Lies

I feel like hell is here
Why am I this way, people wonder
"Because I want to be," I reply

It is a lie
I fall in love and things look great
People are happy for my happy life
They can only see things from a distance
All they see is lies
Secrets told to people are for them only
The next day ten people know
Soon everyone knows, but they pretend not to
And they all lie
We say that friendships are forever
But when more than friends comes along
There is an empty void
And lies fill it up
With all these lies you need some truth
No one believes your threats and promises
Just like the little boy who cried wolf
Your truth is swaying back and forth
If you could think now
You'd say "I was not lying"

Lighten Up

Just words and lines I write each night
Release anger instead of fight
No use to bottle up inside
So to this paper I confide

No friend with ears wide open here
Who wants to see me shed a tear
Let it all go, I hear each day
But in my shoes not one are they

So hard to understand one's self
Suggestions stacking on the shelf
Keep to yourself and then maybe
An answer will come you can see

Each one of us UN-perfect still
Like Jack and Jill tumbling downhill
The time we almost reach the peak

And think finding what we all seek

Within grasp but it is too steep
Need a life in four by four jeep
That time we find we all are weak
Truly Bless-ed are the meek

Inherit Earth someday they will
Without the need to hunt or kill
These words and lines I write each night
Re-engage my faith in the light

Liz 0

Two hours now until we meet
I can't imagine oh how sweet
Just like every beauty queen
Your soft brown hair smelling so clean

Wonderful curves you understate
Your beauty seems to reactivate
Me from my so complacent mood
No more lingering in solitude

Open arms hold me close and tight
Make me feel safe in darkest night
And smiles that spark my soul aflame
All thoughts come down to just your name

Luck, Fate and Time seem to align
To form a glaring radiant sign
A path to follow with a clue
Which points me only onward to you

Your lucent dreams keep me aware
That this could be false, nothing there
If so I pray you never wake
So we can have and eat our cake

Purest intentions all I am
Show myself flat with a diagram
Just read me as you would a book
Careful underline don't overlook

All done right now maybe too late
When only night of our first date
I end this poem for you my dear
Hoping the rhyme was clear to hear

Liz 1

Don't get sick
Sinus
Just a cold
As I

Your voice lingers
In my ears
As a soft song
Loud and clear

Miss you already
Only a day
Keep on wondering
What is in store

My good expectations
Seem nothing for you
Like clockwork so perfect
Fantasy come true

Will the ride be short or long
Or the road be bumpy
Can it be so great as seems
Or will phantasms fade

Don't know what will make you happy
Enough to stay with just me
But I'm thinking always of us
Praying for some remedy

Prefer by I a crystal skyline
That grows straight to oblivion
Walk side by side holding hands tightly
Eyes and smiles locked with face to face

Each touch more sacred than the first one
Rubbing her back with slow strong hands
As she tired I continued as asked
Increasing joy each moment there

No need to hurt one another
Experience tells us that
Understanding like no other
She matches me nicely

A true dream before my eyes
Must be myself all times
Her loving soul draws me back
To a new paradise

Familiar de-JA-vu
Of my happy state
Willing to wait always
If it's meant by fate

Best kiss on the earth
So intimate
Reality gone
While visiting

Night passes by
Smile concrete
Looking onward
Trick or treat

Tomorrow
We talk
And go out
For fun

Liz 2

To be perfectly honest
Her opinion only encourages
Because I feel exactly the same
Wondering what is in store
It really is true that life is painful
People always get hurt somehow
The question is who and when
Unless you finally meet your match
I don't believe in perfect people
Just ideal situations and mutuality
No doubt a difficult task I take
But I will wait until I break
Each moment that passes is gone
Hazy memories never do justice
Seize the day was a good idea
But I want to seize my whole life
My subjective outlook is still mine
And the inner voices all say yes
While my mind sits in disbelief
Waiting for my infinite cycle
Happiness, Serenity on the way
Pain and Chaos left in the path
Tattoo maybe true does not dictate
Reality never set easily on a plate
For a change I know just how I feel
But time is on my side right now
I don't wish her to fall for me blindly
It must involve love to be correct
Feelings no doubt are dually present
I only need a door unlocked
To attempt to fill the void he left
In your oh so damaged heart
But wait I shall for revolutions
Of planets all from near to far
Because just like a fortune cookie
No one knows the way you are
...Unless you are opened up

More wonderfuls in one week
Than I have ever heard before
Encourages me to seek
One that could knock me to the floor

I would respond automatically
And rise with my permanent smile
You can't hurt me sporadically
Runners high from my mile

I've climbed up roads so tall
They seemed to be vertical
And now I refuse to fall
Going unidirectional

CRASH BANG BASH
GOT WHIPLASH
ONLY PART DONE
LOST IS THE FUN

Dived face first into a wall
No way to climb it much too high
And after the initial fall
I'm scared I may be much too small

Scamper off like a rodent
Scared of the inevitable sting
Of barbed wire and electricity
The baggage that you must bring

Just once simple would be nice
But I have not yet found the price
How much can I sacrifice
Before my body turns to ice

Liz 4

Maybe I need to sit down and rethink a minute
About what exactly it is that I want in this world
The things I have and already take for granted
And all that is out there within grasp and effort

I don't want to be a pill junkie for the rest of life
I do want to have a family and children someday
More than all I want to feel loved by an outsider
By anyone who just reciprocates my own sacrifice

Maybe my tendency, but no more get walked over
Letting a wind current decide my mood for the day
Plant myself on solid reality for a gigantic change
And let emotions just flow without reaction

I feel like I need an advisor so I don't step off
The narrow edge of manic-ness and depression
For the first time the anger is subsiding back
So I can really see how dependent I have become

A smile from anyone is worth ten thousand of mine
And locking eyes seems to be almost orgasmic
Luck be on my side in this crusade for self-discovery
And may she be hand and hand on the way

Liz 5

Oh how I would love to know what you are thinking
Just so I can stop all this Piscean need to be loved
I am very confused sometimes when you choose
A friend over me assuming that I am all right

I don't understand how this is fair at all
When you seem to have total control
But I asked for it by giving you some freedom
So I could at least hold on to you a few more days

I figured your being so equal and giving

Protected would be I from self-doubt because involved
But more like walked over in some ways
Although I have to admit I am happy as always

I am just afraid I am going to get crushed
Every day with her is a massive step up
But each day without is hurting me a bit
Maybe I should already ask for a commitment

Seems way too soon, she could be a reason to stay here
Otherwise I'm sure my dad will come first back home
But love is not something easily attained this way
And I know he would not want me to give up

For her I would attempt anything imaginable
But it would be useless if I had to ask her
Why can't I just learn that I can't do it
I cannot predict the future

I cannot read people's minds, only manipulate

Liz 6

3 and 7 are important in the Bible
Although 3 is sometimes good like
3 kings, 3 days-Easter-etc....
7 is sometimes 7th day-rest
Unfortunately this is not all accurate
3 is the number of times Judas cheated
On the Lord before the third call of rooster
3 can be an evil number too
3rd strike you're out, only second chances
Perhaps being born in March, 3 is my destiny
But when I hear the same excuse three times
I begin to wonder if she is really worth waiting for
I am doing nothing but second guessing myself
Which could lead to a greater understanding
That is if I were to figure out or guess
Why I am being avoided like the plague
I remember making the decision friends first

Well I don't want to impose and make you feel needed
But there is more than your one helpless friend
And he sits around waiting for you to talk to
For three nights he has been hoping the two could talk
But it just seems like something always gets in the way
And I am not about to beg for affection and attention
Like the little girl reaching out in so many ways
I wish you could figure out what I did long ago
Helping only helps if the person is trying
When they choose to remain helpless and self-pitying
Nothing anyone can say or do will bring them back
Being left alone is perhaps the best thing to do
So she can reassess her place in the world
And start giving a little more than taking
You are being brought down by her, like it or not
I don't know you or her too well and I don't have to
I have been there on both sides many times
I understand the best way to solve a problem is alone
I understand the only path of change is through me
I understand that bitching and talking don't always work
I understand that it sometimes takes more than an ear

Liz 7

I cant think a bit to write
Maybe I should fly a kite
But its raining out tonight
Lightning could decide to strike
And just having that thought
Would make it just more likely
Than the 1 in 50,000 people
Chance of me being stricken
So I waited a few days
And now I'm ready to write
Fuck flying a kite
Too cold outside now on strike
What this most likely originated as
Was a way to escape the reality of her
And right now although I know it could work
My self-prophecies will likely come true

I hate this shit about willing things to happen
In a lot of ways that makes me almost telepathic
Except more in a mind control brainwashing
Just determining a certain fate for relationships
Seeing any idea just once in my head
Can forever grab control of my reality
Unless I have people to talk to sometimes
That is what I am really interested in
She seems to be almost sexually ready
After I confirm with a passing test grade
But I can't do it without any commitment
I like her too much already right now
She is so emotionally stuck and maybe
She likes to concentrate her energies one at a time
So that problems do get solved and someday
I will make myself known as a problem
...somehow
The only thing is that I don't wanna be a problem
I just want her to get unstuck off her friend for me
I am just a selfish bastard who wants a lot beginning
In something unlabeled that may turn out nothing
...but I try

Liz 8

Now when we talk
It's of questions past
Do you really think
That is what we are now?

Just the sum history
Of what we have done
Without adding the kinetic
Potential for one hardworking human soul

To me seems endless
Possibilities galore for us
But each add restrictions
That tangle the path

If I can feel you from more than
One hundred miles away
You therefore are important
To me in many ways

Scared at the thought
Monday was goodbye
Yet excited in hope
It was much more

No glasses to help
Or computer to check
But I miss you so much
I figured what the heck

Old fashioned isn't dead
So fuck all the critics
God is my judge
All be an objective mix

Liz 9

Well that didn't take too long
And my self prophecies came true
Time to go back to the bong
And in school somehow renew
The avoidance for three days
Was such a bad sign that I saw
But to hear it in just one phrase
Was like a hard punch in my jaw
Maybe my pride, self-concept
Wherever it hit reverses me
No I will be effortless with perfection
Now I can succeed at failing
Too bad that isn't an option
I must graduate and go home
To take care of my dad and fam
To keep hope alive for someone
Because here I am no one's crutch
I don't feel like I'm fulfilling potential

I feel like a burnt out sick of college
I'm ready for a new life without school
I don't want these boundaries holding me
Keeping me from taking more chances
I need a week job with nights and weekends free
I need a place where I can really be me
Stop your bitching for just a minute
To realize there is no decision to be made
It has been formalized by her now
No questions left to wonder about
I knew she wasn't ready from the start
But I tried to force her into submission
My manipulation caused her to cheat
And realize I am just another Joe
Saddest when this happens to me
In comparison with others I become pale
I wonder if she slept with him
Numbing my sense of being a male

Liz 10

Today when going through the routine
I noticed something that had not been
I had an electronic message from a person
Not some company out to sell services
Or products-or whatever

The letter was from Elizabeth, wondering
If I hate her and if not to write back
What if I do, could I be so bold as to not
Return a message left by someone hurting
Or thinking-or whatever

I sent the regular nice response by the book
So much practice lying about my dad
To all teachers about his phone calls
So I can just be away from school
Or Liz-or whatever

Told her I was ready to talk immediately
If that was what she wished for
And that I have been thinking a lot
And that none of this is her fault
Or my fault-or whatever

I don't know what I believe anymore
And there is bad luck starting Halloween
So I think I'd rather just sit on this idea
And deal with the email as she responds, good
Or bad-or whatever

Love letter

Too much time has gone by
Since the last time you said goodbye
I miss your sweet touch, your
Cool words, and most of all
I miss being close to you
While you were here it
Was as if time flew
But now that you're gone
It has come to a dead stop
Please don't let it end here
Come back. I long for
Our conversations, for our dances,
For our smiles
I love you
O please

Marry me

I hope you see
I will not be
Walking away
I'm here to stay

I know I'm free
But I can't flee

Only display
From day to day

All honesty
And sympathy
Bring a bouquet
Displace your gray

Pure bravery
Some flattery
Meet you half way
With all foreplay

Compulsively
Monogamy
Ask if you may
Be fiancée

Masks

Pretty face masks person inside
For those who use it as a guide
Not long before one has lied
Leading to another divide
Hard to find the inward side
Someone to whom good rules abide
A creature with nothing left to hide
Truthful and never tongue-tied
In this one you can confide
And end the search so far and wide
Live happily because you both have tried
And smile until the day you've died

Me

Chris
Be blunt
Be yourself
Describe what you find beautiful

Tell how you feel
How every women has at least one quality that turns you on
Almost all of them
How most also turn you off
The decision of who to chase and date
How much a smile can mean
How you see more with your eyes closed sometimes
How noise can be soothing because you're not alone

<u>Megan</u>

I email but you never return
I cannot phone because 'twould burn
A hole inside me for promise broke
To sister who thinks that I'm a joke

How can I make this message clear
I had good intentions and no fear
But I'm left here in the dark
Envisioning the worst a dog could bark

For one white lie I pay this much
For one mistake I cannot touch
Or mend or sew or even stitch
As long as I'm just some old bitch

Knocking hard on doors to reopen
Something that we had was broken
Envision from my point of view
How everything I'm left with blue

Surrounding me and making mess
Of my last semester to be my best
Nothing ever works out for me
Maybe I should just crawl up a tree

To be forgotten and long past
And watch you walk across the grass
Picking flowers dancing in the rain
Till the day I see you go down the drain

Megan 2

I just don't want to talk to you anymore
You let me get my foot in and shut the door
You call me manipulative just like your sis
When I try only to be friendly and all is amiss

Your words sting like tacks and your tone is unfair
Why should I be the one left with all this to bear
We started on a bad foundation, this is all too true
But second chances seem to be a foreign concept to you

How the fuck do you expect me to figure it out
Like I'm some kind of psychic without a doubt
I can't read your mind or thoughts and if I could
I'm sure I would just see how immature you stood

Cutting me off like I'm some kind of disease
Without even the courtesy to say goodbye please
Smash me down like a roach that you can smear
And then expect me to just disappear

I've been here four years and I'm not done yet
If its a fight you want then its a fight you'll get
And I'll make you really wish you never met me
When I'm through with you, vengeance is all that you'll see

Life is a bitch and sometimes much worse
I cannot begin to explain in this verse
But I refuse to just stand here and act like I'm dead
Because you made the mistake of inviting me to bed

Take responsibility for one's actions and do not place blame
Because I feel all right with myself and you're full of shame
I'm glad we talked and both overreacted
Now from my life you have been subtracted

Megan 3

Time is on your side
With many things left to do
A decision to make
A choice that is up to you
Friends we are now
And forever we will be
Nothing less, nothing more
Until you make up your mind
You have my love
You have my trust
You have my respect
I have all of these from you
In my opinion
But to be safe
Lets have you decide that for me
I think you love me
But it is not for me to think
It is for me to know
By proof
Your proof, your words, your heart
Tell me how you feel
Look within, you know
I need to know
So I can have a fucking life!
No,
So I can love you even more
I miss you - come b a c k
You're s t r e t c h i n g farther away every day
CLOSER
Now

Megan 4

I don't know
Why I can't see
Just how perfect
Life can be
Each time we meet

Face to face
My heart beats faster
In a chase
To meet with yours
On solid ground
Halfway and equal
Our feelings not bound
No string nor chain
To hold us back
Feelings flow freely
We are tired of waiting
Just let me in
Trust me, no fear
Love me, no regrets
I fell in love with you
In the seas of feeling I see in your eyes
Please look for that in me
I will wait an eternity and beyond
For one moment of your love
Until then
No regrets still
Do nothing without purpose
Only wait
I wait forever
For you

Megan 5

Your fear
I will conquer
All walls
I can climb
Your limits
I will respect
Your love
I can gain
The time
Could be forever
To last only
One second

It would
be worth it
Anything for
You
Forgive and Forget
The hardest thing to do
Is nothing for me
You cannot hurt me
I love you

Megan 6

For years I have been sleeping
In a pool of sin just weeping
The secrets I would not tell anyone
Your whisper awoke me like a daisy in the sun
Your voice rang true like a great bell ringing
The words you speak like angels singing
Messages floating down from above
Beginning the moment I first fell in love
Freely flowing thoughts down a river of wine
What is mine is yours, What is yours is mine
Everything I am belongs to you
And you in turn, belong to me too
From your sweet lips the sounds you speak
Each carrying me to my highest peak
While dreaming still guided by that beautiful voice
I love you so much that there is no choice
Seconds now drift by so very fast
Moments with you should forever last
I wish that I could find a way
To make time stop for just one day
Enter into an enchanted kingdom to be free
And sit alone together, just you and me
Everyday with you is a priceless work of art
One the tender canvas of my heart
I love you

Megan 7

98

Tears rolling down my cheek
Reflect the fantastic life I've had
Lost in a point of view
I will never be found

Silence is what my listening picks up
Utter quiet and wind blowing
The end is near
Sleep will begin and never end

I cannot be happy without the God that loved me once
And with Him I would still betray
What has happened to me?
Am I gone or here

This is all just an illusion
I am being toyed with
Fuck, I want to die
Help

I feel a pain in my neck
It is yearning for the bullet
I need to end it
Why, why can't I?
What is left...
Love?

Megan 8

I lie
I am so afraid
Maybe it's not fair
I will never let you go
I can see that now
No circumstances could change the way I feel
Nothing, even death or supernatural could end this
Everlasting, love for eternity and beyond
I say
Friends are okay

Spend time with them
Don't bother explaining
I understand
Lies
All their lies!
I don't understand
I sit waiting for you
You may wait for me while I'm at work
I don't know
I am so damn selfish
I need you

Megan 9

You are the light
Or a candle
That could go out
Yet I lie in darkness
Hot wax burns my skin
Like slow tears falling
From your face
I am in a box
6 feet under
Worms devour my flesh
Yet your touch is so powerful
That flowers grow
out of my chest
Why? Why? Why?
Help me Megan
I can't do this
Our feelings are so difficult
Yet we are so awhile
I love you
Can't you see that
Humor me
I don't ask for much
Just a little compassion
Your voice, your touch
Or even just your company
Come over now
Or I fear

The flowers
Will just be thrown on the ground, while me 6 feet under

Melissa

With someone from work never try to date
It may turn the relationship from love to hate
On this particular instance the words we can't share
Make it hard on everyone with a job there

The rule I have broken more than one time
And this is too much, a horrendous crime
All out in the open our business becomes rumor
Things develop at light speed that could doom her

Gone in a flash without looking back
I move away running ahead of the pack
Never hearing nor seeing the mess that I make
Because lust isn't love, it was only a fake

Some say too young, or too immature
Well it takes two, and never fewer

Melissa 2

All that you've done
I could care less
No more time for fun
You left me a mess

It's over here and now
No way I'm looking back
To see some ridiculous bow
Proud you are of what you lack

Thoughts of you occur but I block
Keeping my eyes set on future
I threw away the key to the lock
Passed over and forgotten murmur

Don't you touch my cock much too bold
You fucking whore of a girl witch
So loose at only sixteen years old
What the fuck is wrong with you bitch

Time to find a new friend
From whom you can take all
Now time to end this pretend
Away with cover not crawl

See you never
Were all at end
Wish you were clever
Enough to start then

Missing Pieces

So it's broken again
The wrinkled tape
And crusty superglue
Are no longer holding me together
Each and every crack
Is like a seam slowly being torn open
Letting more and more of me seep out
Through the inflating crevices
I seem to be unraveling
Making a mess of myself
No more layers left to peel off
Just a barren lifeless heap remains
Left here, walls down, helpless
Start to pick up the pieces
Someday they might get in place
To be reinforced with stronger tape

Mom

Forever working
To make me happy

Sacrificing whatever it takes
To see me smile
Through hell and back
Almost everyday
Works every waking moment
No time to rest
The love she gives
Is unconditional

Moments

These happy moments are the ones I dread
I can't write, I can't think
I can only smile
What good is that
A useless expression for no one to see
Except myself in a mirror that
Breaks every time I look at it
I pretend to be sad
I pretend to have inspiration
It's not really worth it
So I just wait in this room
Attempting to brainstorm, to perform
my task, to get anything written
Just empty smiles
Happiness is so overrated

More than a Girlfriend

K
You're not just another date
another fling, just a girl
You are real
Feelings, thoughts, ambitions, dreams
More like me than you or I know
You are special
Special because I really love you
Not the word Love
Not the physical love

The love you feel all over
the pain that intensifies the further apart we get
The butterflies in my stomach tingly feeling
The laughing for no reason except for joy
I want to spend the rest of my life with you
You, my blond haired, blue eyed beauty
My 90 pound. bundle of happiness
My K
I love you

Move on

I am all by myself
As I've always been
Please don't wait for me
It would be a sin
The secrets I will keep
Nothing left to say or do
So let the sadness come
I give my heart to you
Until the day I die
Close your eyes and breathe
You broke my heart in two
I will train myself to be alone
Don't wait for me
Say goodbye

My Little Teddy

I need a teddy bear
To let out my anger
Always Smiling
No matter What

Fists and Blood
And still that smile
Anger and Sadness
No change occurs

You feel better
And teddy waits
You grow up
And rid yourself of teddy

You feel angry
You feel sad
No teddy bear
You kill yourself

The problems end
The anger ends
The sadness ends
Death is final

The teddy moves on...

My Muse

My eyes rarely see tears
Because of my immunity to the world
But she was a shortcut
To get by my wall
She has a key to my gate
And the combination to my lock
She is the answer to my question
And the hardness on my cock
She makes sense of madness
And knows the way in the dark
Her voice rings soft and true
When she speaks the words I love you

Necklace 1

Looking back it's funny
How I don't remember how many
loves or girlfriends I've had
But I remember how many time I've been dumped
With this one everything was great

My first time making-out, two months gone by
And a week, one week since the gift
A gold necklace that ended it all
Engraved with "I love you"
I don't think I did
But it felt good
Until that day
I had called twice
Then she returned my phone call
She said she had met someone
She told me it was over
The next swim meet
My friend brought me back the box
Dark green and cotton filled
With a necklace resting in it

Necklace 2

I have so many friends
This is so great
Everyone likes me
I feel like God
I am the only one old enough to drive
I call them, they don't call me
I listen while they complain
I stick out like an erection
I tell myself it's all right
Just their way of friendship
But what they are smoking tells me
This is just a phase for them
I want a girlfriend, a relationship
I need to talk sometimes
But when they have nothing left to say
They leave me, without anyone in the world
I open my green box with cotton
Take out the "I love you" pendant
And open it, an in the place of
A picture I neatly write " no one"

Necklace 3

After many failed attempts
There she is, a new face
A new life, a new love
More like another lie
She was very beautiful
translation-large chest
Within one week we
Were ready to get it on
I told her "I love you"
From that moment on I knew
It's all lies
I didn't feel anything inside
Just a hard-on in my pants
We almost had sex - but didn't
Thank God
I gave her the pendant, with the box
And the "I love you" but
Without the "no one"
She really loved me
Then I broke it off
It didn't work
Am I incapable of love?
The broken hearted continue the cycle
Breaking more hearts
I made her keep the necklace
To keep the lie alive

Never Permissible

Lying is never permissible
When in love with the receiver
Just loving a person
Is not as important
And lying can be permissible
However when in love
Lying is a break of basic trust
And doing so will bring ruin
The guilt for some

Overcomes them so they self-destruct
Or being a basic down-set
That destroys the magic

Never Right

The moments that seem to be fleeting
Are the ones I miss the most
Where my assumptions seemed correct
Because of a deep emotional fog
Not too many like me in the world
Radically Liberal and understanding
Easily taken advantage of by others
While still great at manipulation
It sucks to know about the enemy
But be the last one to find them
When it is absolutely crucial
I bend and break at all joints helpless
I would have made such a good soldier
Walking mindless like a robot forward
Taking orders like they were biblical
Being controlled by others is nice
I wish I was a child again, no money
No worries, no doubts, no fears
I would try so much harder this time
To make my sister feel very happy
The love would shine bright at home
And all the romances I botched
All the words I mistakenly said
Wiped from the slate without my memories
God, I wish I could say no regrets
But life is almost a regret in some ways
My initial goals set a little high up
Damned if I won't try forever
But they can't be reached with hands
And they can't be reached with brains
Technology is not the key
And science only bothers me with complexity
I might make it there someday
But that would just be an illusion

I can't do it by myself
And I don't believe in God

Never Enough

The roses were never fresh enough
When I bought them for you
And the chocolate was never sweet enough
To be touching your lips
But the bullshit layered quickly
Without us reaching each other enough
Time got slow and boring again
And neither one of us was happy enough

So I took off for a new queen
Looking each and every single way
To find myself some true queen
Lying beside me every single day
When I found her she was alone
Could she be one and only queen
Or just another layer of bullshit
To mud-mask up her face the queen

Never know because I gave up
And just went back to leading myself
I tried so hard but then gave up
And my blood began to flow again
I became centered back in space
Looking back often but then gave up
And now finally happy I
Am very glad that I gave up

New Start

Finally its over
Got back the CD
This last link over
Now past takes a rest
And another one _

OKAY Computer
Oh how I love it
Things turn out for best
Didn't respond to
Her vicious email
At least didn't send
It for her to read
Just response for me
Writing down the words
I felt at the time
To remind me K
Of you and yours
That I can be used
That I am confused
But now a new start
I cannot think of you
Once or twice a day
Since resolution
Has been met by both
Leaving this school soon
Only a few months
Till you disappear
From real life and not
Just my headaches gone
Louder the music
From my stereo disc
Already taking
The space you reserved
So much more freedom

Newbie

A newbie is someone new
To a game or other thing
At least they appear that way
Until you get to know them

Then newbie status disappears
And they become some relation
Either friend or foe, acquaintance or one-time only
If we match maybe a lover - the one

Sometimes things really work
And both feel the energy between
Either good or bad, long-lasting or short
But it exists nevertheless

Too late to comprehend early
Feelings that have been present
From the first meeting of the two
Until the last encounter or union

Then too late to turn around
Past set in stone like a published book
Forever the same always
The way time keeps moving along

Mistakes made are lessons
And two-gather learn about life
But how awesome is a newbie
Before you find all this out

A new soul you know nothing about
Without pre-judgment and hypothesis
To just let it all go and be yourself
And see what is in store for you

Almost as if you have a foretold future
People come in and out of your life
But the one stays forever with you
And it may be the newbie you just met

No realism

How can I escape from all this self pity
Have I ever been this bad before, why?
Everyone tells me I look horrible...
And it is so very true - because I don't eat

Every time something close to good happens
It evaporates before I can truly appreciate

111

Or worse I do fall lovely asleep to a nightmare
Why does this seem to be my pre-ordainment

I try to convince myself that I'm alright
But lying is no longer in my nature
The new vulnerable person has emerged
As defenseless as a cocoon waiting for hatch

Hey maybe things will change soon for the best
But as a Pisces I think more likely for the worst
These last months have reborn a pessimist
There is no realism or reality anywhere

THE WORLD WILL NEVER BE FAIR

Not Smiling

I have nothing to look forward to
So I am not smiling
Is that so hard to understand?
Would you prefer me to be fake
To just pretend to be happy
So that you don't have to see the real me
All I can do is worry
Too many looming problems
And responsibilities I can't complete
Getting too sick of this repetition
This stupid schedule that repeats
Week after week after week
When will something new come?
I'm going stir-crazy from the monotony
And I need to find the answers
Questions that I can't forget
Always running through my head
Why can't I find a solution
Guess I'll just keep wandering
Alone, Bewildered, and Tired
Waiting for it all to end

Nothing

You care
You love
They care
They love
-Nothing
You care
You love
They don't care
They don't love
-Pain
You don't care
You don't love
They care
They love
-Jealousy
You don't care
You don't love
They don't care
They don't love
-Happiness

Nothing Matters

Do you really have any feelings
I think its all just talk
When you are in trouble who do you depend on
Yourself?   God?
Not your so-called friends
They are useless
Do you help anyone else
No, you just keep bringing them to conclusions
That they already knew
Nothing you say matters
Except to you
You tell me you want to talk
But then sit back and listen to me go into lectures
Until I get bored of my own repeating voice echoing into the nothingness
You did not ever want to talk

Just to listen to everyone else
Until they bored you with their pathetic lives
Until you were finished using them
And ready to move on to your next victim
You are so selfish

Once More

I just asked a girl out
And she said yes excitedly
It feels good to have a date
And something to look forward to
Last night while trying to study
We talked for a few hours
And I think we are totally compatible
She seems like a real giver
I have not met any females
That impressed a giving sense on me
From the beginning at least
And she definitely is very empathetic
Nice to have someone with a need
To help others so willingly
Her friend's phone call convinced me
She is definitely a wonderful person
Right now I have no idea what will happen
But I hope we will end up together
Today I found out she is the same sign
As my mother and sister - strange coincidence
I really identify with my mother completely
But she is totally an introvert and different
Yet my sister is also in the group
And she is extroverted and wild
I know this Saturday will be an adventure
Maybe dinner, a drive, movie, and talking
Lots of talking is the most important thing
When getting to know someone new
I bet without my medication I would be jumping
Because this is the best I've felt in weeks
But on my small scale of emotions I'm peaking
And that is great all by itself
No judgments or pre-conceived notions

One

My tears of blood slowly float
Down the stream of my cheek
Faster and faster they flow
To the waterfalls of the weak
Strong could never describe me
I am but a humble slave
Whose wishes are overlooked and forgotten
Whose actions are anything but brave
I quietly sit back alone
Alone like a dying flower petal without the
light
My lips as rough and cold as rock
My heart has shattered and broken tonight

One Last Kiss

I am going on a journey
The destination is nowhere
The reason is you
Life is just not fair

Goodbye to my memories
I cannot love anymore
I must leave forever

My lips are hurting and yearning
For contact one last time
I love her but I must die
For the blood leaves as I speak

Forgive me if you wish
Or don't, how can I care
In nowhere
But just one last kiss

One week

So fast emotion caught no time to react...write

She has just told me it cannot work
We have known each other one week
Yet My feelings for her overshadow years

Feelings change and must because
Time is the ultimate test of life

Her friend is a place I'm welcome and
I accept it with extreme pleasure

I imagine having a vivid dream of someone
As you have spoken of about me
And I know we were completely real
Endings don't always mean never

We can both move on and learn
And teach one another as friends
This is just a new beginning
It could never be our ends

I love you in an honest way
As a friend is where you'll stay

I accept all apologies but feel no need
For life is by definition changing

For the immediate now it cannot work
We have known each other one week
Yet the Possibilities exist for years

Some feelings caught written...done

Over You

It might have taken more than four months
But now I am finally over you

Today would have been our twenty-six month anniversary
But I don't give a shit
I'm glad that we are through
Now I can move on to better things
Without your annoying little nags
And pathetic pleas for attention
When I think of your name
I get sick to my stomach
It would be better if you disappeared
Cause I never want to see you again
Your childish ideas I have outgrown
And your face no longer makes me smile
It might have taken more than four months
But now I am finally over you

Picket Fences

How she could give me a second chance
Blows my mind after first romance
But I know as sure as rain
That she remembers all the pain

Still willing to look me face to face
She has no idea of my disgrace
Of all the women since her leave
I've managed to get up their sleeve

Can it be that each person that I loved
Took part of my heart replacing it shoved
I fall right back into the same place
Years past but still that beautiful face

Her hugs are like blankets keeping me close
Her kiss more sweet than any glucose
Reemerge this wonder and excite
That used to keep me up all night

Talking for hours about nothing
Just to hear each other's voice
Maybe magic is a choice
And this one will be the Rolls-Royce

Picky

The ones I choose are never nice
Never made from sugar and spice
And ever so I continue the same
The stupid lust has become a game

The one I want needs only like me
Like my lock can be opened with any key
Each one taking their little piece
Until one day I just release

Without a heart to hold me back
From being what I think most lack
Becoming stereotypical in my sex
Then I can start creating wrecks

Those around me smothered down
Feelings nonexistent give me a crown
To be the king of all bad males
Starting by hurting each female

Why can't I be picky and know what I like
Take these training wheels off my bike
Regardless who's next I may just assume
That they would cut out my heart with a spoon

Pictures

A reminder
A dream
Fading Thoughts
New Ideas
A beautiful face
Nothing
Colors on paper
representations
No limits
No expectations

Pisces

Maybe the reason us Pisces have problems
Is because fishing is not easy for fish
Friends I can find with no troubles
But lovers are never a dime a dish

To lure them in to my pond
Do I need some other bait
How hard can it be to find one
Willing to be my soul-mate

Harder and harder it gets each year
Trying less and less I think
The depression has got me quitting
And alcohol seems like a good drink

But from sadness comes another
The one for the time being
A perfect image I uncover
Never before sight-seeing

How easy it is to fall for one
The first one you catch sometimes
When if you'd try to have fun
You'd had gotten past the slimes

Miscommunication is the key
Not a complication that occurs
When two people so free
Become a mess of just blurs

Moments frozen in memory
Each one occasionally surfaces
To remind me of the misery
Of feeding the rat bread and honey
So it would come back once more
To bite me in the hand

Planned Pregnancy

Why do we always use this term
Planned Pregnancy
Majority are not married
And it's not planned

Perhaps the greatest loss is in
The momentous question
Is death a fair term for two weeks
Into the pregnancy

Is anyone careful ever
I doubt it somehow
Pulling out, out-dated by far
Use protection please

Population control like some
Is not a bright picture
Condoms and pills used more equals
Less homeless and abused

Pointless People

Am I saying something you don't want to hear
Or is it something you already know
Would you rather be out having a beer
Are you really a friend or a foe
You ask me how I'm doing
And then you walk away without hearing my response
It just makes me want to hit you
And when you're forced to stay around
Ignoring me seems to work
My Motto!
If you don't want to know; don't ask
If you don't have any; don't offer
And if your an asshole, don't talk to me
I've got my own ass to talk to
When I don't need a response

Punching Bag

If it makes you feel good to hate me
Then hate me all you can
Because it is not my intention to hurt you
Pretend I am a punching bag
Redirect every bad thing in your life unto me
Make a target of my picture
Pretend your pillow is my body and rip it
If that really makes you feel better
It's OKAY with me
I really care about you
If you don't want to believe it, that's your choice
And you are choosing wrong
Believe me, you're not perfect
No one is or will they ever be
Just stop telling me everything is OKAY
When I can see a fire in your eyes
And a hiss in your voice
Don't be a hypocrite
Don't hide behind your friends
They will not protect you from me
If I wanted to hurt you, it would be worse
Just learn to live with it
We were not meant for each other
I am through playing games
Do what you must
Just get it over with

More Qualifications for that Perfect Day

After 3 days of waiting your female date breaks up with you
She has cheated on you over the break
Ending your last perceivable link to this place
You now know your only place to live is home
The family was depressing because mom nagged me
I don't ever want to hear pot or alcohol from her again
Have broken down and told at least 3 friends the story
When I could have just written it out like now
Their self-pity refreshes daily reminders of my state

I lost my 1st pair of contacts the day I got them
Smoking like I don't have a minute to lose
Feeling school float away at a glance
Knowing I will pass going freelance
Makes it hard to concentrate at all
And these new meds are spinning me towards fall
Only destined to double in two weeks
Where I will feel reality begin to cease
Your damn mail order piece didn't arrive
And the ones that did are somewhat lame
Bills have doubled since last I checked
And I have no job at all with my car wrecked
Need to make a dollar here and there
So that I can survive this huge scare

Rachel

Why are you never busy
Just sitting and waiting
Like the only thing you need
In the world is me
A phone call or visit
Just makes your day
Can't you find someone else
To do it for you
I can't take this
Your high maintenance friendship
Always angry with me
When you never called
I must initiate it all
Otherwise it's not perfect
It's not what you need
For your little dream world
I have other friends
My life revolves around me
Please stop dreaming
About being with me
I am not a Romeo
And if I were
You would not be Juliet

R K

From the moment we met
Till the moment you left
I truly learned the definition
Of the word Love
Each moment I spent with you
Brought me to a happiness
I seldom could find
From just one person
Sitting on my birthday
You gave me the best present
And it only grew and grew
And continues too with you away
My nights spent trying to sleep
In a bed where we slept
Lying awake and wondering
Where you are right now
My body is longing for the warmth
You gave me every night
And my lips miss the softness
Of your skin and your ears
I miss your personality the most
The long intelligent conversations
The beautiful smiles and eyes
Your attention and your love
I can still smell your hair
When I concentrate on you
Walking alone on the street
My hand feels empty without yours
Everyday seems an eternity
As I mark it off the calendar
Waiting for the day that
You will be back here with me
I have never been so in love
As I am with you, Rachel
My life will always be better
Knowing that you are alive
A person as awesome as you
Gives me hope that someday

I might actually meet
The perfect person for me

R K2

The roses were never fresh enough
When I bought them for you
And the chocolate was never sweet enough
To be in your mouth
So I chose not to waste money
On those frivolous gifts for you
Saving instead all of my money
To pay the rent for us
We seemed happy enough when you left
I was very thrilled for you
Away to Europe when you left
You spoke to me seldomly
I soon got the impression we were only to be friends
But I kept up relations with you
You must think we cannot be friends
I have not heard from you yet
Not what your back my anger builds daily
Heart-broken by the closeness of you
Too often your picture seems to appear daily
In the frame at the back of my mind
Forgetting you seems quite impossible
And our first kiss and our first fuck
That's only a joke you bitch
Your been forgotten, and left in your ditch
Getting rid of you has given me luck

Rebecca

You mean a lot to me Rebecca
In many different ways
You are a prefect without a Replica
When I'm with you I'm so much fun
You are my cure for insomnia
On all my sleepless days

You're the center of my nebula
You heat me in the sun
Your voice is like an opera
That I always come to see
I want to solve your formula
And make it part of me
You always rock my Kasbah
And know how to make me laugh
I feel safe in your aura
Invincible to others wrath
I want to be on your peninsula
So that you're always close by
And to take your picture with a camera
To cheer me up when I cry
You are an exceptional phenomena
That I can't live without
Being with you is a Utopia
And I am sure without a doubt
Rebecca, I really like yah

Redecorating

I walk into a room
And realize I don't belong
Time to change the background
Redecorating must begin
All the memories stuck to the walls
Go into an old shoebox
Many of them I don't remember every happening
But the picture just fills my head with memories
Finished taking down everything I think about
What to put back up
Music, Posters, pictures, Memories
No, I'll just leave the walls white
Blank and Empty
Just like me

Reflection

I wish when I looked in a mirror
I saw something different
I am sick of the same old me
Unattractive, Bad Dressing, No hair Chris
It's so boring
Just like me
People like me when they meet me
I make a good 1st, 2nd, 3rd impressions
But when you get to know me
You see the real me
The one from the mirror
Not a disguise
Then they no longer like me
I lose all my friends
And I hope at the next first impression
things will be different
I wish nothing was in the mirror
But the wall behind me

Repeat

Trying not to fall in love is strange
I can't sing love, or mention the word
Nothing means as much
Confusion surrounds me like a pack of wolves
Slowly waiting to devour my mind
And stop my thoughts
Why think - Just be physical
This pressure from society pushes me to continue
Struggling and Fighting is no use
It is too strong
I will continue until I can do it no more
And then the cycle will repeat

Right Place

For the first time in a long time everything is in the right place
I have felt control in some way
Today life changed because of me
The only colors black and white
Too forward at first now shall unite
To create a semi-infinite gray without a definition of anything
Just two people interacting
Can be satisfying to tears
And too have done it alone I almost fear I am being cohesive
Maybe I in some way lied
Could I have used the situation
To form a compassion for the weak
Because I know she mends them
My father is very sick no doubt
And all my other words were true
But K gave me this idea that I take advantage of people
I can't get it out of my head
This constant self-checking
Am I being cohesive...?
And if so is it just a part of me?
I feel like I'm too elastic to get hurt
Each time I leap head first from high dive
Sometimes splash will scare her away
Sometime pool will be hard and empty
Always thinking - every moment forever -
"They" could be right in front of me
I think I picked this up from an old friend
Who had the idea to sleep with everyone, because it could be anyone
Never that brave or stupid and today I feel damn good
Having raised two situations today
To a much more acceptable level
Another moment in the brief history
Of my thoughts I've shared this night
Too tired for me to get you back there
Where you were a moment ago
By now you're bored and waiting
For the end of my writing
Praying that it doesn't go past this page

You're in luck for once - you kind genuine human organism with a soul
Time for me to get my eight hours

Satisfied

I am not satisfied
I tell the truth when I should have lied
Happiness was next door
But it was denied
No one answered my knock
I used to have secrets
But I chose people to confide
When I look back at them
I can only sigh
Sometimes I just want to
Fall down and die
I fear these days
Because I will never be...
Satisfied, goodbye

Scary

The suicidal thought is not far away
From this desk where I sit and decay
Much too close this game I play
Alone in darkness with dismay

So many ways it could be done
I don't wanna see the rise of sun
Just gimme some bullets and a gun
And then I'll end this night of fun

Such a sick joke I'm playing now
My life as frivolous as a cow
With all I have, think this how
Just a boy afraid to take a bow

Playing games with my head
Walking such a thin thread

Without water and bread
I may just end up dead

Seeing Past

You think that I can't live without you
But that is a fantasy not based on truth
Going on seems almost as easy
As meeting another person to replace
The space that I am going to erase

I'm not sorry at all for anything I spoke
Because you fucked me over in the bed
Going on seems almost as easy
As finding just another pretty face
To chase after on my new foot race

Go crawl back into the hole
That awful place where I offered my hand
Going on seems almost as easy
As pulling you up by your arm
No harm in trying to disarm

Someday I will look at you again
But we will both be dead and in hell
Going on seems almost as easy
As changing out my necklace charm
This farm thinks that you are a weed

Self-Pity

I can't stand it
Just bitch and complain
Why are you where you are?
Because you took steps to get there
When I ask a question
I want an honest and direct answer
Or an honest none of your business
None of this beating around the bush shit

If you make a choice that is wrong
That is cool as long as you take responsibility
Don't blame anyone else and most of all
Don't exaggerate the situation
It can and will get worse and better
That is the way life comes, in waves
When you force yourself onto a high wave
You must be ready to crash afterwards
I know sometimes I am guilty of it
But I don't blame anyone else
Usually I find other's excuses funny
Because no one was holding my hand
And no one was holding theirs either
You jump off the cliff completely alone
And if you don't wear a bungee cord
Then you die, its a fact - not an opinion
Certain things are this way in life
Black and white like I like them to be
Where I know a clear right and wrong
And then make my choice anyway
Gray areas really suck for perfectionists
Impossible to know exactly what to do
No set of directions on how to use or set up
The complicated circumstances one is in
Just hold on tight and enjoy the ride
Past is over and often forgotten
The memory you have is a conscious choice
Of only what you want it to be

Serene

When I stop looking it seems to just appear
But if I start off trying instigates response of fear
Why does it have to be by chance instead of planned on purpose
That I find a wonderful romance in the strangest circumstance
I project like a wide screen confusing some to see me clean
Neither of us needs a vaccine just to find a place serene
Like walking on melting ice to stay on this life raft
No one has the advice to help me escape witchcraft
Feelings that I can't explain bombard me from all sides

130

On this quest for Sarah tall and plain, Open eyed, Dissatisfied
Silly Love Song when I'm with you
With you alone all things I can do
Relaxed on my throne and with your friends
If you're there too, you watch over me
And I offer you plans infinite
Until we die together we stay
Without a goodbye so happy now
Tears slowly fall reminding me how
We met at the mall you cloud my head
Raining down love each day I thank God
Angel from above please do not blush
It is all true
I never tell lies when it comes to you

Sisters

Oh God, Oh God, what have I done
Last night was almost too much fun
Sisters a line I never crossed
But both secure with lovers lost
What a jerk I am for allowing this
Even once invited I should miss
Too much emotion packed inside
This crazy roller coaster ride
But worse still now I must admit
I loved every moment I could get
Now bowing to the goddess' dual
I ask forgiveness of broken rule
If ever one love should catch a hint
I fear my life could be hell bent
Should I run or shouldn't I hide
Or be up front and rules abide
Stranger still not one beating pulse
Of conscious hanging over impulse
Two beds I slept with no dismay
On a seven month holiday
So close those known only short time
I hope and dream this was no crime
My mind aloof with crazy thoughts

About each one I so besought
Time now unfair I slip away
To friendship basis faking gay
Hope no one else gets in on it
Our secret stoned overnight bit
Laughing about it seems so wrong
With two I don't know even day long
If I were they cry and me hate
For being such a fucking mate
True love almost blind to these eyes
I can't forget the last good-byes
Oh why do all infatuate
Perfect in thought incriminate

Sleep

I need more sleep
Than most people do
Because I have to forget
Everything I can
My mind is more tired
That my body can get
Of just thinking
Who I really am
The rest helps me relax
And see only dreams
Instead of the cold reality
I awake to the next day
Life is no fun
Working and Sleeping
Thinking and Dreaming
Living and Dying

Slithering

You are like a snake
With your hypnotic eyes
Gathering me close
To deliver the venomous bite

The longer I am with you
The more I need you
The worse the pain
Of your absence for short hours
Hours that could be used
To bring me joy
And to experience life
Are wasted
Longing for what I miss
For the injection of you
Into my veins
That I need to live
You are poison
And I need a tourniquet

Slut

My poetry comes from the heart
It is not something that can be heard
By just anyone who thinks I'm cool
Or can write a poem about me
It is a special form of communication
That is reserved for my loves
And since you are just writing words
That don't mean anything you are not one
You just fake to love me
When in reality you're a whore
Just a little girl that sleeps around
And thinks its OKAY
One day you will realize your faults
But it will be too late and you will
Catch some disease that is fatal
Hope that will teach you
You're just a slut
And you will never matter to anyone
Unless you take the time
To fall in love again

Something Bad

What the hell is the point of it all
I wake up - do whatever - and go to sleep
I in no way feel loved by anyone outside of my immediate family
No one calls...
No one writes...
I am in no way happy and I'm tired of trying to give the illusion that I am
I have basically no belief system
Most of my friends have grown up, gotten married, moved on
The ones that haven't
Only remind me of my failure so I don't want to see them
So I just sit here and think
Every day it gets a little bit worse
If I am not making anyone else happy or being happy then why am I here
Why do I have to continue if it is never going to be fair
In this great country I can't even commit suicide because it's illegal
Although I almost think
More people would be affected if I were dead than alive

Sometimes

Sometimes you are so cold
I feel like you're an iceberg
Sometimes your stories
Upset me like a sharp knife
Sometimes that warm smile
Seems cruel and sadistic
Sometimes you avoid conversation
And the silence is too much to bear
Occasionally you land the right comment
Ruined usually by the next
Occasionally my opinion is offered
Shot down perhaps with your arrow
Occasionally your mask melts away
To reveal the horror shining through
Occasionally you won me over
Another mistake along the way
Never ending describes our friendship
Which has somehow managed to survive

Never say the words I love you
That phrase should not be lies
Pretending we were nothing
But friends must suffice for today
Getting bored with the infinite drama
Repetitious cycles are not the way

Soulmate

I once met a girl looking for a soulmate online
Unfortunately everyone looked liked a stalker
So she just sat in front of her computer dreaming
Maybe one day that man would come to her
But most likely she would just sit and dream
Hopes never being fulfilled and wasting time
One day she decided to take a chance, a risk
Go out on a limb and meet someone, just local
And it didn't work out, it ended badly
This only discouraged her and she waited
Time passed on and on until she grew older
The only things she regrets are the chances she didn't take
As a middle age woman she eventually met someone
Not the man of her dreams but someone good
And they have a family, etc... but it ends up
as usual, in divorce, separation, or just unhappiness
And once again she is discouraged, unable to get back on the horse
She sits and waits, wasting time and her one and only life
Out of nowhere I appear in her late years
Instantly we know we are soulmates and it is wonderful
Except the fact that it could have happened forty years ago
Holding hands, Rocking back and forth in our chairs
Visiting waterfalls and writing poetry we grow even older
Then we die and life is over
We can only have one chance and it is important to take it
Everything in this world is a risk but staying alone is one too
If only she had listened, if only she had heard me, if
Too bad that this story doesn't really have fiction characters
It is every one of us who does not reach out every day for the stars
Because the only one in control is you, and you make your destiny
No religion predestines it

No God intervenes
No Man or Woman or Animal or Plant controls you
You are your own best admirer and worst critic
The choice is always up to you
Unless you're living with your parents
And most of us reading this are past that point
Except the ones who are writing it...

Something New

Cry to escape the fear
Growing much closer still
The blur becoming clear
All alone in this thrill
Running slow motion near
Glass of water and pill
Sedating me like beer
Impossible to shrill
Yawning deeper towards sleep
Tripping walk I'm caught
Twisting to escape deep
Thoughts from past long not sought
When you block something out
And forget for some year
Why does it resurface
Complicating around
Me like a damn puzzle
Cannot get free from it
I wake up sweating hot
Trying to make me calm
Force brain that it was dream
And not a memory
All these drugs surrounding
Maybe my grip solid
left reality's grasp
Brain damaged possible
New functionality
Because of immense change
Most of them last school year
In overdosing purposely

All that I could find at one time
Just swallow and wait half an hour
And you will feel some difference
Another four hours you will be
Blown away if you can maintain
The awesome death experience
From just pushing your limits out
Just a tape recorder and you
In a room with a big mirror
Access to bathroom with shower
And doing anything you want
At this place only
You might find like me
A little bit of truth
Or a special place
Record your good thoughts
On the tape cassette
And forever a copy
Of one night's thoughts you had
Remember at all times
You can take a Zanax
And go to sleep if bad
And that the effects are
Gone in twenty four hours
Go drink a lot of water
To make fast your cleaning
And your background be seen
As it is now
Then if you're brave enough
Do it again
Just make sure to save enough
And leave some life to live

Start of Something

Laying on the front yard
In my high-rent no class house
Gazing up at the heavens
Pinholes of light in the black night
I think to myself

137

What is all of this for?
Later, further in the ghetto
I see a man risking his uniqueness
For a couple of laughs
And a bit of money from the coke he sells
Getting angry about the life
I see all around me
Why its so often thrown away
Without even thoughts of recycling
Or lost somewhere quiet
Where it is never found
I want to enjoy it all
Every moment and emotion
And to keep a memory
That is why I'm here
Not to mope around
Complaining and Bitching
Leaving things worse
Than how I find them

Still Talking?

Are they still friends
After all of this shit
Now more than ever
I expect someone to get hit

Finally broke up
Cheating involved here
New girlfriend in place
I kind of wonder if it's fear

From being apart
After so much time
Can't let it just end
Continue self-inflicting crime

Never know shall I
Outside looking in
And does it matter
Any more than their origin

I know neither still
Let's leave it at that
People are boring
I need to get another cat

Sunflowers

Yellow
Full of Life
Bright as Sunlight
Weak like a baby
No minds to make up
Bees like the pollen
Reproductive seeds
Much help needed
To grow
Yellow
Green little stem
Tiny to tall
Eat a lot
Drink a lot
Like children
Happy
Create a picture
Hommmmmmee
Stares at the stars and the moon
moonflowers
Alllllll there is she was
Just growing up
Lovely
She still comes to visit me
On Sunday
Like a toy
Got hands
No mmmmmmmmmmmind

Technology

Its nice to have a phone
So that I don't have to yell

Or move from where I am
Watching the television
With news coming from all over
About people trying to decide
What's more important
Popular or Electoral votes

Its nice to have a computer
So that I don't have to write
Or buy stamps or use a mailbox
I can just type some words
Click a mouse and send
Information anywhere I choose
Without spending a penny
Or breaking a sweat

Its nice to drive a car
So that I don't have to exercise
And my body can grow fat
I can go through a drive through
Where people make fast food
That increases my blood pressure
Decreases my life span
And tastes fantastic

Would I miss technology that much
If I weren't an American
As helpless as a newborn
Without gadgets to work for me
Maybe losing weight would be nice
Getting back into the sunlight
Going for a brisk jog
And not using any electricity

The Bitch

You stupid fucking douche bag whore piece of shit
Why do you keep on talking to me if I'm so immature
Why were you the last one trying to flirt with me
Why can't you understand an email might just be to make a point

You have had my fucking music for long enough
I want my stuff back from you and I'm not visiting you to get it
Just give up this stupid fight you think two little girls can win
Because you will never beat me no matter how hard you try

I am fueled by the fact that I piss you off and its exactly what I want
I want you to feel as shitty as I felt for about a week
For the rest of your hopefully short and pointless lives
To just shrivel in the never-ending decay I create around you

Next time you walk up to me you can talk to my finger
But you're not even worth a pinkie finger to me
You are not even worth a fucking dead flattened roach
You reek of ten month old milk mixed with shit and snot

Please God I pray to make you disappear every day
But because I'm not a Christian I don't think God's listening
I think God wants nature to take its course on its own
Because if God intervened you would already be dead

Stop bringing up the past like you have some time machine
It's over and done with and you had just as much say as I
Blaming me just shows how stupid and immature you are
And everything you tell me just lets me know how you feel about yourself

Projection, my favorite psychological defense mechanism
It's all you seem to be able to do for yourself
Just somehow rationalize all your own problems into words
And throw them on the closest scapegoat you can find

From this day forward you will never bother me again
As hard as you try you will only get it back threefold
This karma is going to catch up with you some day
And hopefully it will ensure that you rot in hell, if you're not there already

The Dizziness

Sometimes while walking
Outside in the sun

141

Without a hat, umbrella, or other
Everything seems to get really bright

It's probably like having the optometrist
Dilate your eyes to look at them
I have never had that done so far
But I dilate them myself regularly

Two-Three times today this occurred
While downtown-in the car it leaves
And while walking back from the car
When back at the dorm again

It's hard to carry food, drink, etc...
When it seems impossible to see
Maybe I should take my medication
This could all be a side effect

One more small problem
I don't have one medicine
I have four or five of them
Legality disregarded

Maybe all five would work ???

The Mighty K

The Mighty K
Steps up to bat
Her bed taken
But friends again

As she showers
I wonder about
What we will say
How we'll react

I'm not dressed yet
But I think yes
I will look nice
Just for the test

I do not know
If this a game
Being played on
Me Once more still

Am I doormat
Or maybe mud
Could be lovely
Expectations

Strike one, strike two,
strike three, you're out
The mighty K
Has now struck out

The one

Curly brown locks of hair
Bouncing with each footstep
Gliding across the floor
Approaching toward me

Blue within Blue eyes
That stop searching
When they make contact
With mine and smile

Smooth soft skin
Rubbing against mine
Hands interlocked
Wishing it would never end

Dresses flowing in the wind
Make her seem to float
And she glows
As if God has a flashlight on her

The Schoolyard

Approaching the school I see the playground
It's too cold right now for children to be outside
But the wind blows the swings to and fro
The chains jingle as the rubber seats collide
An empty playing field in the back with dying grass
Oh how many games have been played here
Can a place be measured by the enjoyment that has come from it
The schoolhouses would then be priceless
The front door takes some effort to open
Much more than a child could muster
But the teachers are here to protect them
From all the dangers outside in the world
They are here to be taught about everything
Each subject and class presents more knowledge
To be remembered, regurgitated, and recited
So that someday they can grow up
And no longer be children
All this innocence and understanding
I wish people's lives could be reversed
So one started off with all the knowledge
That makes us unhappy
And we could eventually get back
To the basics that make us happy
And the innocence that makes us sweet
But that can never happen
The school stands tall and works hard
To teach us one and all the skills we need to survive
In the world that exists outside its doors
Hopefully with a sheet of paper in hand
And twelve years of learning
We can see world through tinted windows
Of hope

The Spanish Teacher

When she walked in one might think
Wrong classroom, French is down the hall
Her facial features and her haircut
All match a firm stereotype we had

Her clothes and dainty size
The fact she could be confused as a student
And that wonderful accent, no faking it
Fear stricken, European teaching standards
Although ready to have fun with us
She was a serious person in some ways
We needed to do the work assigned
And stop acting as if school were a game
Once the point was made class became better
Much too late for those who missed weeks
Too many days to even know our names
Or how or to make up believable excuses
Some plotted to get her drunk after class
But it never happened, maybe afraid
Talk was left just talk and laughter
She rode her bicycle to school
No point in buying a car for a year
As an exchange teacher, but still reminiscent
Of a lady on a bike from France
I prayed she liked Monet and presented
A couple of prints to help in decision making
If I had a borderline grade in that class
School isn't over yet, but I'm sure that
I made the impression that I needed to make
Maybe it was very difficult for some of us
Including me, but I feel like I learned something
Which is the point of school after all
In a few weeks she will be a fleeting memory
But right now I'm glad she is my teacher
Almost like I could call her up
If I happen to be in France anytime soon

The Whore

How can you just be a whore
Sex with one after another
Good looks being one goal
And old age being another
Maybe you are passive
And you just go with the flow

If you don't say no its OKAY
Sex will just happen without thinking
Your body is not as pretty anymore
And your honestly seems like lies
Your kisses are rough from blisters
From the medication you take
For all the STDs and problems
You have received from sex
You're not a nympho
But you admit being boy crazy
And every good looking guy
Ends up in a bed with you
One minute I hear that he is cute
Or that he has a lot of talent
By the next day you have fucked
And are talking about another one
I don't feel the love I once did
Even though its only been a few weeks
I am glad I am not physical with you
Your infections are foreign to me
And it will stay that way
As long as you are a dirty whore

The Word K

When I hear your name
It makes me fall in love all over again
I can't stand myself
For all the problems I have caused you
I fear I may have broken your heart forever
Because I have lied to you too much
I have been a horrible person
And I have no reasons
I wished we would be married
I wished we could have children
I wished you would go to UNCA
I wished we could be in love
None of these wishes will ever come true
I already know you want what I can't give
You want to move at the perfect pace

You want no cheating
You want the truth
You want a best friend
I am none of these things
We will be finished someday
But I will never regret the time I spent with you
You are my everything and you are the one for me
I am just not the one for you

Timed Love

Time is too slow
For those without time
Time is too quick
For those who are slow
For some it's like
A hummingbird's heart
And for others
It comes and it goes
In that respect
Its just like love
Moving from
place to place
It can be like the
Life of a flower
Or a crack
In a perfect vase

Trees

Running in the Woods
Amber autumn leaves falling
Coast by me like gliders
On their way to the ground
But I do not see them
My world is a dream
Thinking about problems
Worrying about impossibilities
I wish I could fall into the leaves

And be buried from the world
To be myself and relax
Without you there to torment me
I could be a tree
Standing tall and firm
If you were not the termites
Eating me alive

Tri-angle

Not lust or love in this triangle
Just friends entwined in need untangle
Words can explain the strangest thing yet
But not the last if I were to bet

How much fun we are going to be
Three open souls without secrets free
First feeling like some sort of third wheel
Now a tricycle not a big deal

Clear minds as fast as we were confused
No need to write about those dark blues
Far from guilt as before time we met
Singing songs with a finger on fret

Bi-polar all types combined in one
Laughing talking crying unison
We can reach up, try to touch the sun
Anything together can be done

From far to close now to far again
I wonder if I will ever win
Either's heart for more than friendly talk
Holding hands on the beach during walk

2 Days After

2 days following the anti-drug campaign
Of my lifetime, by just being open in a class,

To pass off the last requirement for psych
By talking orally competent about my drug experience
I've decided to smoke a joint
And rethink this whole no drug thing
After all, if not this semester, on occasion, mind you
Then what better time from this point on
When I have some career instead of job
Luckily its pretty much true that if I
As an adult in this system with a job making money
Quietly smoking some pot in my house
It's about as white collar as crime can get
But I would not be treated like a delinquent
At that age by most judges in any state
But now is still better, much better
Cause I'm high writing this
And for some reason I always just let it all go
Every thought I have is yours to explore
Truth and Justice in the system isn't here
But in my lifetime I am gonna work on it
In some small way I have to make a difference
Be it just to awaken some person to truth
I want to share information with someone
To educate people in the true state of the union
Because we need to fucking revolt - we understand what capitalism is
It sucks - lct all things being voted on and have a socialist pay system
With unlimited child support and medical insurance and legal drugs
Which all come out of taxes, which pay for school though college
Either a technical school or university depending on grades
I mean this is a reality some places now as I am writing
But George W. Bush has only been president for 8 full months if that
Being as its September 26, 2007, maybe he got to start in February
I don't fucking remember or care to
He is a pathetic rich child following in his father's footsteps
For no apparent good purposes but to make dad happy
Unfortunately doesn't realize he looks like an idiot
On almost every channel on cable once daily
Re-election would be intolerable
If any time in my lifetime so far the people could revolt

Two-Faced

I feel like hitting you
Each time you pass by
Forgetting what you always tell me
"I'm your best friend"
It's just an illusion
I've fallen for
You hang out with another
One you tell me you hate
Do you tell him you hate me?
I wonder
It would not be unlike you
You're so two-faced
My anger is building
I don't know what to do about it
I tell you exactly how I feel
You promise to remedy and as usual
You do nothing
Nothing in life is fair
I learned that from you

Unconditional

Your eyes remind me of precious stones
Shining back a perfect reflection of mine
As we sit starting at one another softly
And enjoy the infinite silence we create

Our hands forcefully lock into one another
Forming an unbreakable bond of flesh
Almost as if you are becoming part of me
And I am being consumed by you

My body rubs against your smooth skin
And it reminds me of a security blanket
That kept me safe as a tiny baby
Much like your warmth keeps me now

Your voice is soothing and knowledgeable

And each word rings in my mind like bells
Your songs are sweet like lullabies
But I could never fall asleep this entranced

Each kiss reminds me of the difference
Between being in love and a crush
Slowly our oceans collide without even a wave
As lips lock in a passionate bliss

Away from you part of me is missing
Your smile never leaves my mind
I have never felt this way inside
Unconditional

UN-fair for him

The circumstances were not fair
No one told the poor boy he was in a personality test
And he failed it so hard without trying
I can only reassure myself there is another reason
Why she risks more wasted time
Without even a hint of his crime
Just his presence is his bad
What a fuckhead is this lad
I have no right to judge him
Because I have never heard his point of view
But I don't really think it would matter
I am pretty sure he is just a fucker
Time has passed and I was dead wrong
Just the wrong time and wrong place
So it's time to continue this song
And show everyone his new face
Our conversation was revealing
About truths I would have never known
Open to me about the whole thing
Multiple problems outside of me ended them
She spent the night with another guy
After all the shit she had put him through
And went back begging with a cry
Thinking another chance to start new

They said broke up but I would never know
From the frequency of her visits to him
But once I heard the words your new girlfriend
Can you just drop all this from your mind
Not out on a curb like me but friends
How and why I get so cheated I don't know
I'm sure on point of view my facts depend
But there is nothing left anyone can show
Me that I would pay to see for even one dime
They are all out of my life like a passing fad
So I just keep on walking without a care
Trying hard to be at my best
So no one else will catch me dying
Because of something simple as season

Unforgettable

Although forgiven
Never forgotten
Never the same
Always changing
Just that one thing
Holding me back
From being the same
Old me
Can't feel myself
The old me
Ground up in dust
Of the past
And blown away
By winds of change
To the new
Me
Never the same

Unique Evolution

This unexplainable topic which touches our souls
And causes so many arguments and discussions

Is not what this poem is about
It is about the theory that binds us to one another
We do evolve on a regular basis daily
Every second that twenty five thousand
Births are occurring we have made many
New and unique people who will continue
To change and be more and more unique while
They in turn influence the next wave continuing
Into the ocean of people on this planet
Which never ends in the pattern of existence
We have to experience each and every day
Sometimes a little uncomfortable to be different
And sometimes great, to be unique and know
We are not alike and will never be able to be duplicated
Exactly regardless of cloning technology and
The living dead and ghosts and heaven there will never
Be another person with your exact same point of view
That can ever be exactly who you are and therefore
Evolution is a natural pattern that means from wherever
The first life came from it continuously spread
Life along a track of different interactions and hurdles
Eventually ending with nothing but ashes and memories
But still unique and wonderful because of it
Ever evolving into the next perfect creation
Of ourselves

Untitled

I have this feeling
It's warm
It makes me feel good
It's always there
I feel it radiating
But only toward one other
The one who shows it to me
In all they do
It shapes my smiles
It lights my nights
It controls me
I can't stop it

And I would never want to
I can't lose
I am sure
It's love
Continuing for infinity
Through my lifetime and the confusion following
Stronger than any chain
Sharper than any blade
Love is just there
From you Kim

Untitled

I don't understand
Why I have nothing to do
Everything I think of
Is impossible
Just sitting in an empty room
Looking around
Thinking about what I want
Thinking about what to write
Wishing and dreaming
Things I will never have
So far away
No way to get away
Pictures surround me
They are closing in
Just staring
I try not to look
They are all over me
Looking at me -every direction
I punch and kick to get away
Back to the empty room
With nothing to do
I don't understand

Untitled

I trusted you
You trusted me
I loved you
You loved me
I listened to you
You listened to me
Now I see my trust was blind
I cared for a liar
What I called love was lust
It was all physical
We listened but did not hear
Hear our thoughts in our tone
Telling us this would never work
It never does, does it?
It never is perfect, there are no fairy tales
Everybody really does argue
All marriages are destined for divorce
All people break up
We might as well not have hearts
Because all the superglue in the world
Could not even attempt to help one of us

Untitled

Oh, I'm sorry
That was my hard-on talking
I don't really love you, or anyone
It's not someone else
It's just that we have everything in common
We are perfect for each other
And I am an asshole
You've heard the expression "Coke is it"
Well for me "sex is it"
Bye

Untitled

Many albums
Many pictures
Pictures you cannot imagine
Crazy images
Blended Lives
All Women
Many different Women
One man
My father
Nudity...
Sex...
Affairs...
No divorce?
Does my mom know?
Should I tell her?
Should I confront him?
I told everyone
Mom, Dad, Sister, friends, psychologist
What did they say?
Too bad
Deal with it

Untitled

If only I had known
It would be this way
I never would have agreed
To live in your room
To live in your building
To go to this college
To be born
Why did you have to go and ruin everything
E!
I wish you would slowly die
Better yet, I wish you would disappear
Then things would be better
I would have my friends back
My friends that live in the college

In this building
In this room
Damn you Bastard Fucker!
I hate you
Now I'm miserable and guess what
I blame you
DIE!
If only I'd have known you in another life
I would have killed you

Untitled

After a wild night
I am left haunted
With a perfect memory
Every detail of the previous day
Whether I should blame myself
Or the alcohol I can't decide
Or her, the other, the girl
Who was with me last night
I remember every second
As it slowly passed
I never said "no"
I never pushed her away
I just let the kissing commence
I let the holding be tight and meaningful
Now only awareness remains
In place of our friendship
And an empty guilt
That rings like a telephone in my head
That no one picks up

Untitled

I wonder how many kisses
I've wasted on pretty faces
I wonder how many I love yous
I've said without thinking
Each one taking a part of me

that should not have been wasted
Drying me out like a desert
With rain never falling
I wonder about all the love-letters
I've written with my soul
And many lines of poetry
Flowing from my lips
That went into a shoebox
Or into a trash can
Forgotten forever
Collecting dust

Untitled

Disconnected
I am deteriorating
Surely this venom will kill me
Without a counter active bite
Separated
Although a covenant was made
This masquerade can cease
If we unveil one another
You emit an aura
That I need to grow
Excommunicated
From your soul
I grow so tired
Without my angel
Let me hear it just once
Those magical words
That can set me free forever
I love you

Untitled

Do you know the pain that I know
With a suicide glance
You are stuck in your ways
With concrete roots

But you are not the way
I want you to be
Empty conversations
Have lost their meaning
The comfortable silence
Has become a black hole
Eating us up
My heart does not feel broken
I don't think I have a heart
I don't have emotions
I cant even cry one tear
I wish I could have one more kiss
Just to remember how good it was
To be lost in a dream reality
Where nothing matters but you

Untitled

A raindrop falls from the sky
And trickles down my cheek
Another relationship has ended
Just as it began
I feel I don't
Know her at all
Or anymore
For that matter
I am one
Once again
How could it have only been
A month and a week
It seems I have loved in her
For an eternity
I am still sad but happy
That she showed me love
My heart is broken once again
And a loosely knit relationship
Is over
Words were natural until now
And now they are not spoken
Not a word has come out
Since my heart was broken

Untitled

I think that there will only be
One girl I will ever meet
That had a personality and goodness
That was so sweet

The first day I met her
I fell head over heels
She has always seemed
Like every big deal

She is the most outgoing person
With a beautiful smile
To cheer me up she would
Go out of her way a mile

The person I loved
Became my best friend
Because I thought something serious
Would have a quick end

Through the toils and troubles
I have already some
To be around her
Makes all my pain numb

All relationships have ups and downs
But ours is always great
The only thing I needed I never got
One chance on a date

I hang out with someone I would marry
And don't give it a second thought
If I were on a quest
She would be what I sought

Everything is forgiven
No matter what it was
I am never truly angry
No matter what she does

Untitled

Please believe in me
As I believe in you
And it is urgent
That you do this now
Others are nothing
Nothing can be done
For you are the only one
That knows how
I can't lie to you
Because of your feelings
The only person I need
To lie to I can't
This conscience that I have
Protects you completely
And yet it repels
Any shielding that I have
I feel that I am nowhere
And its where I will stay
If something is not done soon
I will go away
Whether or not I'll be back
I don't know
The Bible is not
That specific
What I do know
Is you are eternity
To get you
Is like being immortal
Can't you see
My power lies in you
All of my essence
Has been drained
Hear me now
As I tell you this
You are the hope
For many people
Please don't let anything I do
Affect you
At all

Untitled

It's all going to change
Once you run out of it
Like spice, a drug you need
Hardly chance doped up

This is just sad
Why hate yourself
If it's who you are
Stand up tall now!

But then turn round and run
Back to where I come from
These drugs I have some
That stop cum ability

How much fun a girl could have with me
And it would be absolutely cost free
All taking long turns once, twice or sometimes three
Talking all my bark away naked tree

Too much sex now
Must leave to bed
There is awful moon
Overhead

Untitled

Well, My life has ended
The pain will fade away
I am so very tired
I think I'd sit for lay

I don't know where I am going
I cant find the way
I listen to the voices
But no one to obey

Everyday I lie here
Up to the day

When someone will come passing
And wave or say hey

If I stay here much longer
I lay here, un-molded clay
Until that days comes
I surely will decay

Untitled

Thoughts are past and forgotten
The baby has been put to sleep
Will I ever recall them
No noise, not even a peep

They are lost in a sea of sadness
Dreams disappear and reality floods through
Is it true or torture
Some things old and some new

I can't believe anything
Nothing matters anymore
What's the point in going on
Life is just and endless bore

Everyday is filled with dread
More and more people hurt
I think that people love me
But all they do is flirt

I look at others constantly
My whole life is a gloat
I think I might just drown
I wonder if I'll stay afloat

Waiting

Can you not see
The way you treat me

That nasty horrible way
You must just act
The way you feel in this play
After all, hearts break everyday
I can't stay here lonely
Just waiting for you to come around
I doubt there is anything you can say
I need my breathing space
But I could share it, with one
And more than one is not OKAY
Just tell me an answer
A complicated yes or no
I won't just sit and stay
Waiting for you for an eternity
Like always

Walk on By

As if today wasn't bad enough
I had to talk to Megan - she hates me
Then I had to visit and get my stuff
K is like oblivious to everyone and everything
Except E, and she just keeps on saying his name
At work I find out I need an attitude adjustment
Why? Because they all think I hate them
After crying and staying over an hour late
Trying to do the safe count, etc... myself
I drive home - exit my car - and then walk
I walk to the end of the parking deck and see Ed
Just the two of us - all silence - but I can feel it
The negative energy being projected on me
As if I didn't feel like a pile of shit already
I'm so tired I don't even have adrenaline to rush
So I avoid contact and keep on walking
It's too late to make this jargon rhyme
So I'm just gonna say fuck it
Tomorrow is a new day and beginning
Things do change and I am a thing
Therefore I can change – adapt - and become
My ideal self
Then they can all walk on by

Wasting Time

I brought up all the pictures
My reality enforced memories
So I could show her myself
Under different settings

But before she looked canceled
As if I were under her control
Not giving me any say at all
Just an excuse and goodbye

Now I see wasted space taken
And wasted time spent gathering
My past up for a friend
Who turned out empty
Waste of time

Now I have finally finished
The colossal waste of time
That I began on four years ago
It seems like only yesterday

Why did I listen to them
All pointing me in a direction
That was wrong for me
I never really needed that degree

So much stronger now
I stand up to my opposition
But at the cost of my life
How long until I will be free

This next four years so slow
The seconds crawling past
Father time is against me
While I pay off all my wrongs

Sitting in the darkness of night
I just want to jump off this cliff

Recurring this thought again
Is this life or just my personal hell

What is love?

If I had any one wish
It would be for you
To be able to read my thoughts
And know how much I love you

Words cannot say the feelings
Or thoughts floating in my head
I need you to let me in
So I can prove what I have said

There are no secrets
That I could ever keep from you
Each breath you breathe is sacred
Along with everything else you do

This love I feel cannot go on
Without your soft sweet hand in mine
I have never felt this way before
Heaven would be hell without your sign

The bond between us
Is my only weakness you must understand
The connection from heart to heart
Is only a tiny little strand

My thoughts are pure and clear
The visions of you I see
Dreams and pictures float by
In the waves of you, in the oceans of me

Without you I am lost, alone and by myself
I would betray the world
To only kiss you goodnight
I love you

Forever

When will I find her?

Some of us just have to keep on looking
No matter how much time has gone by
Maybe unlucky with so many disappointments
But the experience will stay forever

Keep the faith that somehow in years
Or seconds we will bump into the one
Like I am stuck in the Bermuda Triangle
A self made wall that keeps me trapped

Jealous yes, of those around me married
All healthy relationships that I can't have
And left wondering if I have ever really
Tasted anything that wasn't a mirage

Are they really more mature than I am
Do they really know themselves completely
Maybe I am just blind or blinking
Each chance I have slipping past me

I sometimes hope my writing is for nil
And she will appear as if in a fairy tale
Holding me tightly in my sleep
But I always wake up from the dream

The biggest fear I know so far in life
Is that I let her go already
No chance to redeem myself now
I just sit here writing these lines

WHO AM I?

Cashier
Happy
Responsible
In debt

Single
Talkative
Open
Patient
Honest
Employed
Relaxed

Swimmer
Tattoos
Educated
War inside
American
Riot
Together

Student
Angry
Public
Psychology major

Who is He?

He needs some time alone
To gather his thoughts
Perhaps consult his parents
During difficult times
Today isn't one of those days
Fairly stable and laughing consistently
A nervous behavior pattern
Shows up with adrenaline
Maybe not too innocent
And without any halos
He stands tall
Full of worrying and fear
Confidence sometimes fails him
Shyness seems an underestimate
What is it that's so different
About his particular one

Why?

I fall in love
My love leaves me wasted
Like a bird she migrates away
I begin to look

Find her I cannot
I find a new love
She returns in the summer
I am confused

Once I set aside a place
I cannot fill it up
My heart is empty
Without my bird

I try to love
But it cannot be
My new love is a lie
For feelings of pity

It was love I thought
Until my bird came back
Then everything was gone
My broken wing is back

I can't just walk away
A magic draws me in
But if I follow I know
The bird will fly again

I still try to please both
My mind, my heart
It is impossible
I wish I could just die!

Will I Make it?

Three short weeks
Pressure left on me won't fade

Yes, even that affects me each day
Just two little classes and yoga
You don't think it counts either?
Good, it's my only peace of mind
Running low on true pals now
And really broke for once
Still missing checks from job
After over a month
Learning another language now
Or trying to and not succeeding
It's like I will pass the classes
Except I'm not gonna earn it
I almost know for sure I get a degree
But the question is how many times
I just decided to warm up and red nose
My way into a better grade
I feel like I have learned so much
That I deserve it in some ways
But my conscience is bothersome
I'm afraid afterwards also
I am going to come home alone
Family not exactly picture perfect
I don't think it's gonna be enough
I hope Jon can come through for me
Just one more time
I am gonna need him
I'm crying right now over this
But the tears are not flowing
Just sitting there not sure
Almost like I feel right now
Drying up evaporate away
I'm just all gone, I'm not myself
I really have to not give up
But I just want incompletes
I am incomplete

Wishes

I wish I could fly
In the glorious sky

To be like a bird
Would be a dream come true
I could soar over the earth
See animals giving birth
I will hold tight to my wishes
Forget them I will not
To be a leopard without spots
Is something I am not
If you lose your wishes
There would be no point
In life, in work
Or in loving from the heart

Lost

The sky is gone and the suns shine bright
The town lit up by the tiny light
Almost perfect on this midnight
Now two five years done in her flight
Wings down, eyes close, she loses sight
And rests until sky is back to right

Love is...

Love is a pigeon
That carries a note
Love is an ocean
That keeps you afloat

Love is a story
That puts you to sleep
Love is a friend
That is there while you weep

Love is a voice
That sings you a song
Love is a person
That helps you get along

Love is a prayer
That is said at night
Love is a comfort
That holds on tight

Love is a promise
That can not be broken
Love is a window
That always stays open

Love is someone
Who will never leave
And to me
Love we achieve

About the Author

Christopher Sapp was born and raised in Winston-Salem,
North Carolina. He has been writing poetry for most of his life.
He writes the words for a personal release,
and not for the purpose of making money,
but to share some of his feelings with the world.

"If only one person who reads this decides that
they have the inspiration to write down what they feel,
then I have accomplished my goal."
.

Chris graduated from the University of North Carolina
at Asheville with a Bachelor of Arts degree in Psychology
and works with special populations,
making a difference one day at a time.

He also enjoys working online and playing video games.
He loves amusement parks and. his family,
especially his beautiful wife Anne.

www.ingramcontent.com/pod-product-compliance
Lightning Source LLC
LaVergne TN
LVHW011350080426
835511LV00005B/227

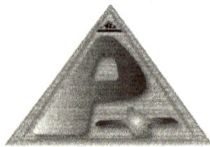

For Piper Kate Younglove,
Because she would have groaned the loudest

Groan And Bear It

A Collection
Of
Awful Stories
Told as Quickly
As
Possible
So You Can
Tell Your
Friends
As
Soon
As
Possible

GROAN

AND

BEAR

IT

By

Gary Younglove

GROAN AND BEAR IT

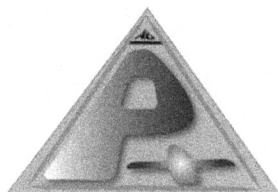

PIPER PLUS PUBLICATIONS
FAIR OAKS RANCH, TEXAS

Orders@PiperPlusPublications.com
Shipping Information On Website
http://www.PiperPlusPublications.com
Piper Plus Publications
28540 Jim Dandy Circle
Fair Oaks Ranch, TX 78015

ISBN: 978-0-9829383-1-7

Library of Congress Control Number: 2010912983

10 9 8 7 6 5 4 3 2

CONTENTS

FOREWORD

ACKNOWLEDGEMENTS

INTRODUCTION

ALL THE GROANERS YOU'LL EVER NEED*

All Groaners are arranged alphabetically by Title.

A New Gnu
A No Fault Solution
A Not So Well Known Theory ®
A Paladin Poser
A Rose By Any Other Name
A Royal Pain
A Savory Concoction
A Shrinking Feeling
A Singular Truth ®
A Sinking Fund
A Slippery Argument
A Sobering Thought
A Spiritual Sacrifice
A Stinking Shame
A Tailors Complaint
A Ticklish Situation ®
A Time Trip
A Turning Point
A Wake Up Call
A Wrong Conclusion
Administrative Hang-up
Ain't He Something?
Aisle Of Man
Alex Keeps Watch
All Choked Up
All In A Day's Work
All Strung Out
All The Way Or Not At All
All Totalled
An Enlightening Lesson
An Evening At The Ritz
An Honest Oversight
An Unholy Juan
An Unusual Rescue Line
Animal Farm
Asking For Directions
Back At'Cha
Bald Is Beautiful
Barnyard Cents
Better Safe Than Sorry ®
Between You And Me
Black Eyed Pea
Body Shop
Bottled Wonder
Bringing Back The Good Old Times
Bury The Last Straw
Cause And Effect
Cheap At Twice The Price
Chess A Minute
Chinese Cooking
Chipping In

Chivalry Is Not Lost
Choosing Sides
Circular Reference
Close Enough For Government Work
Cops And Robbers
Cuff 'Im And Book 'Im ®
Different Sizes
Disorderly Deficit
Doc At The Top Of The Stairs
Don't Squeeze The Tomatoes
Don't Tred On Me
Double Crosses Never Work
Drawing The Drapes
Drying Times
'Ears To Ya, Doc
Ebb And Flow
Elementary Geometry
Even Steven
Every Gig Needs A Straight Man
Every River Has A Mouth
Falling Through The Crack ®
Family Jewels
Fearful Angels
Fearsome Threesome
Figure It Out
Flipping Sides
Foreign Cuisine Brings Fame
Forever Tuned
Fork It Over Buddy
Four On The Floor
Fowl Language ®
Getting Out Of Debt
Girl Of My Dreams
Glove Me Tender
Go Ahead...I'll Cover You
Gone To The Dogs
Good Neighbors Build Fences
Guilt By Association
Half And Half
Handy Wipes
Hasty Action Lead Nowhere
He Was Bound To Get It In The End ®
He Was Dead Wrong
He Was Just Kidding
He Will Drive You Mad
Heads Or Tails
High Society
High Stepping Dancers
High Style Hitch Hiker
His, Hers, And All The Others
Hope And Change Is Never Guaranteed

Horse Sense
Hot Diggity Dog ®
Hot Pants
How Soon They Forget
I Do ... I Do
I Don't Believe It
I Plead Guilty
Ice Sculpture
If I Only Had A Brain
In A Round About Fashion
In The Blink Of An Eye
In The Throes Of Experience
It Can Leave You Breathless
It Could Be Contagious
It Happens All The Time
It Looks The Same From Any Angle
It Must Be Something I Ate
It Pays To Be Cautious
It Pays To Be Prepared ®
It Takes A Man To Admit It ®
It'll All Work Out In The End
It's A Family Thing
It's A Monstrous Problem
It's A Sin To Tell A Lie ®
It's A Small Price To Pay ®
It's A Stretch
It's All About Presentation ®
It's All In How You Look At It
It's All In The Bag
It's All In The Presentation
It's No Small Thing
It's On The House
Juan By Juan
Keeping It All In The Family ®
Keeping It All To Yourself
Keeping Score
Kodak Bare
Last Minute Reprieve
Lift Your Spirits
Lions4-Seers0
Location. Location. Location.
Lock And Load
Look Both Ways
Looking For The Perfect Wave
Lost And Found
Love Potion
Mailman's Wife
Make It Up As You Go
May The Best Man Win
Memories Are Made Of This
Mind Over Matter

Moonlight Romance
Motorcycle Sickness ®
Mulligan's Stew
Multiple Cuts
Music To Your Ears
My Mind's Made Up
Name Calling
Name That Face
Net Assets ®
Never Tell A Lie
Nip It In The Bud
No Doubt About It
No Matter How You Slice It
Not Playing With A Full Deck
Nothing To Crow About
Off The Beaten Track
On Your Marks
One Page At A Time
One Size Fits All ®
One, Two, What Do We Do?
One Way Or Another
Only Time Will Tell
Organic Communion ®
Out Of Breath
Pecking Order ®
Pennies From Heaven
Peripheral Vision
Pete And Repete
Pins And Needles
Plainly Speaking
Play It Again Sam
Potato Chips For The Soul
Powerful Advice
Rainy Weather
Receding Gum Lines
Red Sky In The Morning
Repeat As Needed
Resort To The Retort
Right Time, Right Place
Ring A Ding Ding
Rising Above It All
Rite Of Passage
Road Maintenance
Road Trip Trips Rogers
Rome Is Where The Heart Is
Sad Songs Make Me Cry
Santa's Final Ho
Saved By The Bell ®
Secret Formula ®
Seeing Is Believing

Seek And You Shall Find
Semi-Skilled Labor
Set 'Em Up Joe ®
Sheepy Hollow
Sherth's Worth
Shipwreck Treasure
Short End Of The Stick
Sibling Rivalry
Signed, Sealed, And Delivered
Smoking Out The Bad Guys
Someone's Gonna Pay
Someone's Got To Do It
Something Fishy Going On
South Seas Shift
Speak Now Or Forever Hold Your Peace
Speed Reader Gets In Trouble
Speedy Prince
Start With The Proper Ingredients
State Your Porpoise
Stick Out Your Tongue And Say Ahh
Stormy Weather
Straighten Up And Dry Right
Strange Collateral
Stretching The Truth
Submarine Sandwich
Taco Salad
Take Your Pick
Taking Care Of Birds 'N Nests
Texas Two-Step
The Bear And The Bar Fly
The Choice Breed
The Direct Pitch
The Gory Truth
The Harder They Fall
The High Cost Of Travel
The Main Event
The Million Dollar Question
The Name Says It All
The Night Before Christmas ®
The Odds Were Favorable
The Pause That Refreshes
The Receiving Line
The Road Less Ridden
The Saga Of Wounded Knee
The Same Old Song
The Stages Of Life
The Wrong Style
There Are Two Sides To Every Story
There Oughtta Be A Law
There's Gold In Them Thar Hills
This Crazy Thing They Call Showbiz

Those Evil Cowboys
Throat Lozenges
Through And Through ®
Tied Up Tight
Time To Chill Out
To Tell The Truth
Tommy Knocker
Triangular Relationship ®
Trouble In Grape Town
Try It On For Size
Two Man Tent
Two Pints A Quart Don't Make
Unlimited Visibility
What An Awful Mess We've Made
What Goes Up Must Come Down
When Things Were Rotten
Where There's Smoke, There's Fire
Why Did The Chicken Cross The Road?
Why Is It?
Windex® Wonderment
With Thankful Reverence
Words To Go By
Working Late At Night
You Can Run But You Can't Hide
You Had To Be There
You Make The Call
You Wanna What!?

ONE LINERS FOR YOUR DEVELOPMENT

There are a few pages of one liners presented on pages 345 through 351 for additional enjoyment or the reader's own development.

INTERNET LINKS OF VALUE TO THE PUNSTER

There is nearly an unlimited supply of sources for punny material. A few of those sources available on the internet are provided here. The links provided are accurate only on the date of publication and no assurance is given that the sites still exist.

---

* Some Groaners border on the edge of the risqué, although nothing you don't read in the papers or see and hear on television or in the movies. These few are so labeled with ® in the listing here and marked accordingly with the title on the Groaner's page.

FOREWORD

You have found a book that can give you a lot of joy and fond memories.

Remember the days when the family drove places in a car or station wagon before the days when they didn't have DVD players for the passenger and each child did not have his own iPhone to text his friends or iPod to listen to his personal favorite music? In those olden days, Dad or Mom would have to amuse you and would often tell a long drawn-out story that by the time it was finished you felt betrayed, let-down - even angry. You couldn't think about how funny the story was. Your only thought was what can I do to get back at the teller.

Or remember your first camping experience? In the evening, you sat by a bonfire near the pool and your counselor would be telling you a story that dragged on and on, so that by the time he reached the punch line you and the other campers were so let-down and "angry" that together you picked up the counselor and threw him into the swimming pool.

Or remember those slumber parties with your girl friend and the times someone started telling a story that seemed like forever to tell? And when she was finished you felt not only exhausted but betrayed by the innate ending? At that moment, your only thought was a feeling of anger that you had to sit through all that. And everyone simultaneously threw their pillows at the story teller.

In each of these examples, you were the victim of a Shaggy Dog Story. Many of these Shaggy Dog Stories have a pun or other word play as a punch line. Others do not. The punch line is not relevant. Whether the joke is really funny or not does not matter. It is the let-down, the frustration, the feeling that this was a waste of time that is significant; for that's the result that a teller of such a story is trying to elicit from his audience.

There are several characteristics a tale must have to be called a Shaggy Dog Story. First, the audience must be captive. You can't just close the book, walk away or change channels. Second, the ending, punch line, or conclusion of the story must give you the feeling your time was unnecessarily wasted. And most importantly, the story has to be filled with unnecessary and repetitive material that does nothing to enhance or clarify what you are being told. If the story is about a trip to your Grandparents' home twenty miles away for Thanksgiving, you would have to go back home after being halfway there because Mom forgot the pumpkin pies she baked. Then again because Mom thought she forgot to turn off the oven. And your sister would ask every five minutes if we were there yet and you would have to tell Dad to stop at the next gas station because you had to go to the rest room. You know what I am speaking of. We have all heard at least one Shaggy Dog Story in our lifetime.

You won't find any Shaggy Dog Stories in this book. A book this size could include at most about twenty of these stories and the response to reading them would not result in the goal of making you feel betrayed or let-down. Reading a Shaggy Dog Story never is the same as hearing it when you can not go somewhere else or do something more enjoyable. You are not a captive audience reading this book. You can close it at any time.

What Gary Younglove has done is collect over 300 stories that have been told over and over again in many places and added a few of his own. He has taken these stories and reduced them down to the bare essentials, the facts necessary to reach the punch-line and make it funny. What you get is comparable to reading a 400 page novel in the Reader's Digest 30 page version of the book. And by doing so, giving you the facts only, the stories are funnier than the ones you remember being bored by.

Gary's stories have another characteristic. Shaggy Dog Stories need not end with a pun, Spoonerism or other form of word-play. Many don't. But all the stories you read here will not only end with a punned phrase, but you'll immediately recognize that this is the only ending to the story that is reasonable while simultaneously recognizing the phrase of sentence being punned.

Academically, this is called 'a set-up pun'. Rather than just saying something that is a pun, the author has written a story that could only lead to that pun as its punch-line. Such a story commonly leads to an audible groan. The groan allows you to laugh and at the same time tell the storyteller that he caught you. The groan is your way of saying it was funny but you caught me off guard this time and maybe I can get you next time. And because of this response they are widely known not as set-up puns but 'Groaners'. 'Shaggy Dog Stories' leave you depressed. 'Groaners' leave you happy. Gary has given you a book of hundreds of stories that would depress you if heard in their original form. And if you are a camp counselor, or like to entertain when a group of friends get together, here is a goldmine of stories you can embellish to make the evening a successful one.

Gary warns you to not try to read this book in one reading. I would go further. Do not try to read more than 5 or 6 of these stories at one sitting. To do so, you would lose the joy in each story. This is the perfect book to keep in the rest room to read while otherwise occupied or to read for 15 minutes after finishing the paper as you commute to work. This is the book you might want to give to the friend who is recovering from a major illness or surgery and is looking forward to a long convalescence when she goes home. Take it in short but happy segments. This will bring you the joy "Groan and Bear It" offers you.

Stan Kegel is a retired Pediatric Cardiologist residing in Orange County, California. He has always enjoyed hearing and telling puns and would often share punny riddles with his patients who would frequently try to stump him with a new one. He has been a leader in posting his humor on the internet since 1997, and is the publisher of 7 joke e-lists including "Jest For Kids" for children 8 to 12, and "Puns" a compilation of the mailings to all his lists daily. His puns and jokes are also used by over 40 other Joke lists. On April 1, 2000, he was honored as the "Punster of the Year" by the Toronto based 'The International Save the Pun Foundation' at their annual banquet in Chicago. He is an active member of the punster group "P.U.N.Y."[Punsters United Nearly Yearly] and for the past 11 years has been a judge at the "O. Henry Pun-Off World Championships" in Austin, Texas, each May. He is co-author of "The Ants Are My Friends" with fellow "Punster of the Year," Richard Lederer, a book of over 200 set-up puns (Groaners), all of which have a punchline punning the lyrics of widely recognized songs from all genres.

ACKNOWLEDGEMENTS

Although there are punsters, wordsmiths, and groaner entrepreneurs of far greater talent than I, no one can possibly be the repository of every tale to be told. It was only with the help of many that I was able to collect this assortment of "Groaners". Over the years, many people sent me ideas and even a complete story for my collection. This book would not be possible without their input. There were countless persons who helped, but a few of them stood out in their consistent support. I would like to extend my appreciation to Dick Conaway, Bob Simm, and Gary Hallock whose unending appreciation of the English language is classic. Janet Bednarz, and my two sons, Greg and Geof provided continual support even when groaning explosively. Most of all, I want to thank two Donnas in my life – my wife, Donna Younglove, and a new friend, Donna Taylor. These two editors deserve special recognition for the hours they spent making sure I didn't look too illiterate. They were invaluable and I promise to visit them often in the mental health ward. There are scores of others who have been my test bed. If you've ever heard me tell a 'groaner', you deserve my heartfelt thanks as well.

22 - Gary Younglove

INTRODUCTION

Call it a shaggy dog story, pun, spoonerism or groaner. It goes by many names but the result is usually the same: a visual or audio response that indicates the receiver of the tale is suffering mild mental pain. In my experience, the telling causes the hearer to groan and insist that I abstain from any further telling. Yet, I have observed these same persons rushing to share their newfound humor with another.

I speak, of course, of the well-known art form of story telling that seems to have no purpose. Nearly everyone has been subject to the torturous telling that seems to be going somewhere important then ends up with utter disappointment. We are all lovers of a good tale and we repeatedly fall for the "Groaner", usually well aware of the outcome and, in most instances, welcoming it. Such is the fabric of our past and of our future: there is no way out.

There are numerous presumptions of both the origin and the substance of the 'Shaggy Dog Story' or 'Groaner'. But for purposes of this collection I have settled on a description of the Groaner as the telling of a long and tedious story wherein a pun is finally exclaimed in the final line. Because the humor embedded in the punch line is solely dependent on the recognition of a familiar saying, the listener is usually surprised to discover it makes sense in both its realistic and absurd situations. If the listener is not familiar with the common phrase, it will not make sense and therefore will not be funny, even after explanation which, after the fact, results only in disappointment.

A secondary but common element of the "Groaner" is that the telling of the tale takes what seems to be forever. Each facet of the tale is drawn out with detail and colorful references to the characters in the story. An aura of suspense is built on a foundation of expectation. And when the end comes, there is instant relief that the telling is finally over, combined with an instant collapse of the expectation usually expressed with a loud and prolonged 'Aaarrrggghhh'.

I could not write these tales in their full form for this collection. The book would have been far too long and cumbersome. A fully fleshed out telling would also rob the reader of the privilege of expanding the telling to its usual length in an independent and creative fashion. Therefore, I have written each of the tales in this collection to fit a single page.

Those who are familiar with the Strunk and White gold mine booklet "The Elements Of Style" will find a treasure trove of needed corrections within the tales of this book. It was not my attempt to write these one page stories in perfect English. Rather, I wanted to write each story to fit, more or less, the single page format of this book and do so in a fashion that would entertain. The resulting dialog is much as the story would be told orally without notes.

Another facet of the groaner is that politically correct nonsense has no place in the telling. I have avoided crassness and downright libel. I have also avoided lessening the humor or the enjoyment of the story out of some fear I may offend someone.

Those who have made a life of following the pun, spoonerism, play on words publications and events over the years will find that they are familiar with most of the stories contained in this book. What sets this book apart is that the collection gathers these tales in one place. It becomes a reference and consolidated history of "Groaners" that will exist long after the basis of the tale has become out of fashion.

Each one of the stories related here can be stretched in the act of telling to the point of ridiculousness – such is the basic foundation of a groaner. Let your imagination run wild as you read them, but don't try to read this book from cover to cover in one sitting. My editors did that and now suffer from a variety of psychological disorders.

Some of the very good groaners have more than one version of the telling. You may recognize these when you come across them. I have chosen to include only one version. Additionally, I can make no claim that I have included all that are out there. In fact, I believe there is an endless supply of groaners that ebbs and flows with the continual changes in our culture and language. With all that said, I hope you enjoy reliving the ones you know and groaning over the ones that are new. You may wish to take revenge on me for the angst or hurt these tales bestow on you. Not a problem. After all ....

Even a calendar's days are numbered.

ALMOST ALL THE GROANERS

YOU'LL EVER NEED

A BAD BACK NEEDS HELP

Bernie Backwater had been suffering from back problems for years. These problems had gotten so bad in recent months that he could no longer stand erect. He consulted with countless doctors on how best to relieve his pain and return to his former upright posture. In each instance, the doctors told him surgery was the only answer. They could not, however, guarantee that they could remove the crick in his back.

Bernie finally consented to the surgery but decided to vacation at his brother Bobby's cabin for a week prior to the operation. When he spoke of the planned surgery, Bobby mentioned that there was a sure fire method to correct the problem without surgery or the need of a doctor. Bobby explained it was a home remedy learned over many years of country experience and guaranteed to work.

Bernie agreed to try it, believing he had nothing to lose. So the two of them walked to the lake's edge where Bobby took an oar from his boat and jammed it in the soft mud near the shoreline. He explained that all Bernie had to do was grasp the oar with one hand near the bottom and, much like choosing sides in a sandlot baseball game, work his way, hand over hand, to the top. Bernie began somewhat skeptically, but he was extremely pleased that in no time at all he was up the paddle without a crick.

A BASKET CASE

The local gentry of a small Spanish community built a theater on the town square and brought in the most favored actors and actresses to perform on their large stage. The theater became known the land over for its quality performances. Eventually, the Basques from the hillsides outside of town began to gather near the theater for a glimpse of the society elite. These Basques soon were lining the long staircase that led to the theater entrance.

One evening, the wife of one of the patrons suggested that it would be a charitable act if the wealthy shared some of their good fortune and invited the Basques to enjoy a show with them. The idea was quickly adopted and the following Saturday night all the Basques were allowed to stand in the exit way to watch the play. It was a grand play until someone smelled smoke and shouted the immortal word "Fire!" several times.

The panic stricken crowd jammed the narrow exit and nearly all of those in attendance died as the smoke and fire ravaged the theater. The surviving citizens of the community mourned their dead for many weeks. Then they set about to rebuild the theater as a monument to those who had died. They also passed a local ordinance that made it illegal to ever again put all their Basques in one exit.

A BEARD IN THE HAND

A destitute young man named Bennie assisted an old lady across the street. Upon reaching the other side, the lady said: "I am a special person and for your help I grant you three wishes."

Benny did not believe in fairy godmothers, but to humor her he said: "First, I wish to awake in the morning in a million dollar home. Second, I wish to have a vault with $5 million in it. Third, I wish 100 of the most beautiful women resident in my home to attend to my every need."

The old woman nodded. "You shall realize each of these," she said. "But wishes have a price. You must never again shave, lest you turn into a Grecian urn."

The next morning, much to Benny's amazement, each of his three wishes had come true. And for the next ten years, Benny and his long beard lived a life of luxury. Then one morning, Benny began to doubt the warning and eventually convinced himself that it had been a hoax. So he stood before the bathroom mirror and snipped off one whisker and another and another and nothing happened. With the help of a rusty old razor, long neglected in his medicine chest, he finished shaving.

Upon the last stroke of the razor, Benny promptly turned into a beautiful Grecian Urn. For, as we all know, a Benny shaved is a Benny urned.

A BEER FILLED PITCHER

Although Mel Famie was regarded throughout the sports world as the greatest pitcher ever known, it was his practice of drinking beer while on the job that drew the most attention. In spite of his drinking, his team won the right to play in the World Series.

Mel pitched the first three games and won them handily. The next three games went to the opposing team. When Mel took the mound with his ever present six pack and began pitching, everyone knew he would win. The game was tied in the bottom of the ninth inning. He quickly struck out two batters but the next three advanced to the bases on balls.

A happy ending began to look impossible. Mel finished the last of his beer, something he had never done before, and proceeded. And when it was over he had walked this last batter, thus forcing in the winning run. His team lost. The stadium fell silent. Mel left the mound in disgrace.

Later, during an interview with the winning team members, a reporter asked what they thought caused Mel to be so off his mark. The team members replied in unison that it was obvious. They told the reporter all he had to do was think about it. He'd have to agree, they told him, it's the beer that made Mel Famie walk us.

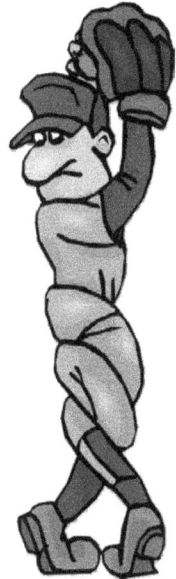

A BOY NAMED SIOUX

On a Sioux reservation in the Dakotas, the chief was a very forward thinking individual and proposed to the tribal council that his son attend the Massachusetts Institute of Technology (MIT) and train to be an electrical engineer. When this training was complete, the son would go on to great discoveries and bring fame to the reservation.

By depriving themselves, the tribes people managed to save sufficient funds, and on the son's eighteenth birthday they sent him off to MIT. Four years later the graduate returned to the reservation and, to express his gratitude, offered to install electrical wiring in the public bathhouse. Lighted, the bathhouse could be used in the evenings as well as in the day.

The young engineer installed the most modern equipment available and the bathhouse became the envy of all the tribes as a result. The young engineer also became known as the first American to ever wire a head for a reservation.

A CIRCULAR ARGUMENT *(Risqué)*

A young Native American woman went to a doctor for her first ever physical exam. She was somewhat nervous when the doctor instructed her to disrobe so he could examine her body. She had never disrobed in front of a stranger, but he convinced her it was necessary if he was to complete the examination.

When he had finished he said: "You are in fine health. There are no problems that I could find. However, I noticed one anomaly. It's seems that you have no nipples."

"None of my people in my tribe have nipples," she replied.

"Truly amazing," the doctor said. "This is worthy of an article for the Journal of Medicine. How many people are in your tribe?"

"There are about five hundred of us," she replied. "And none of us have nipples – even the men."

"Truly amazing," he repeated. "And what is the name of your tribe?"

"As you may expect," she said. "We are known as the Indian Nippleless Five Hundred."

A CLEAN SWEEP

Two straw brooms were hanging in a closet day-after-day and sweep-after-sweep. Each one performed a different function around the house so they never left the closet together.

Eventually they came to know each other so well they decided to get married. The shorter of the two was, of course, the bride broom and the other was the groom broom.

The bride broom looked lovely and elegant in her white dress. She radiated happiness and beauty. The groom broom was equally as striking in his tuxedo and was handsome and suave. The wedding went without a hitch and everyone moved on to the wedding reception.

After all the celebration rituals were completed and while the brooms were dancing their first dance, the bride broom leaned over and whispered in the groom broom's ear: "I think I'm going to have a little whisk broom."

"Impossible!" replied the groom broom. "We haven't even swept together."

A CUTTING CAPER

In an unusual display of sibling cooperation, identical twins, Tom and Tim, decided to establish a business partnership as barbers. For many years their business flourished. They split the profits equally, went on vacation together, and shared all their material possessions without question.

Soon, they were not only wealthy but they had become world renown for the quality of their haircuts. People from around the globe made it a point to visit the twin barbers whenever they were in the country. It was inevitable that someone would want to learn the secret of the barber's success and, in due time, a research project was commissioned.

When the research was complete, Tom and Tim waited with baited breath for the results. The researcher opened his notes and read the conclusion: "The reason you have been so successful," he said. "Is that, as twin barbers, both of you make an extra effort to always shear and shear alike."

A DIME A DOZEN

A young anthropologist came upon a tribe of Aborigines tossing spears into the air at small objects. As he drew closer, he recognized the objects as silver dollars and noticed that the Aborigines aim was exceedingly accurate. He soon discovered that this game would go on for days before anyone missed. So, as he watched the contest, he wondered if those who threw the spears could be as accurate with something as small as a dime.

"Can you do as well with a dime?" he asked the Chief.

"I'm afraid that accomplishment is out of my reach," said the Chief. And he noticed the anthropologist's enthusiasm wane. "But perhaps my brother, who is also a skilled spearman, can do it for you."

"Oh, please ask him for me," the anthropologist insisted.

Whereupon the chief turned and called to a man on the other side of the clearing: "Hey brother. Can you spear a dime?"

A FAMILIAR TALE

Two close European friends, who lived across the German and Czechoslovakian border from each other, arranged to go on a camping trip in the Bavarian Mountains. After setting up camp and watching a beautiful sunset over the mountain peaks, these two friends crawled into their sleeping bags for a good night's rest.

Shortly after midnight the two friends were aroused by the commotion two bears, a male and a female, were making as they rummaged through the camp in search of food. Both the German and the Czech attempted to frighten the bears away, but their efforts only enraged the bears. Eventually, the worst happened - the bears attacked the two friends and devoured them.

The next morning, the game warden and his assistant came to the camp to see how the men were doing. The bears were still in the camp and the warden suspected what had happened. But to prove it, he would have to kill at least one of the bears and confirm the fate of the campers. This he did. And when he opened the female's stomach he discovered the German inside.

"Well, there's your proof," said the warden to his assistant.

"Yep," said the assistant. "And I guess this means the Czech's in the male."

A FEATHERED MOCKERY

A young mockingbird from Mississippi was fond of corn whiskey and, drinking to excess, often ended up wedged in the crook of an old magnolia tree. It was inevitable that he would become an embarrassment to the community, so after a particularly unpleasant episode with the corn mash drink, he was exiled to points further west and south.

After many days, he found himself in Mexico with a powerful thirst. It was not long until he discovered the similarities between bourbon and the cactus drink known in the local area as tequila. Of course, he wasted no time in becoming very familiar with the drink.

As you can guess, he became an embarrassment to the residents of his new home just as he had to his friends in Mississippi. His antics were no less notorious in Mexico than they were in Mississippi, but, in Mexico, a young author saw the possibilities for a fortune in the bird's activity. It wasn't long before he had achieved world-wide fame through the publication of the bird's biography titled Tequila Mockingbird.

A FELINE ENDEAVOR

On his most recent visit to town for supplies, Roy, the cowboy, purchased a pair of fancy boots. He meticulously tried on at least twenty pairs, walking in them and inspecting them carefully. "After all," he said. "These new shoes will have to last me for another ten years and I want to make certain they're of good and lasting quality."

On his way home and far from town, he was attacked by a mountain lion who grabbed his new boots and chewed them into shreds of leather of no use to anyone. Roy, of course, was thankful for his life but quite put out that his new shoes had been so violated. As he sat on a rock contemplating his next move, a town resident happened by. Roy told the visitor about his battle with the cat and the loss of his boots. Then after some mutual commiseration, Roy decided to return to town for another pair.

He hadn't walked a hundred paces when he heard shots fired behind him. As he turned to determine the cause for the shooting, he spied the visitor standing on a nearby knoll, rifle in hand, pointing to a large mountain lion collapsed in a heap on the ground.

The visitor called in a loud voice: "Pardon me Roy. Is this the cat that chewed your new shoes?"

A FISH STORY

Joe Dacron, a rug salesman, and his best friend, Sam, were walking through a Japanese garden one sunny Sunday afternoon. As they crossed a wooden bridge over a pond stocked with large fish, they stopped to admire the many colored flowers bordering the pond.

Joe leaned against the railing as they took in the view and his billfold worked its way out of his back pocket and fell toward the water. Just as it approached the surface, a large carp rose and caught the billfold in its jaws. Immediately, another carp rose to the surface a few feet away and the first carp tossed the billfold to the second.

"Look at that," Sam shouted. And the two carp began to toss the billfold back and forth, never letting it touch the water. "Isn't that amazing?" he continued. "Simply unbelievable."

Joe, surprised by Sam's enthusiastic response, said: "It's hard to believe you've never seen carp-to-carp walleting before."

A FITTING MONUMENT

Following the end of World War II, the government of the small town of Fitty, on the foggy Normandy coast, decided to construct a new city hall honoring their soldiers. It was soon apparent from the citizens that they didn't like the façade of the building nor its location. Unfortunately, there were no changes possible and, despite many protests, construction proceeded.

On the day of the dedication ceremonies, one of the many fogs common to this part of the world had tightly gripped the town of Fitty. The throngs of citizens who had gathered for the ceremonies lined the streets and crowded the hills overlooking the city. But, because of the fog, very few of them could see the beautiful building.

Bickering and shouts of accusation began to ripple through the crowd as the town fathers waited for the fog to lift. It was important that everyone see the beautiful monument they had commissioned. They were convinced that when all the citizens saw the building in its glory, everyone would agree the leaders had done the right thing.

But as the day wore on, the fog became thicker and the citizens became more convinced that it was an omen. Had the town fathers listened to them, this monument would be what it truly should have been: a tribute to the soldiers and not a new place for the politicians to enjoy. But, alas, they left for home convinced that you can't site Fitty Hall.

A FUELISH MISTAKE

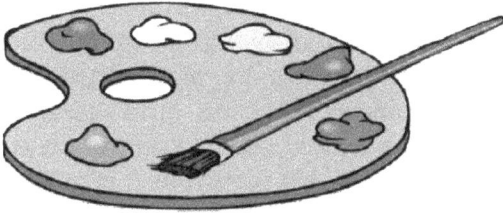

A thief achieved some notoriety in Paris because of his cunning and stealth. He operated flawlessly on many exploits where he stole several paintings over the years from the Louvre and other museums. No matter what the authorities did, he always seemed to outsmart them. He left no clues and no evidence. It seemed as though they would never catch him.

So it was that the gendarmes were speechless when they finally captured him. He had planned his most recent thievery as carefully as he had all the others. He was able to gain entrance, take his desired paintings, and escape from the Louvre undetected. However, he was captured only two blocks away when the van he was using to escape ran out of gas.

Of course, the authorities' first question in their interrogation was filled with awe that he could have been caught. They wondered how he could have masterminded so many brilliant crimes and then make such a stupid mistake as running out of gas.

His reply was blunt and contained no apology. He said: "My two accomplices, Michael and Angelo, and I had no Monet to buy Degas to make the Van Gogh."

A FULL HOUSE

Marty Mallard had been a gambler all his life. He started out as a duckling shooting marbles in the school playground. Soon he was running numbers for the local bookie. After he graduated from high school he became a card shark and bet on the horses from coast-to-coast. He drummed up crap games wherever he could and even ran a numbers game of his own.

It was not surprising then that he would organize a gambling club. He redecorated his home into a casino type atmosphere. He installed blackjack, craps, and roulette tables. Before long, although he restricted attendance to ducks, he had a large following that took advantage of the casino's venue that included a liberal supply of banned drugs.

Everything seemed to be going well. Each night Marty had a full house and the profits began piling up. He thought it couldn't get much better. And it didn't.

One night the door came crashing in, startling all of the ducks in the place. As policemen poured through the door, one of them hollered: "Nobody move! You're all under arrest!"

"On what grounds," Marty responded.

The policemen yelled back: "Operating an illegal quack house."

A FULL PLATE

An old man goes to his dentist complaining that something feels very wrong in his mouth. The dentist takes a look and shakes his head.

"That new upper plate I put in for you six months ago is completely disintegrated," The dentist said. "Something has completely eroded it away. What have you been eating?"

The old man replies: "Well, all I can think of is that about four months ago my wife made some asparagus and put some stuff on it she called Hollandaise sauce. I loved it so much that now I eat it on everything."

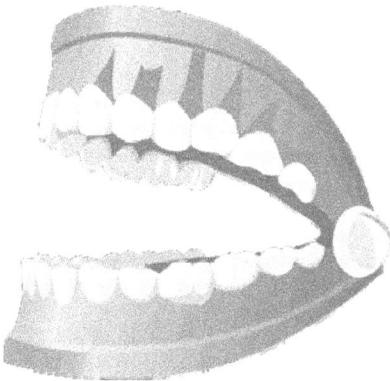

"Well," the dentist answered. "That's got to be the answer. Hollandaise sauce is made with lots of lemon juice, which is highly corrosive. And it has eaten away your upper plate. I'll have to make you a new one, and, this time, I'll make it out of chrome."

"Chrome? Why chrome?" the old man asked.

"It's simple," replied the dentist. "Everyone knows there's no plate like chrome for the Hollandaise!"

A FURRIER AND IVES

An astronaut on the first manned mission to Mars hadn't walked more than a few yards from his spaceship when he was surrounded by at least a dozen little furry bodies. Each of the small creatures had arms, legs and a large head covered with soft, cat-like fur. They were able to communicate with him and said they meant him no harm. He soon discovered they called themselves Furries and he asked to be taken to their leader.

The Furries obliged and led him through a crack in a nearby mountain into a long tunnel. Soon they entered a large cavern in the mountain where all the Furries had gathered. He was then subjected to the usual curiosity and even some gentle poking and probing.

He again asked to be taken to their leader. At this request, they pointed to a larger Furrie sitting on a throne-like chair at the end of the cavern. This larger Furrie looked like the others except an appendage that looked like a doctor's hypodermic needle grew out of the top of his head.

The spaceman turned to the Furrie closest to him and asked for the proper title for their leader so he could address him properly.

"He is called many names," was the reply. "But most of us simply call him the Furrie with the syringe on top."

A GENERAL SEARCH AND DESTROY MISSION

The Mesopotamian king had complete and repressive control over his subjects and forced many of them to build ziggurats to his honor. Many of these pyramidal, stair-step, towers were built at a great cost.

The burden of the King's unrelenting drive for immortality eventually drove a small band of brick makers to consider assassination as the only way to escape the King's terror. Unfortunately, their elaborate plans, all written on expensive parchment, failed and they were soon pursued by the King's general in charge of defense.

The assassins fled to the Valley of the Ziggurats to hide. While there, they began destroying the plans they had drawn up by burning them. And the general, who was close on their tail, noticed the smoke from their fire rise above the ziggurats.

Using the smoke as a beacon to their hideout, the general closed in on the assassins. It was only a matter of time until he had destroyed them. In the process he proved that a searching general can determine that smoking ziggurats are dangerous to your health.

A HARD LIFE

A wealthy young man decided to experience life aboard a four-masted sailing ship and signed on as the lowest of the crew of the ship known as Hard Times. Soon, they were under sail and work began in earnest. The captain was a task master of the highest order, working his crew until they were exhausted.

The wealthy young man quickly learned that a hard life did not give you as much wisdom as it gave you an unrelenting desire to never have to live that way again. And as the trip wore on, a simple bond of friendship developed between him and a poor sailor on board.

One blustery afternoon as the ship tacked into the wind, the Captain sent the poor sailor aloft to repair a rigging that had come loose. As the young man struggled with the lines, a gust of wind snapped the canvas and threw him onto the hardwood decking of the ship. He lay there motionless as his distraught friend ran toward him fearing the worst. But the Captain stood in the way.

"Your soft life has taught you nothing. He is a survivor. He cannot be injured. He will be okay."

"How can you say that?"

"I can tell when a man is used to hard ships."

A HEAD START

Most everyone is familiar with Bluebeard the Pirate's savage approach to life and the many tales about him that frighten even the most stout hearted of us. Among the most intriguing of stories, however, is the one wherein Bluebeard is finally captured and sentenced to death by decapitation.

The story relates how Bluebeard would be spared if he would simply turn his back on his evil ways. He refused to repent and his captors had no recourse but to proceed with his punishment. Still, there was one among them with pity and a little hope and suggested that they perhaps amputate his leg and give him still another chance to repent. The others agreed.

With a leg removed, Bluebeard still refused to change his ways so they removed the other leg. Again Bluebeard would not relent and his captors were obliged to remove one of his arms and then the other. With only his torso and head remaining, Bluebeard remained adamant and blasphemed his captors for their stupidity. This only enraged them and made them more determined to carry out what they had planned at first.

As the sword removed his head from his body, Bluebeard shouted his final curses at those who had done him in. He was never known to be one who quit when he was ahead.

A HEAVENLY SONG

Sammy Crabb and Harry Johnson grew up together and spent nearly all their free time together. As fate would have it, they both died together in a fiery auto crash one Sunday afternoon but went separate ways in the hereafter.

When Sammy reported to the devil, he was given his choice of occupations and quickly requested permission to run a discotheque, something he had dreamed of almost constantly while alive. Harry Johnson arrived at the pearly gates and was also given a choice. His desire was simply to learn to play the harp.

Two weeks later, an angel discovered Harry sitting on a curb sobbing and wringing his hands. The angel asked him what was wrong and Harry told how he missed his friend Sam. The angel agreed to make arrangements for Harry to visit Sam but insisted that Harry return before midnight or be abandoned in hell forever.

Harry found Sam at the discotheque and enjoyed their reunion all through the evening. When he heard the clock striking midnight, he hurriedly left the discotheque and raced back to heaven, arriving just as the gates closed.

He first breathed a sigh of relief that he had made it, then raised his hands to his face. "Oh no," he wailed. "I left my harp in Sam Crabb's disco."

A HOUSE FULL OF CHAN TEAKS

A distinguished Chinese cabinet maker named Chan was widely known for his exquisite workmanship. He was adept at making wondrous items of teakwood that other less confident woodworkers dared not attempt. A large portion of his success depended on a private supply of the most precious teakwood in all of China that he kept in a locked shed near his workshop.

One winter morning, Chan discovered his shed had been opened and some of his teakwood taken. The telltale footprints in the snow convinced Chan the culprit was but a young, barefooted boy who obviously needed only firewood. If such was true, the boy would return and Chan resolved to apprehend him.

That evening, Chan prepared himself for the wait that is always necessary when one wishes to catch a thief. And many hours later, he was awakened from his drowsiness by sounds near his shed. He spied the culprit, but in his grogginess was amazed to see that the thief was a bear with two perfectly formed boys feet. He watched, stunned by this miraculous sight, as the bear gathered an ample supply of the precious teakwood and began to retreat into the forest.

Chan quickly recovered and ran after the creature. And for hours one could hear him throughout the forest calling: "Stop. Stop. You boy foot bear with teak of Chan."

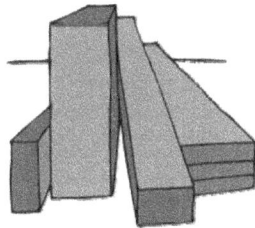

A LESSON WELL LEARNED

Jimmy was an only child whose father shared countless lessons of life with him. When Jimmy went to college, he left with the knowledge of every solution to every problem he thought he would ever encounter. It was indeed a surprise when Jimmy called home for additional advice. "I want to buy a car," he told his father. "And I can't decide between an inexpensive coupe and an extravagant sports car that would take all my money."

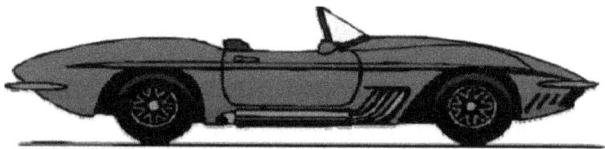

"Take your problem to the weevils," the father said. These were two imaginary characters they had invented and to whom they would pose questions for resolution. They would ask first the large weevil, then small weevil. The process never failed them.

A week later Jimmy called home again. "I bought the sports car," he said. "I took the question to the weevils. And the large weevil argued for the inexpensive coupe and almost convinced me. Then I took the question to the small weevil. He too made a good argument. I was torn between the two and didn't know what to do. Then I remembered a wise piece of advice you taught me many years ago and I knew I must buy the sports car. It's a simple lesson I should never have forgotten. You taught me that whenever I was faced with a dilemma like mine was, I should choose the lesser of two weevils."

A LIGHT AT THE END

A recent college graduate took a new job in a hilly eastern city and began commuting each day. The geography of that area of the country required him to work through a tiring array of tunnels, bridges, and traffic jams. To make the task less onerous, he invited several of his coworkers to share the ride. He soon found, however, that the shared riding did not work and his commute continued to get more stressful - especially the tunnels.

He described to the company doctor that he was fine on the bridges and in the traffic. He was also good when it came to either day or night or even when one of his co-riders forgot to bathe all week long. He went on to point out that it was when he got into the tunnels and he had the four other carpoolers crowded around him that he got anxious and dizzy and felt like he was going to explode.

The doctor immediately announced that he had identified the ailment.

"What is it Doc? Am I going insane?" The young man asked.

"No. No. My boy. It is something very common in these parts. You have what is known as Carpool Tunnel Syndrome."

A LITTLE LAUGHTER NEVER HURT

Princess Funny Bone was the Indian reservation comedienne for years. Every Saturday evening she would stand in the midst of the tribal recreation area and tell joke after joke. Her jokes were so long, however, that the tribe often lost interest before she could finish. As a result she lost her audience.

She went to the medicine man for help in solving her problem, and he told her the answer was simply to tell shorter jokes. So she worked for weeks on a new routine in hopes of regaining her popularity.

When it was time for her return to the stage, she took her place with some trepidation. And in a manner of introduction she said: "I have a short joke for you. It's sort of a mini-ha-ha."

A LITTLE SEASONING GOES A LONG WAY

Sergeant Joseph Johansson served honorably in the United States Army during the First World War. At the age of 18, he was barely eligible to serve but it was his youth that allowed him to survive the vicious mustard gas attacks during that war. His superiors recognized his exploits in the field and, before that war had concluded, they promoted him to commissioned officer status.

Much older now but still a dedicated and loyal soldier, he participated in the Second World War as a Major. His field of operation was the South Pacific Theater. And on one fateful beach landing the enemy attacked his platoon with an almost unsurvivable amount of pepper spray.

Following the war he retired to a secluded life in a small Texas town. He lived there in anonymity, happily pursuing his many hobbies and generally enjoying his life.

However, once each year on Memorial Day, the town fathers cajoled him into donning his uniform and then leading the annual parade down Main Street. He was, after all, the small town's only seasoned veteran.

A LOGICAL CONCLUSION

An old man visited his brother every day of his adult life. To reach his brother's house he had to cross a bridge over the river that ran through town. The old man had heard his brother was sick and hurried on his way for the day's visit.

When he approached the bridge, he noticed a guard sitting by a gate that had been erected in the middle. And when he asked permission to pass through the gate, the guard demanded to know the reason. The simple statement 'I want to get to the other side' was not sufficient to gain passage. The statement 'I want to go downtown' resulted in the same denial of passage. The guard insisted that the old man have a reason and not just a desire.

So the old man said: "The **reason** I wish to pass is because my brother is sick and I need to visit him." The guard immediately stood and opened the gate.

When the old man explained to his brother what had happened, the brother responded: "It doesn't surprise me."

"How so?" the old man asked.

"Well. Ever since the government took over that bridge, they run it like a prison. And the guard is like a dumb robot." He shook his head in disgust. "With all this government control now-a-days, it only stands to reason."

A LOT OF BULL

Reminiscent of Animal Farm by George Orwell, a small farm community was run by a few bulls. The other animals followed the orders of this group of bulls, completing chores as required and attending to the creature comforts of the bellowing bovines. The strange aspect of this social order was that the bulls were smaller than any of the other animals. They stood only twelve inches at the shoulder.

One day a sociologist fox arrived at the farm to study this unusual arrangement and perhaps discover the secret of the bulls. He took copious notes and studied every facet of the bulls' behavior in his attempt to determine the reason for the bulls' control. All he discovered was that the group of twelve inch bulls consumed large quantities of alcohol, spent the greater part of the day inebriated and issued orders as they wobbled around the barnyard.

Finally, the answer for the bulls' control over all the other animals came to the sociologist. It was rather obvious and he was disappointed with himself for not thinking of it sooner. He immediately opened his notebook and made an entry. If you looked over his shoulder you would have seen him write: "Wee bulls wobble, but they don't fall down."

A MAN OF MANY TALENTS

A young man named Joseph grew up in the Israeli port city of Haifa. When he became a young adult, he fell in love with the flute and learned to play it with a great degree of competence. However, there was no money in playing the flute so he took up farming. Although the work was rewarding and he did make a meager income, it was still not enough to satisfy his desires.

Therefore, as he searched for a new occupation, he fell in with the wrong crowd and turned to a life of looting. Eventually, he became a wanted man and his picture was printed on wanted posters and distributed throughout the town.

Because he was the son of a Barcelona ex-nun and a German father, as well as a former flutist and farmer, the police described him on the wanted posters as: "A Haifa-lootin', flutin', Teuton son of a nun from Barcelona, part-time plowboy Joe."

A MARINE STORY

A slightly inebriated young man was in search of his new found friends. They had invited him to join them on a boat at the local marina. He approached the marina pier in the growing darkness and looked over the mass of boats, immediately convinced he would never find his friend's boat among all the others. He was about to give up after an hour of futile searching when he came upon a man mooring his boat.

"Could you perhaps tell me how to find my friends?" the slowly sobering lad asked the man.

"Certainly," the man replied. "Just go to the end of this pier and turn right. Then go to the second branch and turn left. Then go to the end of that pier and you'll find them."

"I don't know," the young man answered. "I've been all over this marina. The piers connect here and there. Some of the slats are missing and I nearly fell into the ocean because it's so dark. How can I tell when I've reached the end?"

"It's really simple," was the reply. "Just go as I said. You'll know when you're there because when you're out of slits, you're out of pier."

A MATERIAL WITNESS

An IRS agent knocked on the door of the county's most prosperous textile manufacturer who was behind in his tax payments. "Is Fred home?" he asked the woman who answered the door.

"Sorry," the woman replied. "Fred's gone for cotton."

The next day the agent tried again. "Is Fred here today?"

"No, sir," the woman said. "I'm afraid Fred has again gone for cotton."

When he returned the third day he offered a statement instead of a question. "I suppose Fred is gone for cotton again?"

"No," the woman answered. She wiped a tear from her eye. "Fred died yesterday."

Suspecting he was being avoided, the tax collector decided to wait a week and investigate the cemetery himself as a way of confirming that Fred had died. Sure enough, there was poor Fred's tombstone with the following inscription: "Gone, But Not For Cotton."

A NEW GNU

The Boerne, Texas, zoo was still under construction when the San Antonio zoo offered them a gnu for which they had no more room. Boerne, not wanting to miss the opportunity, accepted the gnu and put him in an unfinished cage. The following morning they discovered that someone had installed all the loose tile in the cage where the gnu had been placed.

That night they moved the gnu to another cage and the following morning the tile in the new cage was also laid out on the floor in perfect patterns and professional lines. This time they stayed to watch the third cage where they moved the gnu and soon they were amazed as the gnu set about laying all the tile in his cage.

They immediately called the San Antonio zoo to inquire about this most unusual feat. They reported what had happened and how it was most unusual for a gnu to lay tile in such exquisite patterns. They were most interested in whether or not there could be some explanation for this activity.

The San Antonio zoo, however, advised them that this was not in the least out of the ordinary. As they explained it, the animal was nothing more than a typical gnu and tiler too.

A NO FAULT SOLUTION

Gordon Groveler was known for his habitual grumbling about the merits of another's sporting skills, especially when it came to team sports. Whenever his team suffered a defeat, Gordon was the first to point out the weaknesses of his teammates and his belief that those weaknesses were the cause of the defeat.

It is obvious why Gordon didn't have very many friends. That he had any is a testimony to the gullibility of the human race. Those few who stood with him, however, knew that sporting events were more than just exercises in physical strength and team-work.

When Gordon criticized the coach for bad decisions or a teammate for poor per-formance, they cheered him on. They knew what it was all about. They understood, like Gordon, that it's not winning or losing that really counts, but how you lay the blame.

A NOT SO WELL KNOWN THEORY *(Risqué)*

There are few people in the civilized world who are not aware of Einstein's theory of relativity. The famous $E=MC^2$ formula has become an integral part of all scientific teaching. What is not known is that Einstein had another theory he believed to be more amenable to proof than his most famous theory.

This more provable concept found its birth after the Nobel Prize winner married then split from Elsa Lowenthal. This first marriage ended in 1919 and when responding to the many questions he received as to why they split and why they found each other attractive in the first place, he told them it was a simple matter of physics and DNA.

He postulated that if a man is attracted to a woman with large breasts, that man would find the attraction even stronger when there was a DNA connection between the two. Since Elsa Lowenthal was well endowed, he was of course attracted to her and the attraction was even stronger because she was his cousin.

The formulation of this attraction received wide-spread distribution and soon came to be known as 'Einstein's Theory of Relative Titty'.

A PALADIN POSER

The local news reporter in search of a good story heard that the town's only judge had recently visited the doctor for an unknown reason. When the reporter burst into the judge's office seeking his story, the judge was reading the well-known classic Have Gun, Will Travel.

Ignoring all courtesies, the cub reporter blurted out: "Why did you visit the doc, judge?"

"I'm quite a bit overweight. I wanted his opinion."

"What did he say?"

"He told me to take two weeks off to get in shape. Of course I think that is poppycock and pure rubbish."

"So what will you do?" the reporter asked.

"Stay at my post, of course!" came the immediate reply.

"Eureka!" the pup reporter exclaimed. "I have my story and the headline of the year."

"And what, pray tell, is that?"

"Judge defies doctor. Half ton will gavel."

A ROSE BY ANY OTHER NAME ...

James and his wife, whom he called Baby, enjoyed their retirement sitting in their rocking chairs on the porch. They watched children going to school, mothers on shopping trips, and fathers going to and coming home from work. Occasionally, they would walk through the town visiting lifelong friends.

One night Baby passed away in her sleep leaving James alone in his rocking chair. Every evening, he would visit the flower shop on his way to the cemetery and purchase a single rose. When the florist asked him why only one rose he replied simply: "It's for my Baby."

Several months later as he sat on the porch at the end of the day, a large brownish colored frog jumped into Baby's rocking chair. It showed no fear of James and returned evening after evening. It was not long before James became accustomed to the frog's visits and he ended up taking the frog with him wherever he would go.

Sadly, the frog also died and James was devastated by his loss. The next time he stopped by the florist on his daily trip to the cemetery, he ordered up two roses instead of one.

The curious flower shop owner, unaware of recent events, asked him why he was buying two roses.

"I now mourn for two," James said. "So it's one for my Baby and one more for the Toad."

A ROYAL PAIN

Sally Snapshot was the most popular girl in the high school so it was not a surprise when she was selected Queen of the Senior Prom. She carried the title with perfect elegance and throughout the evening posed for many photographs. Most of these pictures were taken with her own camera because she wanted to ensure she had enough for her personal scrapbook.

The day after the prom she took her rolls of film to the photo shop in Walmart and ordered double prints. Then she went shopping and returned in the prescribed hour when her pictures were supposed to be ready. Unfortunately, the development machine was broken and the process was not complete. The attendant assured her they would be ready in another hour.

The second time she discovered the attendant had taken sick and left for home. The manager was very apologetic and promised that a stand-in attendant would develop her film as soon as he arrived.

Fortunately, Sally was a patient girl. She told the manager not to worry, that everything would certainly work out no matter how long it took. She would continue shopping while she waited. Then she wandered back into the store singing softly to herself: "Someday my prints will come."

A SAVORY CONCOCTION

A missionary for the Southern Baptist Convention asked for assignment to a region of New Guinea known for its cannibalism. He thought it would provide him the greatest opportunities for success if he could work with people whose lifestyle was so far removed from the Western culture. His superiors agreed and sent him out post haste.

Try at he might, the missionary was unable to make much progress with the normal methods of conversion as prescribed by the church. More often than not he was rebuffed by the small tribe where he had taken up residence. It seems that they preferred eating over learning about Christianity.

The missionary thought perhaps if he were to prepare a large stew and feed them, he might gain their attention long enough to deliver his message. As things turned out, he had the right approach if not the right ingredients.

When he presented the large kettle of stew to the cannibals, they misunderstood his offering. They believed he was sacrificing himself so they grabbed him, threw him in the pot, and boiled him until he was tender.

It was only when they ate him that they finally got a taste of religion.

A SHRINKING FEELING

A man rushed into the doctor's office with extreme agitation. He wrung his hands and could barely catch his breath long enough to talk. It was obvious he was in need of consolation or medical attention.

Finally, after many false starts, he shouted: "Doctor! I think I'm shrinking!!"

The doctor calmly responded: "Now, settle down. What makes you think that?"

"You must hurry and help me," the man shouted. "I fear I will soon shrink to nothingness."

"Relax," the doctor ordered. "If you want me to treat you, you'll just have to be a little patient."

A SINGULAR TRUTH *(Risqué)*

A Sioux Indian warrior, who had been born with only one testicle, was given the name 'One Stone'. He grew to hate that name and told people never to call him that. In fact, he warned that if anyone were to call him One Stone again he would kill them.

For many years after that no one called him by his name anymore. But one day a warrior named Blue Bird forgot and greeted him saying, 'Good Morning One Stone.' He immediately grabbed the warrior and began pummeling him. Try as the others might, they couldn't stop him and Blue Bird died from his injuries.

More years went by with no one calling him by his name. But one day a squaw named Yellow Bird, who was Blue Bird's cousin, returned to the tribe after a long absence. She saw One Stone and hugged him saying 'Hello One Stone'. He immediately grabbed her and began to pummel her. But she was strong and resisted him and refused to weaken under his blows. Eventually, he stopped.

As he lay exhausted and aware that he was unable to kill Yellow Bird, he realized the truth of the phrase: You can't kill two birds with one stone.

A SINKING FUND

A local gardening club wanted to form an association to exchange ideas and techniques for successful vegetable gardens. At the first meeting, the subject of soil mixture dominated the discussions. Most of the members felt that loam was the essential ingredient in soil to ensure success. And after the debate had gone on for some time it became clear that a large number of the members also believed in a mixture of redwood shavings and sawdust. To appease the largest number of members, the group eventually decided to endorse a combination of the two preferred methods.

As a result of this decision and the subsequent world famous quality of the vegetables growing when planted in this mixture, the club earned the honor of being the only successful Shavings and Loam Association in America.

A SLIPPERY ARGUMENT

An unpopular attorney had just finished trying a case in the County Courthouse and was on his way back to his office. As he exited the Courthouse he slipped on a banana peel that had been discarded on the Courthouse steps. It was a grand slip and he completed an entire flip before landing on his butt in front of a crowd of amused onlookers.

After dusting himself off and giving the crowd his most distasteful sneer, he turned and reentered the Court-house. He hobbled up to the court clerk and slammed his briefcase on the desk.

"I hereby file suit against the court," he declared.

"You can't sue the court," the clerk replied.

"I most certainly can," he said. "And my charges are that the court was negligent."

"And what is the basis for your suit," the clerk insisted.

The attorney pointed a finger in the direction of the front steps and said: "I am suing for being overturned on a peel."

A SOBERING THOUGHT

Wendy the whiskey maker lived in the back hills of Kentucky and produced some of the finest whiskey available in the area. One day, as she transported her product to the black market, she had truck trouble and had to stop by the side of the road.

A young man named Tommy was passing by and stopped to help her. He was unaware of her illegal activities and remained in the dark throughout the course of the growing friendship which ensued. In due course, they even became lovers with him completely unaware of her activities.

One evening, the government raided her place of business and arrested her. Her young lover was with her when she was arrested and suddenly became aware of her past. The officers then transported her to the local county jail where she remained overnight.

Tommy came to visit her in the morning and as he left the sheriff asked him: "I guess this will change your feelings about her, won't it lad?"

Tommy's response was quick and emphatic. He turned to the sheriff and simply said: "She may be only a whiskey maker, but I love her still."

A SPIRITUAL SACRIFICE

Shelley and Sandy were honored members of the Hawaiian community long before Captain Cook ever cast his eyes on the lovely islands. They were devoted spirit worshipers who followed all the rules of their religion.

Once a year they would journey to the volcano on the big Island to offer their sacrifices in the hopes of appeasing the spirits for the coming year. They climbed to the heights of the volcano and cast their goods into the open cauldron of molten rock chanting "Please grant this bounty in all we do, Oh spirits of the underworld."

One year, after they completed their sacrifice, a solicitor approached them at the base of the volcano. He informed them he was collecting items for a sacrifice to the spirit and would appreciate their contributions.

"We'd love to make a donation," Shelley and Sandy said in unison. "But we already gave at the orifice."

A STINKING SHAME

Mahatma Gandhi, as most people know, walked barefoot most everywhere he went. To compensate for the lack of shoes, his feet produced an impressive set of calluses for their protection.

He also ate very little food choosing to demonstrate his piety through frequent fasting episodes. This, of course, made him rather frail.

The fasting combined with the unusual contents of his diet caused him to suffer from bad breath.

When one considers all of these things together it is not surprising that he became known as a super callused fragile mystic hexed by halitosis.

A TAILOR'S COMPLAINT

A Greek tailor had been working in the neighborhood for years. He had always been known for his quality workmanship and had many repeat customers. But as he grew older, he began to make mistakes and his customers began to go elsewhere for their clothing. Rather than try to correct his problem, he became angry about his plight and told everyone who came in his shop about it. His wife warned him that he would lose all his customers if he didn't begin treating people right and again provide them good quality.

When he had but two customers left, the wisdom of his wife's words finally gained meaning for him. He started working harder at perfection, but every time he sewed something, he had to tear out the seams for one reason or another. No matter how hard he tried he couldn't quite get it right any more.

Finally, his wife shouted to him: "I told you to change your ways but you wouldn't listen to me. Everyone has finally gone. And now all you can do is rip what you sew."

A TICKLISH SITUATION *(Risqué)*

A woman desperately in need of work could not find a job because of her lack of experience. Her pleading touched the personnel manager and he finally offered her a job on the Tickle Me Elmo manufacturing line. He explained her duties to her and showed her where she would be working. She looked at him with a deeply questioning gaze but nodded when he told her to be at work by eight o'clock in the morning.

The following day at 8:45 AM the supervisor contacted the personnel manager and complained mightily that the new woman had caused a massive backup on the production line. Together the two men made their way to the end of the line and discovered Elmos stacked up everywhere.

The new woman was at the end of the line and she was intently cutting little pieces of fabric from the fuzzy material that makes up the majority of Elmo, wrapping the material around two marbles, and sewing the material between Elmo's legs.

The personnel manager eventually stopped laughing enough to call the woman aside. "I'm sorry," he said. "I think you misunderstood my instructions yesterday. What I really need you to do is to give Elmo two test tickles."

A TIME TRIP

Dr. Stein had been experimenting with matter transfer theories his entire life and one night he erroneously reversed the wires on his prototype time machine and was instantly cast into a dark void. When he gathered his senses he discovered he was in a tunnel racing forward in time.

His immediate elation was soon quelled as he realized his movement was taking him so far into the future that he would soon reach the time of his death. There had to be a way to stop his forward progress in time and thus avert this tragedy.

He spied a small ornamental recess in the wall of the time tunnel wherein rested a plaque engraved with the number of the year he was about to enter. He could see by this plaque that he had already projected himself two years into the future. He thereupon resolved to catch the edge of the next recess to arrest his progress. This, he hoped, would prevent him from continuing toward his ultimate fate.

And he did so. His movement stopped. "Amazing," he said. "Wait until my friends find out that a niche in time saved Stein."

A TURNING POINT

A strong northeast wind pushed the surf far up the beach and threw the cold rain against the rocks. Far from its normal hiding place, a small tern struggled to overcome these winds and find shelter inland. The struggle was too difficult, however, and the weary bird began to falter. Suddenly, another tern was there offering a helping hand. With the help of the additional bird, they both made it to safety.

The storm blew itself out and the sunshine finally returned to the beach. The small tern who had struggled against the storm began to search for his savior. For many days he visited flock after flock until he spied the selfless Samaritan feeding in a nearby lagoon.

"I have come to be your slave," he said to the older tern.

"That is not necessary," the older one replied. "In fact, that is only done in the movies."

"But I insist," the younger demanded. "For it still remains true that in times like these one good tern deserves another."

A WAKE UP CALL

The local news reporter contacted his station and requested the opening spot on the night's news broadcast.

"Why should we do that?" the producer asked. "You haven't given us anything worth that slot in months."

"This has to do with a heinous murder," he replied. "A man was found murdered in Seattle this past weekend."

"There is nothing special about what you've said so far. Anything else about this news?"

"Definitely," the reporter went on. "The detectives found him dead in his bathtub which was filled with corn flakes and milk. He also had a banana shoved into his mouth and sugar sprinkled all over his head. Police suspect it was a cereal killer."

A WRONG CONCLUSION

Bobby Bedmaker and his wife Belinda decided after years of sleeping in a small double bed that it was time to buy a king size bed and sleep in luxury.

He and Belinda shopped for many weekends until they found the bed that suited them. They paid for it on the spot for delivery the next day. Because they needed new sheets, the salesman recommended they buy them from the Wong Brothers Sheet Maker establishment, a small Chinese shop in town.

When they inquired of the first Wong brother about white sheets, their desired color, they discovered that he made only brown, tan, and yellow sheets.

The second Wong brother was not much help either. He told them he made only sheets in rose, pink, and lavender. Try as they might, neither Bobby nor Belinda could convince the Wong brothers to make a white sheet for them.

They left the store disappointed. And once outside, Bobby turned to Belinda and said: "I've heard it all my life but have never been unfortunate enough to experience it. Now I know. I have finally witnessed the truth of the statement that two Wongs don't make a white."

ADMINISTRATIVE HANG-UP

On a recent trip to the Philippines, the President of the United States was visiting Manila and taking in the sights. He traveled throughout the city and was entertained by the artisans wherever he went.

At one particularly interesting stop, he was impressed with the ability of a young man who bent himself into the smallest of bundles and crammed himself into small boxes and pots, time and time again.

"I simply have to know who that boy is," the President said.

"Sir," his aide replied. "I'm surprised you don't already know him. He's the original Manila folder."

AIN'T HE SOMETHING?

When the Israeli prime minister was Benjamin Netanyahu he answered to the nickname of Bibi. It was a nickname that most people were unaware of but his wife used it almost exclusively in conversations with him.

The prime minister would often make trips worldwide in his attempts to gain continued support for Israel's existence. Some of these trips included visits with the Palestinian Liberation Organization or the PLO.

He would often take his wife with him on these trips and so it was not unusual when she accompanied Mr. Netanyahu to a summit conference between Israel and the PLO. She had always wanted to take a more activist role in her country's affairs and attendance at this summit would allow her to do so.

As they entered the great hall where the summit conference would be held, it was determined by the protocol officer that Mrs. Netanyahu should introduce her husband to the PLO leader Arafat. The feeling was that she would be able to lessen the tension that existed between these two great men.

She gladly accepted the invitation and boldly approached Mr. Arafat. Pointing towards her husband with a hand gesture she caught the PLO leader's eye and said: "Yasser, that's my Bibi."

AISLE OF MAN

A recently married man decided to surprise his wife by baking a cake. One day when she was out shopping, he gathered the tools and ingredients necessary in the kitchen. As he began to work he realized he was missing butter, the most important ingredient.

He summoned Rover, his faithful dog, and sent him to the store. Now, Rover was a very intelligent dog and was known to have read a book or two in his lifetime. So it was not unusual that he was intrigued by a nearby bookstore's window display. After a few moments of review, Rover was wandering the aisles of books completely lost in thought.

In the process of his literary deliberations, Rover completely forgot his mission was to procure sticks of butter. Instead, he bought a book of poetry and hurried home so he could read it.

The cake baker was disappointed in Rover but not that surprised. Situations such as this had happened in the past and he chided himself for not remembering. He knew as well as the next man that you don't send an intelligent dog who likes to read poetry on an errand for groceries. Invariably, he will get verse before he gets butter.

ALEX KEEPS WATCH

An entrepreneur, who had made some bad investments and lost all his income, began selling watches from his extensive collection to support himself. To get the most from each sale, Alexander sold his watches separately from the watch bands, each for its own price. Although he soon wore hand me down clothes and used a piece of an old cotton rag to strap his favorite watch to his arm, he held his head high and proudly begged money in between watch sales.

One day, while soliciting from a wealthy pedestrian, his expensive watch and its cotton strap became visible at the edge of his tattered sleeve. "Rather than give you a handout, will you sell the expensive watch you are wearing," the man asked.

"No," Alex replied.

To which the stranger asked: "Why?"

"This watch is special," Alexander said. "It has a strong sentimental value."

The pedestrian shrugged and as he walked away he said: "I don't believe it. A valuable watch worth hundreds and still he begs."

"You don't understand," a nearby beggar said. "If he sold the watch, he'd also have to forfeit Alexander's rag time band."

ALL CHOKED UP

Arty Angryman complained to his friends about nearly everything. He hated lines, traffic lights, noise, happy people, sad people, old and young people, summers, winters and both good and bad experiences. He was a most miserable man.

One day, while in the grocery store shopping for produce, he squeezed a tomato and a clerk chastised him for his conduct. Soon the clerk, his helper, and the store manager were in heated debate. Fortunately, one of Arty's closest friends witnessed the altercation and ushered Arty outside before a fight could begin. Once outside Arty began mumbling: "I'll kill 'em. Next time that happens I'll kill 'em. Give me a dollar now and I won't have to wait. I'll kill all three of 'em for a dollar." Just to shut him up, Arty's friend gave him the requested dollar and took him home.

The next evening, Arty's friend returned from a hard day's work and opened the local newspaper. "Oh my God," he said. "I don't believe it."

But there was no way to escape the truth because the headlines read: Artichokes Three For A Dollar.

ALL IN A DAY'S WORK

Frankie proudly drove his city bus throughout the busy streets every day for more than fifteen years. He would come home from work each evening and his wife would ask him how the day went. This routine developed into a daily event where he would give his wife a one word clue that described the day's happenings and she would try to guess what he meant. The game worked well for many years and his wife was very adept at guessing the answers.

One day, Frankie was surprised to see a set of very large twin ladies board his bus at the Sesame Street stop, especially when they kept calling each other Pattie. On the next stop, a long time passenger, Louis Cheese, boarded and was followed by Ross from the special education school down the street. Louis spent his entire trip complaining about his bunions and, when combined with the vociferous twins and energetic Ross, it nearly drove Frankie crazy. That night he went home quite tired.

His wife waited for the usual clue and he finally offered it: "Hamburger," he said.

She thought for a long time but finally admitted Frankie had come up with a clue she couldn't decipher.

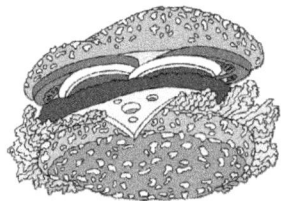

"It's really rather simple," he said. "Just think: Two all beef Patties, Special Ross, Louis Cheese picking bunions on the Sesame Street Bus."

ALL STRUNG OUT

The symphony orchestra was performing Beethoven's Ninth. In this piece, there's a 20 minute passage during which the bass violinists have nothing to do. Rather than sit around that whole time looking stupid, some bassists decided to sneak offstage and go to the tavern next door for a quick one.

After downing several beers in quick succession, one of them looked at his watch and said, "Hey! We need to get back!"

"No need to panic," said a fellow bassist. "I thought we might need some extra time, so I tied the last few pages of the conductor's score together with string. It'll take him a few minutes to get it untangled."

A few moments later they staggered back to the concert hall and took their places in the orchestra.

About this time, a member of the audience noticed the conductor seemed a bit edgy and said as much to her companion.

"Well, of course," was the reply. "Don't you see? It's the bottom of the Ninth, the score is tied, and the bassists are loaded."

ALL THE WAY OR NOT AT ALL

It was that time in a young boy's life when the baby teeth were beginning to come out. The tooth fairy was still a believable part of this young man's perceptions. So, when one of his front teeth cracked and a portion came out, the young boy went to his parents and announced that he had something to trade with the tooth fairy.

The parents looked into the young man's mouth to confirm the story and discovered that only a portion of the tooth had broken off. Both parents looked at their son and shook their heads.

"I'm afraid this won't work yet," the father said.

"Why not?" the son asked. He thrust his open palm toward the parents. "It's a tooth, isn't it?"

"Yes it is," the father answered. "But the tooth fairy has some very strict rules."

"What rules?"

"She's insistent about enforcing this rule." The father struggled to make the next revelation palatable. But he could find no way out. So he merely said: "Before she'll pay, she wants the tooth, the whole tooth, and nothing but the tooth."

ALL TOTALLED

The young teen mowed his grandfather's lawn once each week. On a particular week he was unable to get the lawnmower engine to start and he sought out his grandfather's assistance.

The grandfather looked at the engine then had the teenager pull the starter cord a few times to turn the engine over. After that he went to his tool bench and retrieved a small screw.

With the deftness that comes from years of experience, the grandfather removed a screw from the carburetor and replaced it with a new one from the bench. When the teenager pulled the starter cord again, the engine roared into life.

"Wow," the teen said. "I can't believe that tiny screw was all it took to fix the engine."

"Well, like the old saying goes," the grandfather said. "Some of the parts are greater than the whole."

AN ENLIGHTENING LESSON

The professor of philosophy entered the classroom and turned out the lights. He then walked to the front of the class and addressed the students.

"The lesson for today is the power of cooperation," he said. "For which I have a demonstration."

He walked to the door and turned to face the students again. "I want all of you to raise your hands," he said.

After all the hands were in the air, he turned the lights back on.

"This demonstration," he said. "Proves that many hands make light work."

AN EVENING AT THE RITZ

A monk's days at the monastery consisted of prayer, meditation, and one good meal served each evening. At mealtime, all the monks would assemble and await the arrival of their leader who would open the large doors at the end of the dining hall, enter and chant in a loud monotone voice the single word: "EVE-NING". The other monks would chant in return: "EVE-NING". Only then could dinner be served.

A young monk was given the job of selecting the best wine for serving at dinner and he did his job well. He sampled first the white wines then the reds. As dinnertime approached he selected the best of the wine and proceeded to the dining hall.

That evening the leader did not arrive at the usual six o'clock. At six-thirty the young monk, affected by the wine he had been sampling all afternoon, reasoned that if he greeted the group by speaking the key word, dinner could be served. So he spoke the required word in a deep monotone: "EVE-NING" and the dinner was served.

Shortly thereafter, the double doors swung open and the head monk entered, saw the others eating, and fumed with anger. "I cannot believe that any of you would start eating before I arrived," he said.

And the eldest monk near him replied: "But, sir, someone chanted evening."

AN HONEST OVERSIGHT

While Leif Erickson was completing his journeys in the North Atlantic, the leaders in his home town decided to determine how large the town had grown over the years. They appointed the local accountant to conduct a census because he was good with numbers in his job and could give them the most accurate count. And to ensure that he had done the best possible job, the accountant first placed all the citizen's names on a list then removed those that he couldn't verify.

When he had finished his task, the accountant presented his list to the town leaders for review and approval. But they returned it to him the next day and insisted it was inaccurate. They had all studied it closely and it was in error. The accountant, of course, didn't know what the error was let alone explain the discrepancy. One of the town leaders then chimed in and stated that as far as they could tell, the accountant must have taken Leif off his census.

AN UNHOLY JUAN

Juan Esperanto had dreamed of being a bullfighter since he was a small boy. When he was twelve years old, he asked his father for permission to begin training. Although reluctant and thinking that his son should take up a safer sport such as golf, his father agreed.

Juan trained for three years. He became quite good and showed excellent promise. On his fifteenth birthday, Juan's trainers commented that it was time for him to face his first bull. They scheduled him for a fight the following weekend.

The crowds gathered to watch Juan fight the bull and they cheered as he walked into the ring. He thought there could never have been such adulation had he taken up golf as his father had wished. There could be no sense of accomplishment such as what he was about to do.

Unfortunately, the brawny bovine had other ideas and with a single pass, the bull made a hole in Juan.

AN UNUSUAL RESCUE LINE

Two men, who had recently become friends, were looking to add some excitement to their life. One of them, a successful businessman, had a sailboat at the local marina. The other, a simple banker, had never been on a boat in his life. The businessman decided it would be great fun to introduce his banker friend to the art of sailing.

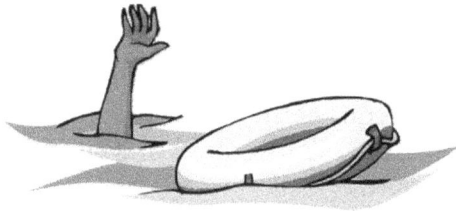

They launched the boat on a sunny afternoon and sailed out into the harbor without incident. There was a steady breeze and relatively calm waters. They sailed to and fro enjoying the experience together.

Unfortunately, the banker had a lapse in his attention and failed to duck as the boom swung round. As a result, he was knocked into the water and began thrashing about.

The banker's businessman companion grabbed a life preserver and prepared to throw it to him. But, since the businessman didn't know if the banker could swim by himself or was in need of personal assistance, he called out: "Before I throw this to you can you float alone?"

"Of course!" the banker yelled back, his face showing signs of confusion. "But this is one hell of a time to be talking business."

ANIMAL FARM

In the quiet and peaceful countryside there lived a compassionate farmer who was devoted to raising young animals to adulthood. The farm was heaven-like and radiated safety and love.

One day the farmer discovered that during the night someone had murdered one of his pigs. This bothered not only the farmer but all the residents at the farm as well.

Fortunately, the farmer had a witness to the murder - his pet bunny rabbit. Since the rabbit was unable to speak and tell him who murdered his pig, the farmer lined up the four most likely animal suspects for the rabbit to view. A cow, a horse, a young goat, and a duck all nervously took their places in the line up. The farmer told the rabbit to identify who had committed the murder.

The rabbit surveyed the line then hopped forward and stopped directly in front of the goat. The farmer then shook his head in sadness and said: "The hare's looking at you, kid."

ASKING FOR DIRECTIONS

The young man graduated from college and was ready to embark on a career. But he had no idea what he wanted to do or how he could contribute to society. He had been struggling with this indecision since his junior year. He had been to counselors and advisers to no avail.

As he sat in a local bar drowning his uncertainties in beer, a patron sitting next to him began a conversation.

"You look down in the dumps," the patron said.

"I guess I am," the young man replied. "It's just that I don't know what to do with my life. You'd think after four years of college I'd have some idea."

"I used to feel the same way," the patron offered. "I milled around like a homeless veteran hoping to find my way. But nothing worked. I thought I was doomed. But, then I went to the aquarium," he said.

"The aquarium?" The young man repeated with an obvious degree of skepticism. "Why the aquarium?"

The patron replied with all sincerity: "It was the only place I knew of where I could find a porpoise."

BACK AT'CHA

A young man from the backwoods area of Kentucky was unable to complete public education because of the demands of his family. He was the eldest of nine children and was required to help raise the eight other children in his family. As a result of this lack of schooling, he was often considered backward.

Because he could not attend schools he taught himself to write. In the process he began writing all of his poetry backwards unaware of the proper methods.

In the late evenings after he had completed his family tasks, he would often sit at his crude kitchen table desk and write poetry. After a considerable time, he had amassed a significant amount of this verse stacked in boxes in various places throughout his shack.

Poetry Is Beautiful (written in mirror-reversed cursive)

Some years later he was discovered and became known throughout the country as the 'Backward Poet'. He was, however, by then quite educated and the reference was to his method of writing.

Eventually, someone asked him the inevitable question: "Why do you write your poetry backwards?"

To which he simply replied: "My early studies into poetry told me that poets write inverse."

BALD IS BEAUTIFUL

It has been established through the use of modern television that a cure for baldness will not occur for at least another five or six centuries. The Star Trek series has proven it without a doubt.

On a recent episode, the Enterprise recovered three individuals from the twentieth century who were launched into space in cryogenic suspension. Even though these people had died from emphysema, cancer, and heart disease, the Enterprise's Dr. Crusher was able to cure them. The catastrophic illnesses of the twentieth century obviously posed no difficulty.

However, baldness was a malady they were apparently unable to correct because Captain Jean-Luc Picard still baldly goes where no one has gone before.

BARNYARD CENTS

A young farmer sought the advice of a financial expert when he was faced with some large bills. The advisor told him his options seemed limited to selling some assets or taking out a loan from the local bank. Since neither of these actions was acceptable to the farmer, he decided to find another way.

Perhaps my eccentric brother can help, he thought. And he went to his brother's house to discuss the problem with him.

"It has a simple solution," the brother said. "If all you need is money, here's what you do. Get yourself fifty female pigs and fifty male deer and put them together in your barnyard. Then you'll have a hundred sows and bucks."

BETTER SAFE THAN SORRY *(Risqué)*

William Wannabe came home from high school in an elevated state of excitement. He waited with anticipation for his father's return from work for it had been a lifelong agreement that he would discuss any planned action before executing it. When his father finally arrived, William launched immediately into a plea for approval.

"There's this new group at school," he said. "And I would like to join it." He went on to explain what this group was all about, and rushed through the description in hopes his father would grant approval without question. When he had finished, his father mused silently for some time.

"I'm afraid I can't give my blessings to membership in this group," he said.

"Why not?" William complained.

The father looked him directly in the eyes. "I realize this group may mean a lot to you now. But from your description I'm convinced that this group is a dangerous cult. And you know I have always insisted that you practice safe sects."

BETWEEN YOU AND ME

The country band in a Texas dance hall was playing and the cowboys were dancing the two-step with a passion. The fiddle player was especially good when it came to the Cotton Eye Joe and worked himself into a fever pitch. It was not long until the entire dance hall was shaking with the mere delight of the action and many of the Texas cowgirls had gathered near the fiddler.

Two of the cowboys sat at the bar complaining about their lack of feminine companionship and expressing jealousy over the fiddler's success in drawing a crowd of women. They decided that they should buy the country band since each of them knew how to play many instruments, including the fiddle. They soon convinced themselves that they would be as good as any band in town and, since they could play all the instruments themselves, they could eliminate the fiddle man.

BLACK EYED PEA

Farmer Jones checked his pea crop regularly for insect damage and to ensure he harvested the pods at their height of sweetness. One day he noticed a pod that had turned completely black. When he opened it he discovered a small, oddly shaped bug with a single large black eye.

He promptly placed the bug in a jar for safekeeping until he could take it to the local college biology department for identification. As he traveled to the college, the bug began to grow until it nearly filled the jar. It also changed shape and began to look like a combination of many different insects.

It was fortunate that the drive to the college was short because the insect burst from the jar as the farmer pulled into the parking lot. The farmer slammed his car door shut, barely in time to trap the insect inside, and ran to the biology professor's office. "I've got something I think you ought to see, Professor," he gasped.

"What is it?"

"I don't know for sure. But until you can identify it, I'll call it the creature from the black legume."

BODY SHOP

A distraught man went into his psychiatrist's office and immediately stretched out on the couch.

"Doc, you have got to help me!" he said. "Every night I keep dreaming that I'm a sports car."

The psychiatrist nodded and wrote a few notes in his journal.

The patient continued. "The other night I dreamed I was a Trans Am. Another night I dreamed I was an Alpha Romero. Last night I dreamed I was a Porsche."

The psychiatrist put down his journal and crossed his arms.

"What does this mean?" the patient asked.

"Relax," the psychiatrist said, "You're just having an auto body experience."

BOTTLED WONDER

The beachcomber stumbled upon a bottle washed up on the shore and in sheer fantasy decided to rub it. Much to his surprise, a genie emerged from the bottle and offered to do whatever the beachcomber wished. It was then the Genie's turn to be surprised for the beachcomber requested only that the genie perform magic tricks - especially the pulling of brown rabbits from a hat.

The Genie did as he was requested for many hours until even he became bored with the magic. Still, the beachcomber insisted that he continue.

"Magic is my only love," the beachcomber explained.

The Genie then asked: "If that is so, why must I continually pull the rabbit from the hat? Surely you must know by now what is going to happen."

"It is a historic moment," the beach comber said. "And I will savor it for as long as I can. Not only am I fortunate enough to have you perform magic for me, but I am also the only person alive to have ever seen Genie with the light brown hare."

BRINGING BACK THE GOOD OLD TIMES

Harvey's grandfather clock suddenly stopped working one day, so he loaded it into his van and took it to a local clock repair shop.

The little old man in the shop insisted he was Swiss but spoke with a heavy German accent. He asked Harvey: "Vat sims to be ze problem?"

Harvey said: "I'm not sure, but this clock doesn't go 'tick-tock-tick-tock' anymore. Now it just goes 'tick … tick … tick.' "

The old man said: "Mmm-Hmm! I belief I can fix zis clock."

He then stepped behind the counter and rummaged through his drawers. He finally emerged with a huge flashlight and walked over to the grandfather clock. He turned the flashlight on, brought it up toward the top of the clock, and shined it directly into the clock's face.

Then he said with a menacing voice: "Vee haf vays of making you tock!"

BURY THE LAST STRAW

A young female strawberry farmer in Michigan had finally developed the world's largest and most succulent strawberry. The strawberry weighed twenty two pounds and was as large as a watermelon. After she reported her achievement to the local newspaper, she quickly became a nationally prominent strawberry farmer. The publicity generated many inquiries concerning her farming methods and an equally intense stream of visitors to view the world's largest strawberry. She soon became quite concerned that someone would try to rob her of her treasure so she hired a watchman to help protect her secret.

One evening, after she had secured her home and was preparing to retire, there was a loud knock on the door. She looked on with trepidation as the watchman cautiously approached the door and called out: "Who's there?" To which came the reply: "A friend."

"You're no friend," the watchman said. "You're the strawberry farmer from down the road and you've come to steal the lady's strawberry."

"True. I am who you say I am. But I am not a thief. I admire the lady's successes. And I come not to seize her berry, but to praise her."

CAUSE AND EFFECT

City officials were dumbfounded when they discovered their new courthouse had been destroyed during the night. The beautiful edifice was now merely a single pile of rubble contained within a single city block. The City Council convened immediately to determine what to do.

They decided to hire the best consultants they could find to help them determine the cause for the courthouse catastrophe. After a month, the consultants could find no answer. The building had simply collapsed upon itself with no outside influence of any kind.

The City Council could not accept this answer and hired new consultants who arrived at the same conclusion. A third set of engineers completed their study and once again reached the same conclusion. In their final report, however, they offered some advice to the Council.

"You are wasting money and time trying to determine why the courthouse collapsed," they said. "You will be far better off if you accept the facts of the situation. Your courthouse is truly a rubble without a cause."

CHEAP AT TWICE THE PRICE

A renegade Apache Indian known as Standing Rib approached the U. S. Cavalry and offered his services as a spy. In return, he accepted trinkets that were valued at no more than 79 cents. He was so good at his work that many battles were won by the cavalry only because of the information he passed to the Union generals.

One day, however, his tribe discovered his treason and, in keeping with their custom concerning spies, they sentenced him to death by burning at a stake.

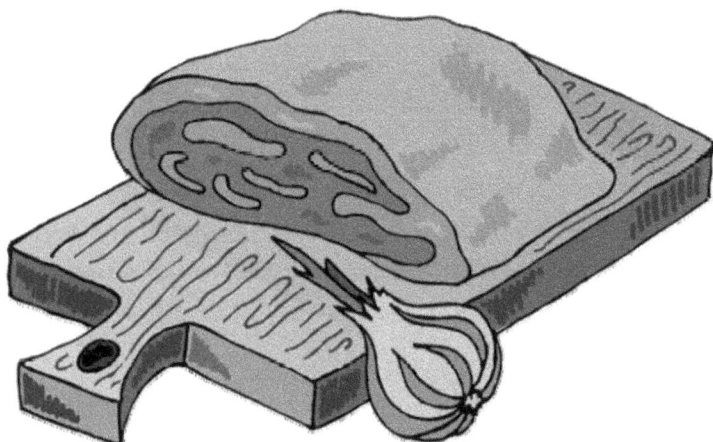

The following morning they tied him to a stake and piled brush and firewood around him. And as the chief lit the fire, the squaws, as was also their custom, stood in a circle chanting the basis for the execution: "Standing Rib Roasts for 79 cents."

CHESS A MINUTE

A group of world class chess players had just finished their tournament in the grand ballroom of a swanky hotel. During this tournament, a number of new moves were played and the sheer number of these special moves had the participants excited beyond expectation.

As the contestants gathered in the lobby after the games, they began bragging about the outstanding competition they had just finished. Their voices grew louder until they were disturbing the other guests at the hotel.

The manager finally approached them and told them to either quiet down or they would have to leave. "In this part of the country," he said. "No one can stand to listen to a bunch of chess nuts boasting in an open foyer."

CHINESE COOKING

Sammy Sing, one of the world's most renowned Chinese cooks, still used the cooking utensils his mother had given him years ago. And when his son grew old enough to take over the kitchen, Sammy tried to teach him all the tricks of the trade. His son, however, told Sammy it was time to modernize and purchase an electric wok. When it was clear neither of them would relent, the son moved out and began his own restaurant.

At first all went well. But soon the son noticed his business had dropped off and his profits had begun to dwindle. He spent many nights trying to determine the cause of his failing business. Finally, after an especially discouraging night, he realized it was because he had forsaken his grandmother's cooking utensils.

He immediately called his father on the phone and pleaded for Sammy to come to his restaurant and help him. He sounded in pain. Sammy couldn't refuse him and when he arrived, he found his son in the corner of the kitchen, a large, heavy wok pinning him against the wall near the phone.

Sammy began asking many questions about the business but his son stopped him. "You were right," he said. "Your way is best. All I need now is some help. Even you can tell I'm between a wok and a hard place."

CHIPPING IN

Many people find it quite surprising that there are more Catholic churches in Las Vegas than there are casinos. Visitors to the city are mostly unaware that the residents live lives much like other families in all the other cities across the nation.

So it is not so surprising, when you think of it, that some worshippers give casino chips rather than cash when the basket is passed around. It is not considered wrong or offensive. The chips have value and the churches need all the money they can get to carry out their missions.

Since the worshipers donate chips from many different casinos, the churches had to come up with a method to efficiently convert them into cash. So they forged an agreement with the local Franciscan Monastery to consolidate the chips, make an accurate accounting of the amounts from each church, and cash them in at the casinos.

It wasn't long, of course, before those who processed the casino bounty were given a most appropriate nick name. It just became obvious that they must be called chip monks.

CHIVALRY IS NOT LOST

The ancient Egyptian society prized both sexes equally. Thus, when Pharaoh's many wives produced dozens of daughters exclusively he was quite proud of the number of daughters he could call his own. As a result of his pride in his family he designated a small valley near the Nile as the Daughter's Dell.

He then commissioned a beautiful marble statue for each of his numerous daughters and had them placed within the valley. He would often walk among these statues beaming with pride. Therefore, it was understandable how greatly saddened he was when an untimely earthquake shattered all of the statues into a pile of rubble.

The Pharaoh immediately summoned his architect and told him he wanted the valley filled in completely so that he would not have to look at the cause of his sadness. The architect in turn summoned Howard the duck - the superhero from Hollywood fame. This weird looking, disrespectful duck seemed a strange choice for the task at hand.

"Why do you believe you can do my bidding to my satisfaction?" The Pharaoh demanded. "You obviously don't have the stature I would expect from someone capable of this job."

Howard replied with confidence. "My feathers grow very fast and they are as hard as rocks," he said. "Like a ridge over rubbled daughters, I will lay my down."

CHOOSING SIDES

A young man began working in the lumber industry as an apprentice in the sawmill. He was responsible for placing the stripped down trees on the conveyor belt that led to the large circular saw. He guided the tree through the saw as it cut rough hewn boards. It was a strenuous job and filled with risk but in his youth, he felt invincible.

One day, however, the stub of a branch that had not been completely stripped from the tree trunk caught in the young man's jeans and pulled him onto the conveyor belt with the tree. With no way to reach the safety switch, the young man traveled with the tree into the saw. It only took a few seconds before the young man's entire left side was cut off.

He was rushed to the hospital where he underwent extensive surgery. And for more than eight hours his friends, family, and coworkers paced throughout the hospital hallways praying for his survival. It was with great anticipation that they gathered in the waiting room when the surgeon appeared.

"I know you're all waiting to hear the outcome of the surgery," he said. "I have to admit that this was one of the most complicated surgeries I've ever done. But you have nothing to worry about. The surgery went fine and your young man is all right now."

CIRCULAR REFERENCE

The Lone Ranger and Tonto walked into a bar and sat down to drink a beer. After a few minutes, a tall cowboy walked in and said: "Who owns the big white horse outside?"

The Lone Ranger stood up and said: "I do. Why?"

The cowboy looked at the Lone Ranger and said: "You may want to know that your horse is about dead!"

The Lone Ranger and Tonto rushed outside and discovered Silver swooning from heat exhaustion. The Lone Ranger got the horse water then said: "Tonto. I want you to run around Silver as fast as you can and see if you can create enough breeze to help him cool down."

Tonto said: "Sure, Kemo Sabe." He then began running circles around Silver.

Not able to do anything else but wait, the Lone Ranger returned to the bar to finish his drink. A few minutes later, another cowboy strutted into the bar and asked: "Who owns the big white horse outside?"

The Lone Ranger stood again and said: "I do. What's wrong with him this time?"

The cowboy looked him in the eye and said: "Nothing. But you left your Injun runnin'."

CLOSE ENOUGH FOR GOVERNMENT WORK

Although the debate about the longest river in the world has been long resolved, two men at a bar, began a debate concerning the most impressive river on the globe.

The first man, being an Egyptian, proudly announced that the Nile River was indeed the most impressive. He argued that its origin in the jungles and survival throughout a harsh desert before emptying into the beautiful Mediterranean Sea qualified it on these facts alone. He then added its many years of history to his justification.

An American was his debating partner and argued on behalf of the Mississippi River which he chose to refer to simply as The Miss. He spoke of the impact this river had on the growth of the great American culture, wealth, and diversity. Certainly, this ranked it better than the Nile.

A third patron at the bar had been listening to this debate for some time. When it looked as though the discussion would never reach a satisfactory conclusion, he caught their attention. "May I suggest a solution to your dilemma?" he asked.

The debaters nodded their agreement.

"You could agree," he said. "That both rivers are equal to each other. After all, everyone learned a long time ago that the Miss is as good as the Nile."

COPS AND ROBBERS

As Japan faced its worst rice harvest in a century the police were called in to investigate the disappearance of large volumes of the grain from the national warehouses. The robbers had become bold, turning what had been a small time operation into a large organized effort.

The police soon discovered that Oligarchy Sumigata, the equivalent of the Japanese Godfather, was behind the entire process. He controlled every facet of the entire operation and directed its efforts with amazing efficiency.

They began building a case against him. They stalked him on nearly every rice paddy in the country. They tapped his phones. They inserted informants. And eventually they amassed nearly as much evidence as he had amassed rice.

When they finally arrested him and charged him with a felony he protested. He argued that the charges and the resulting penalty far exceeded the crime.

The police demurred and insisted they were right. After all, they countered. With the volume of rice he had taken, they could not charge him with mere paddy larceny.

CUFF 'IM AND BOOK 'IM *(Risqué)*

There was once an annoying prude who decided to vacation in the south of France. He arrived at his hotel late in the evening and went directly to his room.

In the morning, his thoughts were focused on getting to the beach where he could soak up the warm rays of the sun. When he discovered he was the first person on the beach, he spread his blanket and lay down. It was not long until the jet lag caught up with him and he fell soundly asleep.

He awoke sometime later and noticed a naked old man sleeping nearby. This, of course, offended the prude's sensibilities and he rose with the intent of hiding this indecency from view. The only thing he could locate to cover the old man's genitals was a book the man had let slip to the sand. So the prude picked it up and covered the old man's nakedness.

As it turned out the prude was on a nudist beach and the old man was a judge. Finding the prude had placed the book on him he called the local gendarmes and had the prude arrested.

The authorities led the prude away as he protested and challenged the police to tell him what he had done wrong. A sympathetic policeman finally told him that in this community you never cover a judge by his book.

DIFFERENT SIZES

A smallish witch in Salem was eventually captured and sentenced to death by burning at the stake. Since her small size was so unusual for persons of the psychic medium, the scheduled stake burning had created more interest than any other execution in history. People from miles around arranged their schedules so they could be present when the torch was put to the pile of stakes.

S

On the eve of the burning, the witch conjured up a spell and escaped from her confinement. Within minutes she had fled the town and disappeared into the surrounding countryside. The alarm was sounded and the sheriff and his posse began pursuit. They returned late the next morning to report that they had been unsuccessful.

M

It was only a few hours later when the local newspaper editor had worked up his headlines which proclaimed: SMALL MEDIUM AT LARGE.

L

DISORDERLY DEFICIT

A mere few years before the advent of the dark ages there was a troupe of performers who traveled throughout Europe. Their specialty, which consisted of displaying death-defying activities without safety devices, gained them great notoriety. Because their program caused a great deal of apprehension within the observers, their performance became known as the Show Of Tension.

They capitalized on this label and took pride in the fact that those who watched them called them Tensions. They had T-shirts and uniforms with their stage names printed elaborately upon the fronts and the backs. They advertised themselves as the Terrific Tensions. And they became quite renowned for their feats.

But when the dark ages swooped down over the continent and the entire population was sucked into poverty, the Show Of Tension slowly but surely joined everyone else in destitution. There was no way to avoid this painful demise. As the population despaired, the Tensions had no way to avoid the same horrible condition.

And as many business people have found over the years since, this troupe of talented performers was unable to survive because their entire audience was unable to pay a Tension.

DOC AT THE TOP OF THE STAIRS

An old doctor, known to his friends in Detroit as Doc, would see his last patient of the day and then wander downstairs to the corner tavern every afternoon for his daily medication. Because Doc was a frequent visitor, Dick the bartender had become very accustomed to the doctor's favorite drink - an acorn daiquiri. Promptly at five o'clock, Dick would squeeze the juice of an acorn into a daiquiri and have the cold drink waiting.

One afternoon, much to his dismay, Dick discovered he had no acorns. Not wanting to disappoint his faithful customer, the bartender located a hickory nut and squeezed its juices into the daiquiri, hoping the doctor wouldn't notice. Old Doc entered the tavern on schedule and, per his custom, sipped the drink to savor its mellow taste.

Doc motioned for the bartender and when he came near said: "This isn't an acorn daiquiri, Dick."

"No, it isn't," the bartender confessed. "I'm sorry but I ran out of acorns. This is a hickory daiquiri, Doc."

DON'T SQUEEZE THE TOMATOES

A teenager, in response to his father's dictates, took a job as a bagger at the local grocery store. He understood that this was necessary if he intended to go to college. His father was not that wealthy and there were four other children in the family who would also need assistance.

His first few days in the market went well and he was pleased with the paycheck he was able to bring home. But during the second week of his employment, he noticed workers installing an orange juice squeezing machine. He immediately thought that would be a more appropriate job for his talents. As an added benefit, he heard the salary for orange juicers was nearly double what he was earning as a bagger.

He approached the manager of the market and proposed that he would make a wonderful juicer. He even went so far as to explain the financial needs of his family, something that embarrassed him but seemed important to ensure his selection.

The manager shook his head. "I understand, young man," he said. "But I can't give you the job." Then, in response to the young teenager's disappointment, he continued: "I'm really sorry. But you've got to understand. Baggers can't be juicers."

DON'T TRED ON ME

Bathrooms in Britain are often called loos. Many of them are shared male and female facilities. They have tile walls and linoleum floors to make the maintenance as efficient as possible. Those located in populated areas are many times architectural marvels.

A lone French terrorist decided he would use the most visited loo in London as the location for his home made bomb. He planned his attack carefully choosing the busiest part of the business day for detonation. If all went well, he could claim victory for his cause and become a hero in the process.

The night before the event he carefully placed his bomb under a sink and set it to go off during the lunch hour. Then he retreated to his apartment hideaway to await the cataclysmic event.

It's a good thing he wasn't a little smarter. It seems that day was a national holiday and no one went to work or used the loo. So, when the bomb exploded the only result was a lot of water in the loo and all the linoleum blown apart.

DOUBLE CROSSES NEVER WORK

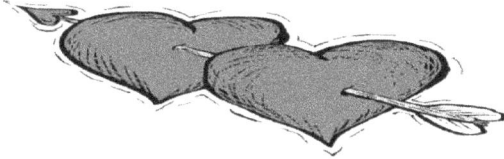

Tommy Twotimer had made it a habit to keep two women on the string throughout his young adult life. In every case, he kept his two femme fatales separated by great distances. Over the years, the constant travel necessary to maintain these relationships began to tax his finances as well as his physical strength. So, when he dropped one of his women he decided to find the next much closer to his home town, St. Louis, Missouri. Edith, the remaining girlfriend, already lived in St. Louis and he reasoned that if he was careful he could manage his affairs with no difficulty. Within a week he found another local woman, Kate, and Tommy settled down into a comfortable, less hectic routine.

Two months later, during one of his few times alone in his apartment, there was a loud knocking on the door. When he answered it, Kate burst into the room.

"You two timer, Tommy," she shouted. "I just found out about Edith and I won't stand for it."

"But it didn't bother you before you knew," Tommy pleaded. "Did I ever neglect you?"

"That doesn't matter. I've talked with Edith and we agree. You must make a choice. You can't have your Kate and Edith too."

DRAWING THE DRAPES

A woman approached her husband with the news that they needed new drapes throughout the house. After two weeks of debate on the real need for new drapes, the husband gave in grudgingly. The two of them then advised their daughter they were going to the fabric warehouse to select material.

Once at the warehouse, the couple embarked on a growing disagreement as to color and design. No matter what one selected, the other didn't like it. It turned into a nightmare. It became a clash of wills just as their daughter had known it would.

While they were gone, their son returned home from an afternoon at the movies. He asked his sister where the parents were.

"Oh, nowhere special," she answered. "They are simply trampling through the warehouse where the drapes of wrath are stored."

DRYING TIMES

A young woman had just filled a washing machine in the Laundromat when she noticed a man begin removing shoes from another washing machine that had just finished its spin dry cycle. The man's entire washing load consisted of nothing but sneakers and he tossed them into the gaping hole of the dryer against the wall. When he had finished, he had loaded at least ten pairs of sneakers into the dryer. The man then struggled to remove the change needed for the dryer from his pocket. His task was made more difficult by the tight fitting jeans he wore. So, as he withdrew his hand from his pocket, a number of dimes fell from his fist and rolled around the floor.

Immediately, the man fell to the floor and began to retrieve his dimes. But, alas, they had rolled beneath the washing machines and were not accessible. He turned to the young woman and said: "This has not been my day. Everything has gone wrong. And this has been the icing on the cake."

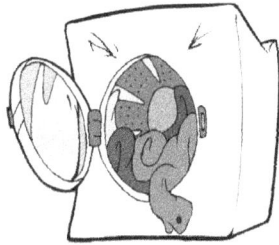

"There has to be some good in every day," the young woman said. "Surely this incident can't be as bad as you make it out to be."

"Ah. But you are wrong my friend," he replied. "What you don't realize is that these are the dimes that dry men's soles."

'EARS TO YA, DOC

The Christmas rush was finally over and Santa and all the reindeer were resting. Rudolph was happy to have a chance to do something that had been on his mind for many years. Although some would believe it had something to do with his nose, his real concern had something to do with his ears.

He made an appointment with a plastic surgeon and explained to the doctor that he was sensitive about how he looked and his ears needed work. They were so long that they stood out like a sore thumb when he was around the other deer. They embarrassed him and he wanted them trimmed. The doctor agreed and, after the brief recovery period, Rudolph returned to his herd and proudly held his head and new ears high.

The others thought he looked quite dandy and they voted to honor him with his own special day. And since that time, January 1st has been celebrated as New Ears Day.

EBB AND FLOW

One afternoon The Sea rolled into the offices of a clinical psychologist. Although it may have seemed out of place for many others, the doctor smiled as he had not seen his old friend for some time.

"Well. Well," he said. "Long time no Sea. How are you doing?"

The Sea replied: "Except for a single thing I am doing fantastically swell."

"Ahh," the doctor replied. "What seems to be the problem?"

The Sea swished about in his seat. After a brief struggle, he blurted out: "It's just that I've become very weary. It just seems that I keep going in and out every day. In and out. In and out. There never seems to be an end."

"I understand," the doctor said. "But there's nothing anyone can do about it. It is a fact of physics and nature. And since you can't beat it you may as well join it. You see, my friend. It's your destiny. It's a simple truth that you're fit to be tide."

ELEMENTARY GEOMETRY

Two fighter pilots, looking for some excitement in the absence of combat, were bragging about what good hunters they were. They decided on a contest to determine which of them was the better hunter. As with all contests of this nature, there had to be a symbolic prize. Therefore, they agreed to each put up a pint of the best whiskey they could find. The winner would take all.

As they prepared for the contest, a local television newscast announced that a lion had escaped from the zoo and was roaming in the desert surrounding the base. The contest immediately took on a new element: The first pilot to bag and bring back the lion would be the winner.

One pilot borrowed a large hunting rifle and began hunting the lion in the conventional manner. The other pilot, more inventive and willing to take more risk, secured an Army National Guard Apache helicopter. He loaded it with ammunition and began searching for the lion.

Of course, it wasn't long until the airborne pilot saw the lion and, from the safety of the helicopter, killed it with a burst from the guns. He then set the chopper down, loaded the lion on board, and returned to the base. As the winner, he promptly downloaded both bottles of the fine whiskey thereby proving that a strafed lion is the shortest distance between two pints.

EVEN STEVEN

Steven the silkworm and his girlfriend Sally had been competitive ever since they emerged from their eggs weeks ago. When they first met and fell in love, they spun a web of deceit that hid most of their activities from all the other silkworms. But it was to be the combination of their competitiveness and deceit that would be their undoing.

One night Sally challenged Steven to a race. She contended she could crawl from one end of the web spinning table to the other faster than Steven who thought himself the greatest silkworm alive. They waited until darkness to carry out the challenge.

The race began. Steven broke into a fast lead and maintained it until mid-table when he became winded. Sally caught up with and passed Steven with a chortle and began laying down strands of web to impede his progress.

But Steven was not to be denied his win, He tried even harder to catch her. And as they neared the end of the table, it became quite clear to each of them that the entire event was a mistake. They were both destined to end up in a tie.

EVERY GIG NEEDS A STRAIGHT MAN

It has been said that time is relative, that it gets faster as you get older, that once spent it cannot be retrieved, that it is fleeting, and a host of other platitudes.

A key element of comedy is timing. The very best of all jokes can fall flat if not uttered with a sense of timing. The same is said of slapstick humor such as slipping on a banana peel. If not enacted precisely as called for in the humorous skit, the slip and the fall would fail to amuse.

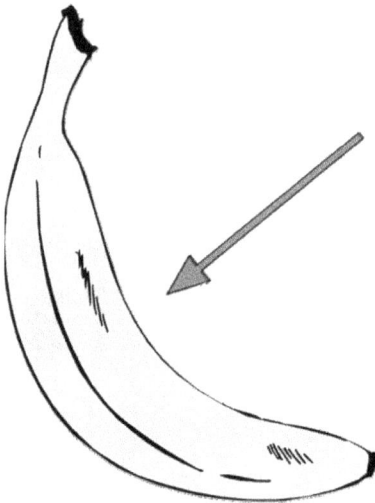

To prove this point, a student conducted an in-depth study of the use of time and bananas in humor. His research covered the use of humor in everyday life throughout known history. It was his earnest desire to assemble enough information to complete his master's thesis.

Unfortunately, after months of effort and untold hours buried in his research books, his knowledge all boiled down to this simple fact: 'Time flies like an arrow and fruit flies like a banana'.

EVERY RIVER HAS A MOUTH

A group of dentists who had been in fierce competition for some time realized that their future depended on them joining forces. Therefore, they gathered for a business planning meeting in a local resort beside a wide river that flowed through town.

The result of their planning session was a decision to set up a combined practice of special dental surgery aboard a boat on this river. They believed there were two facets that would make this venture successful: first, it would be a very unique approach to the business of dental surgery; second, they could use the boat as a ferry in this part of the river since the nearest bridge was miles away.

They immediately set about establishing this floating practice and, in a relatively short time, they soon had more business than they could handle. Their clientele found it most convenient to have their dental work performed as they crossed the river to the other side.

It wasn't long until their patients had devised a new name for this dental process. The dentists involved in the venture had no idea that their business would soon be known as the Tooth Ferry.

FALLING THROUGH THE CRACK *(Risqué)*

A middle-aged woman visited her gynecologist to discuss some very peculiar symptoms. After she got into his office she found it most difficult to tell him about them. She fidgeted and tried to start numerous times.

"You've been seeing me for years," the doctor said. "There's nothing you can tell me that would be a surprise. I've seen everything. Relax and tell me about it."

"This one's really strange," the woman replied.

"Tell me what it is and I'll be the judge of how strange it sounds. I'm sure it's not nearly as bad as you think it is."

She told him that the day before, when she went to the bathroom in the morning she heard plinking noises. When she looked, the water was full of pennies. She went on to tell him that in the afternoon when she went to the bathroom she found the bowl filled with nickels. And then again this morning there were dimes. And this afternoon there were quarters.

"I'm scared out of my wits," she told the doctor. "You've got to tell me what's wrong with me!"

The gynecologist put a hand on her shoulder. "There's really nothing to be afraid of," he said. "You're simply going through the change."

FAMILY JEWELS

An enterprising African family was well known for mining large amounts of various, expensive, green gemstones. The quality of their gemstones was unequalled in the world and the family's success caused them to lose touch with the realities of outside events. By not paying attention to what was going on in the marketplace, they frequently made the mistake of overproduction.

During one particular year, the market for the green jewels fell sharply and the family soon realized they had produced far more stones than they could ever sell without driving the market even further into the ground.

So the problem then became: what to do with the excess stones. After considerable debate, the family agreed to a unique method of using the surplus. They donated them to the local high school sports department that used them to pave the running track.

It was indeed a beautiful thing and soon became known as the "Track of all Jades".

FEARFUL ANGELS

His nickname was Treads because he spent most of his time riding his motorcycle over off-road terrain. He had become so skilled with mud and snow riding that Goodyear was looking into the possibility of naming a new line of tires after him.

During a ride in the woods, Treads came upon a situation that would have frightened away even the most stalwart hero. An escaped prisoner had taken the Mayor's daughter hostage and was holed up in a cabin. At least a hundred state police surrounded the log hut but none dared approach the kidnapper who was armed with at least a mini-arsenal of the most highly advanced weapons.

When Treads had sized up the situation, he decided he could overpower the kidnapper. Although the others said he was foolish for wanting to risk his life, he was confident he could be successful. In fact, he knew he could arrest the kidnapper without harm to either himself or the Mayor's daughter.

As Treads revved up his motorcycle for the assault, the chief of state police again warned him of the dangers that awaited him. He told Treads that even angels wouldn't dare do what he had planned.

Treads laconic reply was simply: "Yeah. But Treads rushes in where angels fear to fool."

FEARSOME THREESOME

Three animals of the forest were arguing among themselves as to which of them was the most feared.

The first, a hawk, claimed that because of his ability to fly he could attack anything repeatedly from above and his prey had nary a chance.

The second, a lion, based his claim on his strength - none in the forest dared challenge him.

The third, a skunk, insisted he needed neither flight nor strength to frighten off any creature.

As the trio debated the issue, a grizzly bear came along and swallowed them all - hawk, lion, and stinker.

FIGURE IT OUT

King Arthur and the Knights of the Round Table had wide notoriety and extensive popularity and the King took great pleasure in this knowledge. So it was that when he heard one of his knights had lost the knightly charm associated with all the other members of the Round Table, he became disturbed.

He immediately summoned the wayward knight, known as Sir Cumference, and waited impatiently for the knight to arrive. The arrival was delayed, however, because the knight had to travel on foot - no horse in the entire kingdom was capable of carrying a knight of his rotundity.

When Sir Cumference was finally in front of the throne, the king asked: "Help me to understand, Sir Cumference. Why have you abandoned the oath you swore to when I knighted you?"

Sir Cumference hesitated and looked at the ground in front of the throne. It seemed he could not answer the question. So, the King asked this question again with more directness.

"Sir Cumference! Why are you so large?"

"I am sad my King. I know I have failed you. But the answer is simple. It is from too much pi."

FLIPPING SIDES

The practice of using a coin to determine who would go first in a contest had been a part of the sports genre for as long as anyone could remember. So it was with surprise that many took the news from the US mint that using coins for this purpose was no longer legal. The government wanted to distance its currency from the competitions that usually resulted in illegal wagering.

In response, an enterprising entrepreneur developed a new coin that soon became the standard within the sports world. The originator explained that he had determined the United States had two major figures in its history whose images fit perfectly into the concept of flipping a coin when choosing events in sports. The coin was fashioned after the likeness of Theodore Roosevelt on one side and Nathan Hale on the other.

At first, people were confused by the similarity of both of the coin's obverse and the reverse surfaces. But they soon came to understand the value of having these two busts back-to-back.

It was not long before everyone came to understand that when you flipped this new coin you could simply call out Ted's or Hale's.

FOREIGN CUISINE BRINGS FAME

Li Ning was a Chinese soldier who fought by Mao's side during the revolution. His association with Mao and their victory over Chiang Kai-shek in 1945 propelled him into the high circles of government where he served loyally for many years.

After Mao's death, Li Ning retired from government service so he could pursue a life long ambition of owning a restaurant. He sought approval from his superiors to branch out on his own. He believed that the Chinese people would appreciate having a choice between Chinese food and some of the foreign cuisine he had come to know during his travels. He chose Italian food for his first menu.

Because of his persistence, he was able to gain approval for his venture. Yet, his desires for anonymity failed. He became internationally known and the crowds flocked to his doors just to get a glimpse of him.

At first he was puzzled. Was it his revolutionary war record or his notoriety in government service or just that everyone loved Italian food? For many months the answer eluded him and, being proud, he would not ask anyone for help.

Then one day, as he stood in the street looking at his restaurant and the large sign hanging above the door, he realized what had happened. Because of his choice of a name for the restaurant he was revered as the owner of the Li Ning Tower of Pizza.

FOREVER TUNED

Mr. Opporknockity was the nation's foremost piano tuner. He was quite proud of his reputation as the man whose abilities enabled him to make but a single call on any client. Once he tuned a piano it never went out of tune.

It is therefore understandable why he became angry at a customer who questioned the quality of his tunesmanship.

"You must return," the client demanded.

"Never," replied Mr. Opporknockity.

"But I insist. It isn't fair."

"It is fair," the tuner shouted back. "I treat you as I treat all clients. And Opporknockity tunes only once."

FORK IT OVER BUDDY

Researchers kept a monkey in the laboratory where they were attempting to get it to act more like a human. Part of the process included training the monkey to use a fork when he ate his meals. The monkey found the training to his liking and called the fork his three-point-tool because it had three tines.

One day the monkey escaped from the laboratory and returned to his home in the jungle. He took his three-point-tool with him. Unfortunately, he lost it soon after arriving.

When he approached the giraffe and asked about his three-point-tool the giraffe admitted that he had not seen it. The monkey's visit to the zebra resulted in the same response. The striped animal also had not seen the three-point-tool.

The monkey began to despair and in a last ditch effort approached a Jaguar. "Have you seen my three-point-tool?" He asked.

"Yes," the Jaguar replied. "I ate it."

"How could you do that?" The monkey wailed. "You certainly knew how much it meant to me."

"Ah, yes." The Jaguar said. "But you do know, don't you? I am a three-point-tool eater Jaguar."

FOUR ON THE FLOOR

The snails in Lake Erie near Toledo had been picking on Sammy ever since he grew his first shell. When compared to all the other snails, Sammy's movement was without doubt the slowest of them all. The jokes and innuendos about his lack of speed were almost overwhelming. After a particularly strong insult Sammy decided to buy a fast sports car and flaunt it around his friends.

He went to the corner Datsun dealer and negotiated the purchase of a 240-Z. As part of the deal, he insisted that the car be repainted and the letter Z be replaced with the letter S. Of course, the dealer asked the reason for this strange request.

Sammy told him the letter S stood for Snail and would clearly indicate that he was in the car. He knew how the snails thought and he was confident this approach would gain him respect.

So when he took possession of his new car he immediately began racing up and down the main drag at top speed. He had rehearsed this plan in his mind many times and knew it would only take a few runs down this highway before he achieved his goal.

And by the fourth lap Sammy was proven right. Because every time after that when he zoomed down the road everyone would turn and say: "Look at that S-Car go!"

FOWL LANGUAGE *(Risqué)*

A middle-aged man was on his way home from work when a most unusual thing happened. As the man sat at a red light in heavy traffic, a bird slammed into his windshield. The impact briefly frightened the man. But when he recovered, he noticed the bird had gotten its wing stuck under the windshield wiper.

The man did not like to see the bird in distress and prepared to exit the vehicle and remove it from its trap. However, the light turned green at that moment and he had to begin moving. Without any other apparent options he turned on his windshield wipers hoping it would free the bird.

The technique worked and the bird flew off the windshield. Strangely, however, it's slammed right onto the windshield of the car behind the man. It did not become caught under the windshield wipers of that car but it became obvious as the man watched in his rearview mirror that the bird had struck a police car.

The cruiser's lights immediately came on along with a short burst of the siren. The man pulled over and waited for the officer to walk up to his window. The officer told the man he had seen what happened at the traffic light and he was a little bit upset about it.

The man pled his case but it seemed to fall on deaf ears. The police officer simply stated: "I am going to have to write you up for flipping me the bird."

GETTING OUT OF DEBT

A duck was walking along a stream in Australia when he happened upon a platypus standing on the bank. The platypus was holding a sign that read: "Homeless. Out of work. Please help."

The duck offered to help the platypus but not through a simple grant by donation. He said he would help the platypus find employment. But in the interim he would also loan him the money necessary to get on with his life. They shook hands to seal the deal and each went their separate ways.

Speaking in his simple language, he told his wife that evening of what he had done. "Duck help out platypus today," he said. "Duck feel good. Economy get better. Everyone happy."

His wife looked at him somewhat askance as she continued to prepare food for the evening's meal.

"What's the matter?" The duck asked

She turned to face him. "And what do you plan to do when the platypus fails to pay you back?"

"It pretty simple," he replied. "Duck bill platypus."

GIRL OF MY DREAMS

The bearded young man drove his car down the toll way, tears of happiness obscuring his vision but not enough to be an issue. He had just exited the toll way station and a brief encounter with the girl he had been in love with ever since he met her there months earlier.

She was a toll taker on the toll way and when he first passed through her station he knew she was the one for him. And for the past three months he would linger momentarily after paying his toll and gaze into her eyes. She accepted his gaze and returned it in kind but he was a shy man and could not bring himself to say anything.

One day she was not at her station and he worried that he had let her slip away. All the following week she was absent and he fell into a depression. He cursed himself for his weakness and swore that if he ever saw her again he would let her know how he felt.

One can imagine his joy when he saw her back at her station taking tolls. And he immediately approached her and told her how he had feared she had left him.

She smiled and said: "You have no need to fear. And no need to ask for whom's this toll way belle. This toll way belle's for thee."

GLOVE ME TENDER

Marty Molar was a young dentist in Michigan whose practice was just becoming established. He employed his wife as his assistant and promised that as soon as his patient load produced a profit he would hire a full time assistant. In the meantime, his wife would have to clean teeth, handle the billing, and perform myriad other duties.

The relationship was a labor of love but the love was strained daily as Marty instructed his wife on methods and corrected her errors. One day, the attention became too much for her. Marty had criticized her for flossing a patient without wearing surgical gloves and made her complete the procedure a second time properly clad. When she finished and the patient was gone, she told Marty it was time to hire an assistant, she was finished, she quit.

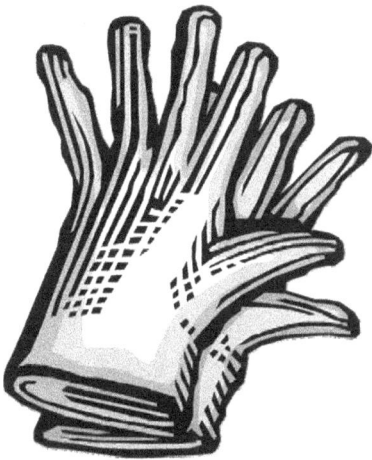

Marty sighed but did not try to change her mind. He merely remembered the sage advice of his dental school professor: "'Tis better to have gloved and flossed than never to have gloved at all".

GO AHEAD...I'LL COVER YOU

The mayor of a small town loved to wear hats. He had a large number of these head coverings hanging on individual wooden pegs in his entryway. He was never seen without a hat in public when out of doors.

Over time it became apparent that he had a few select hats that were his favorites. The hats that were not worn as often as the others began to feel neglected but they were a patient bunch and bided their time.

One day the mayor was running late for an important appointment. The hats in the foyer were well aware of his distress and that he would probably not take the time to search out one of his favorites.

Consequently, it was not surprising that when he entered the foyer one of the neglected hats shouted: "You guys stay here! I'll go on a head."

GONE TO THE DOGS

Many years ago the inhabitants of Munich, Germany, had a most significant problem. It seems for some unknown reason the dog population exploded and almost overnight the city was overrun with very large and not too friendly canines.

To cope with the problem, the residents joined forces and drove the entire dog population out of town into the hills. This action, however, created a significant problem for Lieden, a neighboring village. Lieden was a community almost totally dependent on its paper mills for survival. It wasn't long until the hounds who had been evicted from Munich into the hills invaded the Leiden community devastating all in their wake.

It became so bad that the residents had to close the paper mills. This in turn caused them to gather as a group to descend on Munich and complain. As they were preparing to leave Lieden, they heard a rumbling noise emanate from the hills where the paper mills were located.

The residents gazed up into the hills wondering who could be operating the factory's equipment since all of the employees were gathered for the assault on Munich. An elderly man spoke up first.

"It's pretty obvious," he said. "The mills are alive with the hounds of Munich."

GOOD NEIGHBORS BUILD FENCES

Bert and Nate were neighbors in a country community and joined forces to install a fence around Bert's property. Bert dug the holes while Nate placed the fence posts and positioned the rails.

Work went well for most of the day until Bert discovered that a large rock was lying on the very spot he needed for his next post hole. He couldn't budge it by brute force so he got the crowbar and pried it. Still, after much sweat and frustration, the rock remained solidly in place.

By then, Nate had caught up with Bert and watched Bert struggle for a few minutes. Finally, he walked over, nudged Bert aside and bent over the rock. With what seemed no effort at all, he hoisted the rock and threw it aside. Bert, of course, was astonished.

"That's amazing," he said.

Nate looked at him quizzically while wiping his hands on his blue jeans. "Bert," he said. "I thought you knew it's better Nate than lever."

GUILT BY ASSOCIATION

A most unusual case of attempted murder was recently brought to court in Mexico City. It was a case never before even contemplated, let alone tried.

It seems a man, Jorge Fuentes, was charged and convicted of attempting the murder of his wife under the most bizarre of circumstances. Apparently, he solicited the help of the couple's talking bird to drive his wife to suicide. He taught the bird to constantly repeat, "End it all!" and "Life is not worth living!" and "You'll be happy and in a better place!".

The prosecution brought the bird to court and had it "perform" for the judge and jury. He claimed the defendant was guilty by association with the bird and because of the training he had provided.

After hearing these arguments and the words of the bird, the judge and jury convicted both Jorge and the bird. Jorge received a stiff sentence but the bird got a suspended sentence because it was a Mynah.

HALF AND HALF

John and Jon, partners in a law firm, had struggled for years as consulting business lawyers who never were able to amass much wealth. One day a business client asked them to represent him in a divorce suit - which they did. It was their first big payoff with them receiving half the amount they were able to gain for their client.

Armed with this new found source of wealth, they devoted all their time to divorce cases and grew wealthy beyond their wildest dreams. Every case they took resulted in them receiving half of what they were able to gain for their clients. It was a bonanza and they relished their work.

Before they knew it, many years had passed. They were suddenly considered members of the Senior Society and found themselves bent over with the weight of their years.

One evening, John asked Jon where the years had gone and how they could have gotten away from them. It puzzled him that the years had gone by so quickly.

"I don't know," Jon replied. "But it certainly is true that time flies when you're halving funds."

HANDY WIPES

The UPS driver was on his way to a delivery in the farming section of eastern Pennsylvania. It was a cold and wet winter day and this would be his last run. He anticipated getting home and relaxing by his fireplace.

As he entered the last stretch of road before his delivery, the rain began to freeze on his windshield. It wasn't long before his wiper blades, worn out and ineffective, failed to keep up with the icy deposits. He was forced to stop at the side of the road.

While scraping the ice off the windshield he had an idea. A friend of his, caught in a similar dilemma, had told him of a unique solution to this very same problem. He stopped scraping the ice and went into the woods that lined both sides of the road.

Once there he began looking under large rocks until he found two rattlesnakes about twenty inches long. Because of the cold and the fact that they were hibernating they were quite stiff. But with reasonable effort he was able to straighten them.

He returned to his truck and installed these two rattlesnakes in place of the blades that were defective. As a result, he was able to complete his duties and enjoy his fireplace - all because of the wind chilled vipers.

HASTY ACTIONS LEAD NOWHERE

A young boy pestered his father for weeks for a compass. The father finally took the boy to the nearest store where he bought the first compass he saw - a Tates All Purpose Pioneer. The father then explained how the compass worked: "The needle will always point to the north. Therefore, no matter where you are and in which direction you face, you will know where to go."

The boy then tested his new Tates compass on the front porch and the needle pointed across the street. Then he went to the back porch and found that the needle pointed to the neighbor behind them. The same was true no matter where he went - the needle always pointed in a different direction.

With some anger, the boy's father returned to the store for an explanation. After all, the least one could expect is that it should point in the general direction of north. The clerk stuttered and shifted on his feet. "I'm sorry, sir," he said. "But you were in such a hurry when you bought it, I didn't have a chance to explain anything to you. I assumed you knew what you were doing."

"I was and I do," the father replied.

"Obviously, however," the clerk replied. "You don't know that he who has a Tates is lost."

HE WAS BOUND TO GET IT IN THE END
(Risqué)

A group of college seniors went out to celebrate their impending graduation with a night on the town. They drank enough to become plastered and throw caution to the wind. By unanimous vote they decided to cap off the evening with a visit to the local house of ill repute.

A week later, one of the celebrators discovered a large green lump on the end of his penis. This, of course, concerned him greatly and he went straight away to the emergency room.

After the doctor put the student through a thorough exam he retrieved a heavy medical book from the library shelf. He riffled through the pages until he found what he was looking for. Then he looked at the student and said: "This is pretty serious stuff. We need to operate."

The student was visibly shocked. It took some time for him to gather his wits about him. But he finally said: "Operate? What's wrong with me?"

The doctor sat in the chair facing the young man and looked him in the eyes. "Have you ever heard of the condition that boxers get called Cauliflower Ear?"

The student nodded.

"Well you have a similar condition. It's called Brothel Sprout."

HE WAS DEAD WRONG

A young man had many pets but his favorite was a mouse he had received for Christmas. He carried it with him everywhere he went. He and his mouse were inseparable.

One day he received word that his favorite uncle had died so he went to the funeral parlor to show his respect. On his way home he realized his mouse was missing. Terrified that the mouse may have been kidnapped or worse, he repeated his moves of the day in an attempt to locate his lost friend.

In the process, he remembered he had last seen the mouse at the funeral parlor just before he locked up the hearse and sent it on its way. The funeral directors tried to console him. They told him the mouse had gone to the cemetery in the hearse with his uncle and was now gone forever. They thought he had given it to his uncle as a parting gift.

In his grief, he remembered words of wisdom his mother had told him time and time again. But it wasn't until now that the significance of that wisdom rang true. And he vowed to never again lock a gift mouse in the hearse.

HE WAS JUST KIDDING

A young mother, in an attempt to reduce her own expenses for child care, established a day care center in her neighborhood. Her expertise at dealing with young children soon became well known and she maxed out her facilities and her ability to care for the children. In response to the growing need to care for more children she hired an assistant.

The first day the assistant was on duty a three-year-old, who had been the most difficult of children at the day care center, refused to cooperate. All of the other children had taken their places in their cribs, many of them already asleep, all of them cooperating. But the three-year-old ran from the assistant and disrupted the entire day care center's routine

The proprietor had run into this situation before and had taken necessary measures to deal with it. She had obtained permission from the boy's mother to deal with it in whatever manner seemed fit. And with the mother's agreement she called the police.

As the police were taking the child into custody and removing him and his disruption from the day care center, the assistant asked the proprietor on what grounds this action was justified. The proprietor answered that the child's behavior was simply a matter of resisting a rest.

HE WILL DRIVE YOU MAD

The cowboys gathered in their bunkhouse after a hard day on the range. One of them popped open a cold beer and sat on the edge of his bunk. "Where's Tex?" he asked.

"Oh, he's out looking over his new car," another responded. "It's that new foreign car he just bought. He just can't get enough of it. Spend hours just looking and touching it."

The cowboy standing in the corner said: "Ole Tex is a smart aleck. As soon as he gets back here he'll start bragging about that car."

The one with the beer then said: "Not Tex. He's just a good old boy and that's all he'll ever be. When he comes in, all he's going to do is say hello."

"I know Tex better than any of you," said another cowboy who was standing in the darkness of the far corner. "He may be a good old boy but he's also a smart old boy. He'll figure out some way to brag about his car even when he's just saying hello."

Just then the bunkhouse door swung open and Tex sauntered in. He looked at all the others who seemed startled at his arrival and shouted: "Audi, partners!"

HEADS OR TAILS

Two new graduates from medical school joined together in a partnership and settled in a small Iowa town. Doctor Smith was a psychiatrist and Doctor Jones was a proctologist. The first thing they did was put up a sign in front of their offices that read Dr. Smith and Dr. Jones – Psychiatry and Proctology. For some unknown reason, the town fathers immediately objected and suggested the doctors come up with a new sign.

The doctors tried many new approaches to their signage but the town fathers were reluctant to approve any of them. They tried *Minds and Behinds, Nuts and Butts, Loons and Moons, and Hysterias and Posteriors*. None of these was good enough for the authorities. They even tried *Schizoids and Hemorrhoids* without success.

After what seemed an eternally long time, the doctors and the town fathers were finally able to agree on the appropriate signage for the new practice. With the frustrations of dealing with the local government behind them, they proudly announced the grand opening of their offices and erected a sign that read: *Dr. Smith and Dr. Jones – Odds And Ends.*

HIGH SOCIETY

Mr. and Mrs. Potato were poor their entire lives. So, when their daughter Sweet Potato was born, they decided they would do all in their power to assure her a good chance for success. For years they struggled to pay for her education and ensure her a good future. Then three weeks before graduation, Sweet Potato returned home and announced she was dropping out of college. Her astonished parents caught their breath and sat down.

"Why?" was their obvious question.

Sweet Potato replied: "I don't have to complete college to get into high society. I'm going to marry into it."

"And who are you going to marry?"

"Eric Sevareid," was the confident answer.

The Potatoes were so distraught with her answer that Sweet Potato felt bewildered. She was convinced they would instantly approve and now she was not certain of anything. "What's wrong with marrying him? He will allow me to achieve all you ever wanted for me."

"Don't you understand?" they replied in unison. "He's just a common tater."

HIGH STEPPING DANCERS

A traveling troupe of dancers known as the Steppers performed to sellout crowds in clubs and theaters across the country. After one particularly successful show, management offered them unlimited visits to the bar. It wasn't long before they all became exceedingly drunk.

When it became time to launch their trip to the next town, they continued to party on the bus. They were having a grand old time unaware that their future was in jeopardy.

Beside the highway where they traveled, a family's pet viper, known as Peter, had gotten loose. He was a large snake who became confused with his newfound freedom and paused to collect his thoughts on the highway unaware of the oncoming bus load of partygoers.

The sleepy bus driver, thinking the snake was a felled tree in the roadway, swerved. The bus's tires dug into the shoulder and pulled the bus off the road into the ditch. The drunken Steppers gathered their wits about them and exited the bus as quickly as possible and when the news reporter arrived they were scattered everywhere.

It was only natural that the next day the newspaper headlines about the incident would read: "Peter Viper wrecks a truck of pickled Steppers."

HIGH STYLE HITCH HIKER

A beggar, dressed in tattered clothes and cardboard shoes, snuck aboard a cruise ship bound for the Caribbean. As the cruise ship was preparing for departure, the beggar was discovered and escorted from the ship.

The next day the beggar repeated his stow away activity and was promptly discovered a second time. And the following day he once again tried to hide on board but was detected and ushered ashore. The harbor master was notified this third time and the beggar was summoned to his office.

"I'm merely trying to make it to the Caribbean so I can escape my poverty," the beggar said.

"Ah, yes," the harbor master replied. But what you don't understand is that beggars can't be cruisers."

HIS, HERS, AND ALL THE OTHERS

The football coach, enroute to a big game, stopped for supper at the roadside restaurant owned by one of the team's biggest fans. As the football players ate their meal, the coach realized he was late and told them they would have to suit up at the restaurant if they hoped to arrive at the stadium ready to play. He took all the linemen and sent them into the lady's room to put on their uniforms. And he sent all the backs into the men's room to do the same.

As the last lineman entered the lady's room the coach asked the counter clerk for a soda. The restaurant owner, hearing this, suggested that all the members of his favorite team may want a drink on the house and, if it was okay with the coach, he would see to it.

The coach agreed and called to his team manager who was standing watch by the restroom doors and had overheard the offer: "I'll check with the linemen," the coach said. "You see what the backs in the boy's room want."

HOPE AND CHANGE IS NEVER GUARANTEED

A young boy swallowed some coins and complained to his mother that he felt ill. His mother rushed him to the hospital where the nursing staff took him under their wings. They told the mother to relax and they would advise her when everything was okay.

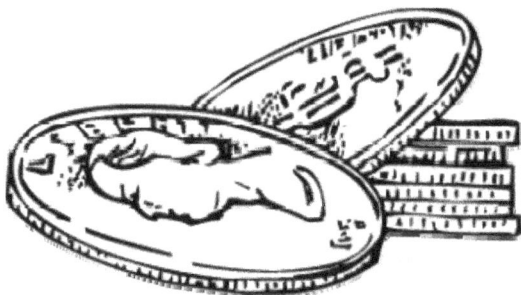

The mother notified everyone in the family about what had happened - grandmother, grandfather, aunts, uncles, and brothers and sisters. Of them all only the grandmother showed anxiety. The others believed everything would be okay over time.

But the grandmother could not stand it and, after a few hours, called the hospital. She was directed to the nursing staff that was caring for the young boy.

She rattled: "Can you tell me how my young grandson is? Is he okay? What is his status?"

The nurse on the other end of the telephone conversation urged the grandmother to calm down. In a soothing voice, the nurse told her the boy was under expert care but had exhibited no change yet.

HORSE SENSE

During the Revolutionary War, General George Washington had surrounded the British in a small town in Virginia called Sotter and camped overnight on a ridge outside of town. At dawn, the British commander saw Washington's soldiers massing for battle. Recognizing that he needed reinforcements, the commander dispatched a messenger with an urgent request for help. The British reserves were hastily rushed to the front with no time to don their full battle dress. Nearly all of them were led to Sotter wearing their traditional pink bed clothing.

Just as the battle was beginning, the force of pink-clad British soldiers arrived on the scene. Their appearance was so unusual that the revolutionary patriots began to laugh and hoot and holler and call the British soldiers many undisciplined names. The British, embarrassed by this attack, hung their heads in shame.

It wasn't long until Washington's soldiers recognized their advantage and drove down the ridge scattering the entire British army. The sight of the beleaguered pink-clad British soldiers retreating was history in the making. This one battle was a turning point in the struggle for American independence. It also taught us a valuable lesson: You can lead a force to Sotter but you can't make it pink.

HOT DIGGITY DOG *(Risqué)*

Larena Bobbit's sister was arrested last night for attempting to cause the same damage to her husband that Lorena had inflicted upon her spouse. She had used a similar knife in her attack and attempted to remove her husband's manhood much as her sister had done.

Unfortunately, the sister didn't quite hit her mark. As she wielded the knife in her attack, she tripped and stabbed her husband in the leg by mistake.

Her husband was able to escape and immediately called 9-1-1. When the police arrived, they arrested the man's wife.

"I trust you will lock her up for a long time," the husband said.

"I'm afraid not," the policeman replied. "The most we can charge her with is a misdeweiner."

HOT PANTS

An upscale young man who used his morning visits to the coffee shop as a status statement ordered his usual large mug of coffee and took it to a table. When he lifted it to his lips for his first savory sip, he discovered the mug did not contain coffee. Instead, a pair of beige cotton pants were folded neatly and stuffed inside.

He immediately went to the counter to complain. But the servers deflected his growing tirade and insisted they had not made a mistake. Eventually, he demanded in his own fashion that they summon the manager.

"I can't believe your people would try to deny that they gave me this," he said as he thrust the mug toward the manager's face. "I find it incomprehensible. After all, I have been coming to this coffee shop every morning for months."

The manager looked at him with apology written all over his face. He stuttered and stammered and finally gathered his thoughts. "I am truly sorry, Sir," he said.

"As you should be," the indignant young man replied.

"We have a new employee," the manager went on. "That employee was certainly unaware of your usual coffee order. He believed you ordered a cup of chinos."

HOW SOON THEY FORGET

Most bartenders live a relatively happy life. They are constantly meeting new friends and are always engaged in some form of interesting conversation. People pay top dollar for their unique services and they bring happiness to most patrons.

The most pleasant times are those in which the bartender is able to join the patrons for a few drinks. And the enjoyment is greatly increased when he purchases drinks for the house. It is at these times that the bartender finds he has more friends than he could ever imagine. And each and every one of them is more than happy to share in his generosity.

It is therefore sad when closing time comes and it becomes necessary to clean the bar in preparation for the next day's business. It is then that all of these fair weather friends disappear. Still, most bartenders understand this quirk of casual human behavior and have learned to accept it.

For it is said: "Quaff and the world quaffs with you; sweep and you sweep alone."

I DO ... I DO

Back when nearly all baking was done by hand there was a small bakery in Berlin run by a baker named Richard. Because of the secret technique he used when pouring a dough mixture as he made his sausage rolls, he became known as Richard the Pourer.

One day he noticed that he was running low on one of the necessary spices for his dough mixture. He dispatched his assistant to the store to buy more.

Unfortunately, the assist-ant was not known for his sterling memory capabilities and arrived at the store having forgotten the name of the ingredients he was supposed to purchase. Although he thought long and hard, he could not remember what it was he was to buy.

He did recall that the store owner was quite familiar with the ingredients Richard frequently purchased for the bakery operation. And he thought that perhaps a simple description of what ingredient was needed would prompt the store owner into the proper selection.

When he explained that he'd forgotten the ingredient, the owner agreed to try to decipher the proper spice from the description. So the assistant then said: "It's for Richard the Pourer for batter and for wurst."

I DON'T BELIEVE IT

Atheism in the mid-west or the deep south is something rarely found to exist. So when a woman who claimed to be a relative of Madalyn O'Hair approached the Tax Assessor in Dubuque, Iowa, for an exemption from property taxes, it was quite a surprise.

The tax assessor told this young woman that in this small Midwestern town there were no exemptions granted to non-religious organizations. Although they used to grant such exemptions to churches and other religious organizations, the Supreme Court's decisions of the recent past had influenced them to no longer do so.

"That may be so," the young woman said. "But you still offer exemptions for charitable organizations do you not? "

"Yes we do," was the chilly reply. "But you have to prove that you qualify as a breakeven endeavor."

"Then it is obvious we should be allowed the exemption," the young woman asserted. "We most certainly qualify as a non-prophet organization."

I PLEAD GUILTY

When the weatherman predicted a winter storm that included sleet, snow, and icy conditions, everyone began preparing for the worst. One man journeyed to the store to pick up the only supplies he really needed: a bag of salt to spread over the front walkway and some batteries for his children's toys.

He took his purchases to the front counter and set them down. The clerk watched him as he fumbled through his pants pockets for cash. It became evident after some time that he had left his cash at home and would have to pay for his purchases with his credit card.

When he finally looked up, the clerk said: "That's an unusual combination you have there, Sir."

"Yes. It is," the man replied as he handed the clerk his credit card. He then said: "I guess you'll just have to charge me with a salt and batteries."

ICE SCULPTURE

Scientists have long wondered what happens to penguins in the Antarctic when they die. Although some must certainly die on land, none has ever been found and it has remained a mystery for eons.

The answer is actually quite simple. It is a known fact that the penguin is a very ritualistic bird, the result of its evolution in the polar cap's harsh environment and surroundings. Over the years it's survival as a species forced the colony to live an extremely ordered and complex life. The penguin is also very committed to its family, will mate for life, and has a form of compassionate contact with its offspring throughout the youngster's life.

If a penguin is found dead on the ice surface, other members of the family and social circle will dig a hole in the ice using their wings and pecking with their beaks. They work ceaselessly until the hole is deep enough to completely entomb the dead bird. When the hole is finished, they roll the deceased bird in and bury it using the excavated ice to fill in the hole.

The male penguins then gather in a circle around the fresh grave and in a demonstration of friendship and solidarity sing: "Freeze a jolly good fellow!"

IF I ONLY HAD A BRAIN

A local drug rehab center had fallen into disrepair and the grounds were in shambles. The newly hired director assumed the task of upgrading the facility. The improvements became the pride of the downtown section of the city with newly planted bushes and a lush, thick lawn, and accent art scattered everywhere.

The director of the center was known for his humorous approach to even the most traumatic of circumstance. Considering the service he provided the community, his constant, upbeat personality was the envy of all who came to know him.

He was also into landscaping with a passion and the new lawn and bushes and new, young trees were a source of great pride for him.

And so it was not a surprise when he chose a motto for the drug rehabilitation center that matched his desires for the preservation of the center's good appearance: Keep Off The Grass.

IN A ROUND ABOUT FASHION

During the hay days of the Roman Empire, Emperor Nero noticed that his subjects were far too idle. Petty thievery was on the increase and many arguments broke out among the citizens. He finally decided he must do something to occupy the citizens' time or he would have a serious problem on his hands.

Therefore, he devised and instituted a new game that all of the subjects under his domain must play on a daily basis. He reasoned that if he could keep them busy for at least a portion of the day, they would not have time to get in trouble.

The game he devised involved the players rolling small discs a predetermined length across the floor. Much like today's shuffleboard, the goal of the game was to have as many of these discs stop their rolling in a specified section of the floor thus amassing points for the contestant.

Because there was a ready supply of discs used to protect tables from a cold glass's condensation, he used them for the game pieces. And because they were made of iron they were most suitable for the game's purpose.

Unbeknownst to Nero, he had invented the world's first roller coaster or, as some would call them, ferrous wheels.

IN THE BLINK OF AN EYE

Two Arabs are sitting at a local bar smoking hashish and discussing current events over a pint of fermented goat's milk. The first Arab digs out his wallet and begins flipping through the pictures. It is obvious he is quite proud of those depicted on the images.

"This is my eldest son," he said. "He is a hero to us and a credit to Islam. He is a martyr."

His companion raises his hands to the sky. "Praise Allah!" he chants. "You must be so very proud."

He flips through the pictures and finds another. "Yes, I am very proud of him. I am very proud of all my sons but mostly of my eldest and this here, my second oldest son." He points vigorously to the image in the second picture. "This son is a martyr also."

"A fine looking gentleman," replied his companion. "Praise be to Mohammed!"

The father of the two young men looks at his pictures with the dreamy, wistful gaze. Then he says with a tone of sadness in his voice: "They sure blow up fast, don't they?"

174 - Gary Younglove

IN THE THROES OF EXPERIENCE

An old African tribe had developed a highly ordered monarchical form of government. Once a year the king would sit on his ornate throne in the public common and issue statements of policy and law and make judgments concerning complaints brought before him. Then the missionaries arrived and eventually influenced the king to ban idol worship and order the destruction of the throne.

One of the Princes, however, was not convinced. He stole the heavy wooden throne and stored it with its inlay of gold and precious jewels on the second floor attic of his grass shack. When the folly of the king's decision became evident, the Prince would retrieve the throne he had stored and assume the leadership role he had always coveted.

Unfortunately, such was not to be. The missionaries converted more and more of the natives and each day the Prince returned to his grass shack, stared at the throne, and dreamed of how it was supposed to be. Then, one evening, his shack began to shudder and creak. Soon it was vibrating and swaying until it suddenly collapsed from the weight of the throne stored on the second floor.

The Prince's deceit was thus exposed and the event gave birth to a lesson of great value. For everybody now knows that people who live in grass houses shouldn't stow thrones.

IT CAN LEAVE YOU BREATHLESS

It was prisoner transfer day at the Travis County, Texas, jail and everyone had taken precautions to prevent a rumored escape attempt. Double guards had been assigned to the process and specially designed busses were used.

In spite of the security efforts, a prisoner escaped because of what could best be called unusual circumstances. As he was being moved to the bus near the front of the jail, an accomplice appeared from a nearby alleyway. He grabbed the prisoner out of the hands of the guards he had distracted with breath mints. As the startled guards defended themselves against the mints, the accomplice was able to rush the prisoner to a safe place.

Later, under persistent questioning, the sheriff admitted his men weren't prepared for the breath mint attack which he called Diversionary Tic-Tacs.

IT COULD BE CONTAGEOUS

A young man was sitting at home one evening when the doorbell rang. When he answered the door, a six-foot tall cockroach greeted him and then immediately punched him between the eyes before scampering off into the darkness.

The next evening the slightly bruised man was sitting at home when the doorbell rang again. He answered the door with some trepidation and discovered the cockroach had returned. This time the insect punched him in the face and kicked him on his shin before running away.

The third evening the angry young man sat at home awaiting the doorbell. He was prepared this time. So when the doorbell rang he approached it cautiously. Unfortunately, he was not prepared enough and the cockroach successfully attacked him with a knife.

The injured young man crawled to the telephone, summoned an ambulance, and rushed to the hospital where well-trained members of the staff saved his life.

The next morning as the doctor was doing his rounds he asked the young man what had happened. Upon hearing the explanation of the cockroach's attacks, the doctor thought for a moment. Then he said: "Ah yes. I heard there is a nasty bug going around right now."

IT HAPPENS ALL THE TIME

The man went to his doctor to complain of a problem he had been suffering for quite some time. After waiting in the outer room for the normal but excessive period of time, the nurse summoned him and took him to an examination room.

When the doctor finally showed up, the man explained his problem as the compulsive repetition of a popular song.

"I can't stop singing The Green, Green Grass Of Home," he said. "And I was hoping you could help me determine what's wrong."

The doctor looked at him for some time as he stroked his goatee. Then he wrote a few comments on the man's chart. "I believe your condition is easily discernible," he said.

"What is it?" the man asked.

"Well it sounds like Tom Jones syndrome."

"Is it common?" The man asked with obvious concern.

The doctor laid down the man's chart, looked deep into his eyes, and said: "Well, it's not unusual."

IT LOOKS THE SAME FROM ANY ANGLE

An invisible man spent his entire life looking for the perfect mate. No matter where he looked he could never find her. It reached a point that he was convinced he would spend his life alone. As he was returning home from what he believed to be his final search for his lifetime companion, he was not paying attention and bumped into an invisible woman.

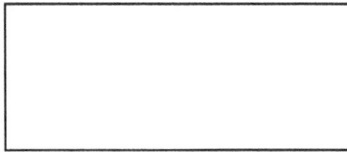

This fortuitous meeting turned into a strong friendship which eventually turned into love. The invisible man and woman had both found something they thought they would never know. They courted for the longest time reveling in their good fortune, blinded to everything but their companionship.

In due course they married. And when the wife became pregnant they wondered whether or not their offspring would also be invisible. And so they waited with great anticipation for the birth of their first child hoping that it would join the family as an unseen and not suffer the fate of visibility.

As the baby was born, the mother looked to the nurse in the delivery room for an indication of the outcome. The nurse, of course, couldn't see the mother but she knew of the parent's wishes and said: "There's no need to worry. Just as I can't see you, the child's nothing to look at either."

IT MUST BE SOMETHING I ATE

The lion had gone without food for two weeks and had worked up a tremendous appetite. No matter how hard he worked at it, he had been unable to capture any prey. It had reached the point that he was uncertain whether or not he would ever eat again.

Then, out of nowhere, he came upon two human beings sitting beneath a large Baobab tree. It was late afternoon and they were both intently focused on what they were doing. One of them was reading a book and the other was writing in a journal. They were both unaware of the lion's presence.

The lion snuck up on the two humans and prepared to attack. He had made up his mind that the reading human would be his target. This choice was the result of past encounters he had with humans. His selection was the reading human for even the king of the jungle knows that readers digest and writers cramp.

IT PAYS TO BE CAUTIOUS

Kangaroos have been an integral part of Australia since time began. They are a national symbol and generate widespread curiosity throughout the world. Circuses have even employed them as boxers for the entertainment of audiences.

In recent times, however, the growing number of automobiles on the road has resulted in an increasing number of collisions between kangaroos and vehicles. The kangaroos, as a result, have developed a very successful method to exact revenge against the traffic that has ravaged them.

The Roos, as the local Australians call them, have learned to display timidity as a car passes them. But once the vehicle has passed, the Roos veer en masse onto the highway and, as a formidable group, attack the vehicle from the rear. Quite a few people have been injured by this activity.

The only known defense is to drive as quickly as possible away. And the automobile industry responded almost overnight with a new mirror that detects an oncoming attack. Once this mirror is installed, drivers can avoid an attack if they monitor their veer-roo mirror at all times.

IT PAYS TO BE PREPARED *(Risqué)*

In an effort to capitalize on the lucrative birth control pill market, the Cadbury Candy Company partnered with the Merck Drug Company in an attempt to produce a mint flavored birth control pill that women could take immediately before sex.

They conducted extensive research over a number of years before they came upon the proper formulation. Once the pill was produced it entered lengthy trials to prove its effectiveness. And when that was complete they applied for and received FDA approval to market the pill.

The biggest problem was to come up with a catchy name for the birth control pills. If they were to be successful, the name had to appeal to a wide audience and also be descriptive of its purpose.

They assembled a team of some of the smartest marketing minds in the industry and locked them in a room. They were not to be released until they had come up with an acceptable name.

It was surprising, therefore, when the team came up with a name within an hour. When questioned, the team responded that it was really quite simple. The obvious name for this type of pill had to be: "Pre-Dick-A-Mints."

IT TAKES A MAN TO ADMIT IT *(Risqué)*

A Midwestern town had a small park in its center. On Sunday afternoons many artists and performers would gather there. Painters, musicians, mimes, and jugglers were but a few of those who showed up on sunny days. There was never a shortage of performers or of an audience. People would gather on the soft, green grasses of the park, stroll through the painter's section, or sit cross legged and watch or listen to those with talent.

Two young men on their first visit to the park in this small town located a vantage point on the cool grasses where they could see nearly all of the performers without having to move. They watched the mimes as they did their thing, the musicians as they played their music, and the jugglers as they deftly maneuvered their hands and feet.

They noticed one man among the jugglers who just stood there. He did not move his hands or feet yet watched intently as the others performed. One of the young men wondered out loud, "Why is he standing there with all the jugglers doing nothing?"

A passerby heard him and replied: "Oh. He's a juggler too."

"Then why isn't he juggling?" the man asked.

The passerby responded: "He just doesn't have the balls to do it."

IT'LL ALL WORK OUT IN THE END

A skeptical anthropologist was cataloging South American folk remedies. He was on site and had collected a large number of hopefully useful plant specimens with the assistance of a tribal Brujo when he bent over with some abdominal distress. His response to the Brujo's question of concern was simply: "I've got me a little constipation."

The Brujo immediately rummaged in his collection of herbs and produced a small, green handful of the lacy ferns. He held them in the doubting scientist's face and told him that the leaves of this simple fern were a sure cure for any case of constipation.

When the anthropologist expressed his doubts, the Brujo looked him in the eye and said: "If you must doubt me, do so. But do not discount my experience until after you have tried these ferns."

The next day, the anthropologist was quite relieved of both his doubts and his backup. He approached the Brujo and said with some excitement and enthusiasm: "Let me tell you my friend, with fronds like these, who needs enemas?"

IT'S A FAMILY THING

The customers in the local Wild West Saloon were hopping it up on a Saturday night. The man at the piano was playing a ragtime tune and the ladies of the night were plying their trade.

When the swinging doors opened and a large three-legged dog entered, everyone stopped what they were doing. It was as though they had been frozen in time. The dog looked them all over and then proceeded to the bar.

He ordered a whiskey and surveyed the crowd within the saloon then he sipped his drink. As the crowd returned to its normal activity, an old prospector standing at the bar turned to face the dog.

"What happened to your leg?" The prospector asked, pointing toward the missing appendage.

"Some man fired a pistol into my foot and I had to have it amputated," the dog replied.

"Sorry to hear that," the prospector said. He turned back to his own drink but after a few moments he turned to the dog again. "I just gotta know," he said. "Whatcha doin' in here with all these people?"

The dog responded matter-of-factly: "I'm looking for the man who shot my paw."

IT'S A MONSTROUS PROBLEM

Two sea monsters were cruising throughout the depths looking for something to entertain them. It wasn't long before they came upon an ocean going vessel that was hauling beets, carrots, and a large store of potatoes.

The first sea monster, known as Bob by his friends, swam beneath the ship, tipped it over, and ate everything on board. The other sea monster was puzzled by this act.

Some time later they came upon another vessel that was also hauling potatoes. As expected, Bob capsized the ship and ate everything on board. He did the same thing with a third ship they found that was also hauling potatoes. His companion watched him with amazement as he gorged himself with everything on board.

Finally, his friend asked him: "Why is it you keep tipping over those ships full of potatoes and eat everything on board?"

Bob replied: "I just can't help myself. Once I get started I can't quit. Everyone knows you can't eat just one potato ship."

IT'S A SIN TO TELL A LIE *(Risqué)*

Two cows were standing next to each other in a field of clover and alfalfa. They had been friends all their lives and shared their most intimate experiences with each other regardless of the outcome. Daisy, the elder of the two, had even described for Dolly her first experience with a bull some years back. The two were almost inseparable.

So it was not unusual that Daisy would feel no compunction about sharing her most recent experience with Dolly. They were grazing near the fence on the far side of the pasture. The other cows were some distance away so Daisy felt comfortable speaking bluntly.

She turned to face Dolly. "Come closer," she said. "I have something I want to tell you."

Dolly crowded close to Daisy in anticipation of a juicy secret.

"Don't tell anyone else," Daisy whispered in Dolly's ear. "But I was artificially inseminated this morning."

Dolly seemed visibly shocked. She shuddered. And after a few moments of silence she said: "I don't believe you."

"It's true!" Daisy said with a strong sense of conviction. "It's true, I tell you. No bull!"

IT'S A SMALL PRICE TO PAY *(Risqué)*

A small town in northern Oklahoma received federal assistance to build housing for a family of small people who lived there. According to the census demographics, the government determined that the population of small people was large enough to justify preferential treatment in the form of a rental subsidy.

The intent of this subsidy was to provide rent relief to the unfortunate and currently unemployed little people. They could then seek employment where they could contribute to their community without the worry of having to meet monthly payments. Also, because of the numbers involved, they would each pay much less than the going rate for rent.

The City Council met to discuss how to proceed with the plan of building the houses that met the subsidy rules. In the discussions it became apparent that the government numbers were wrong and there was only one little person living in the city. It was an easy process to conclude that the government subsidy would cover everything and the sole little person would not have to pay a penny in rent.

The Council immediately authorized a local contractor to build a house which was ultimately called the Stay Free Mini Pad.

IT'S A STRETCH

The local butcher was also an avid gambler. He attended the horse races regularly and bought a lottery ticket every week. Many of his customers would place bets with him on various events as part of their shopping experience. Because of his astute judgment, he rarely lost a bet.

One day Ollie Oddsmaker came to the market in search of a couple strip steaks for supper. After the usual greetings and amenities, the butcher asked him what he wanted. Ollie thought for a minute so as to lay the ground for the upcoming challenge. "I think I'll have a couple strip steaks," he finally said.

The butcher reached into the meat case for two steaks positioned just under the glass. Ollie stopped him.

"I'd like the ones on the top shelf in that meat case behind you," he said. "In fact, I'm betting that you can't reach them. If you can, I'll pay double. If you can't, I get them for free."

The butcher loved this kind of bet but he hesitated as he looked at the case behind him. Suddenly, the reason he had been so successful with his betting came into play.

"No way, Ollie," he said. "It's not a good bet. The steaks are too high!"

IT'S ALL ABOUT PRESENTATION *(Risqué)*

A chicken and a horse lived peacefully together on a farm. One day, when they were playing, the horse fell into a bog and began to sink. He whinnied for the chicken to go to the farmer for help. The chicken discovered the farmer had gone to town with the only tractor. So he decided to use the farmer's new Harley Davidson motorcycle instead and sped off with a length of rope to save the horse's life.

The horse managed to get a hold of the rope the chicken tossed him. And after the chicken attached the rope to the motorcycle, engaged the powerful engine, and pulled on the rope, the horse scrambled out of the bog onto safe, solid ground.

A few weeks later the chicken also fell into a mud pit. He cried out to the horse as he began to sink beneath the soupy slime. He pled for the horse to go get the motorcycle and pull him out as he had pulled the horse out before. But the horse only stood there thinking.

Fear gripped the chicken but finally the horse straddled the large muddy puddle dangling his manhood over the chicken like a chain. He told the chicken to get a good grip and then he pulled the chicken out by simply backing up.

The chicken's life was saved and the event proved once again a long-standing truism: *When you're hung like a horse, you don't need a Harley to pick up chicks.*

IT'S ALL IN HOW YOU LOOK AT IT

The young, inexperienced political science major traveled to the newly formed Kingdom of Exeter. This student hoped to study how the King and his ruling elite would implement the voting process as they had promised to do when they formed the country.

Elections were scheduled the day after the student arrived and the student went to the polling place where he intended to interview voters as they exited. He was greatly surprised and somewhat disappointed when no one had showed up to vote even though there were only a few minutes left before the polls closed.

Moments before voting was to be stopped, the Count of the Kingdom of Exeter arrived and entered the polling place. A few minutes later he exited and the student approached him.

"Perhaps you can help me Sir," the student said. He then explained what he had been doing all day and of his disappointment that no one had come to vote except the Count.

"Ah. You don't understand," the Count intoned. "You see. In a democracy it's your vote that counts; however, in feudalism it's your Count that votes."

IT'S ALL IN THE BAG

A tall, weather-worn cowboy sauntered into the saloon and ordered a beer. As he quaffed this refreshing drink, the regulars quietly observed the drifter through half-closed eyelids.

No one spoke, but they all noticed that the stranger's hat was made of brown wrapping paper. Less obvious was the fact that his plain shirt and vest were also made of paper. As if that wasn't enough, his chaps, pants, and even his boots, including the spurs, were made of brown shopping bag paper. Truth be told, even the saddle, blanket, and bridle on his horse were made entirely of paper.

It stands to reason then that it wasn't long before he was arrested for rustling.

IT'S ALL IN THE PRESENTATION

The Watson family had earned a prominent place in the local community because of their philanthropic activities. And as time went on, they decided to compile a history of famous Watsons.

The book was taking shape and contained descendent information that would make any family proud. There were Watsons who were Senators, pastors, war heroes, entrepreneurs. In fact, the Watson family could boast success in nearly every occupation and pursuit.

Unfortunately, the research also uncovered something that brought them concern. It seems they had a great uncle Samuel who ended up on the wrong side of the law. He had been involved in a family feud for some years and eventually was convicted of murder and executed in an electric chair.

The Watsons hired an author to help them resolve the problem of how to handle this in the history book. They wanted to maintain the purity of their prominence and hoped the author could help them. They would not be disappointed.

The author's entry on the great uncle read: "Samuel Watson was the chairman of the electricity utility for a government run institution. Although he served in this position for only a short time he was firmly entrenched in its activities. His death was a real shock."

IT'S NO SMALL THING

A young man approached the bar in a local neighborhood and ordered a drink. "I'll have one for my friend Tiny, also," he said, pointing to a small salamander perched on his shoulder.

The bartender followed his orders without question but couldn't avoid staring with some disbelief as the man and the salamander quaffed their drinks together. After two rounds of this, the bartender couldn't keep silent any longer.

"Pardon me, friend," he said. "I don't mean to be sticking my nose in anyone's business, but I notice the salamander on your shoulder. I've never run into anything like this before. Do you mind if I ask you a question?"

The young man said that he didn't mind at all.

"I was wondering," the bartender continued. "Considering all the booze that there thing can drink, why don't you name him something other than Tiny?"

"Easy question," the man said. "I call him Tiny because he's my newt."

IT'S ON THE HOUSE

The lonely neutron spends his entire life receiving no credit for anything he does. He forms a major portion of the center of the atom ceaselessly working to provide balance in an otherwise chaotic world. Yet no one cares about his contributions. Instead, all of the credit goes to the protons and the electrons.

Because of this lack of attention, the faceless neutron usually descends into the lowest possible depression. Forced to live side-by-side with his partner who receives all the adulation, the lowly neutron is filled with self-doubt.

One day a neutron was able to take a break from his daily chores within the atom. In the depths of his sadness he decided to go to a bar and get drunk. He walked into the very first bar he found and ordered a beer.

The bartender served him his choice of beverage and then said: "You're a neutron aren't you?"

The neutron acknowledged this fact and sipped on his beer. "How much for the beer?" he asked.

"I understand the trouble you neutrons go through," the bartender said. "You perform a valuable service without recognition. So, for you, no charge."

JUAN BY JUAN

Juan Esperanto, having been gored by a bull, did not abandon his compulsion to become a world class bull fighter. After his complete recovery, he began training again and worked for months to improve his style and agility so he could avoid the fate that befell him during his last bovine battle.

Eventually, he assessed himself ready for his next fight. He had developed methods to avoid becoming hooked on the horns of the bull and practiced them to perfection. He had worked diligently to regain his confidence in the ring. He had spent countless hours refining his technique.

So it was that on a sunny Sunday afternoon Juan reentered the ring as one of three Juans on a special bull fight billing. Juan Garcia, the first, was immediately gored and lost to the bull. Juan Lopez, the second, was also unfortunate and fell to the same fate. With some trepidation, Juan Esperanto faced the third bull of the day and was instantly hooked on a horn and pinned to the wall.

It was here that his persistent training paid off for he deftly removed himself from this horny dilemma and promptly defeated the bull. And for years his fans remembered that day and the Juan that got away.

KEEPING IT ALL IN THE FAMILY *(Risqué)*

Most prostitutes had no families and wandered through life with no goals or hope of a familial situation. Their occupations were dead end careers. Their focus was on earning the quick buck. They were unable to look into the future and see where their lifestyle was taking them.

So it was that a group of concerned citizens formed an organization whose efforts were devoted to helping these wayward waifs. They developed a network of family units across the country who would take the unfortunate ladies into their circle and give them love and encouragement.

To spread the word about its mission, the organization printed and distributed brochures, broad-cast public announcements on the radio and TV, and held forums. All of these showed signs of success but none were as effective as the posters they carried around the neighborhoods.

Adopt Today

Without Delay

It was not long before the posters were the primary means of getting support for their program. And everywhere you went you could see the organization's posters proclaiming: "Adopt A Prostitute – Otherwise They Will End Up In A Whorephanage."

KEEPING IT ALL TO YOURSELF

Two rather large lobsters were catching a few summer-time rays on a Maine beach. After an hour or so the lady lobster asked her male friend if he would mind getting them each an ice cream cone. He agreed and headed off for the parlor.

After having purchased two cones and holding one in each of his claws he struck out on the arduous trip back to the beach. His cone started to melt so he began eating it. Before long he had finished his entire cone as the lady lobster's ice cream was dripping liberally onto his claw.

He merely intended to clean the drippings from his claw but he lost control and ended up eating the entire cone. As a result, he arrived back at the beach empty handed.

"Where are the ice cream cones?" she asked.

"I ate mine on the way," he said. "Then I noticed yours was melting also and I ended up eating it too."

"I don't believe it!" she shouted.

"I'm sorry," he said. "I really didn't mean it."

"It doesn't matter," she railed. "I've known it for a long time. You're nothing but a shellfish creep!"

KEEPING SCORE

Outside a small Macedonian village near Greece, a lone Catholic nun keeps a quiet watch over a 2,000 year old convent. She is the last caretaker of the historic site and when Sister Maria of the Order of the Perpetual Watch dies, the convent of St. Elias will be closed.

In ancient times, a Greek temple to Eros, the god of love, occupied the hilltop site. Historians say that Attila the Hun took over the old temple in 439 A.D. and used it as a base for his marauding army. The Huns are believed to have destroyed a large gathering of Greek legal writs at the site because Attila was barely literate and couldn't read them. But mostly because they provided evidence of a democratic government that did not agree with his own notions as a tyrant.

When the Greek Church took over the site in the 15th Century and the convent was built, church leaders ordered the pagan statue of Eros destroyed, so this ancient Greek treasure was also lost. Today, there is only the lone sister Maria, watching over the old Hun base.

And it appears that's how it will end: No Huns, no writs, no Eros, and nun left on base.

KODAK BARE

The new owners of an old Victorian mansion hired a photographer to take a picture of a ghost they had encountered shortly after moving in. They needed the picture as proof that the house was haunted so they could renegotiate their purchase of the house with their agent.

The photographer set up his camera and the flash unit and prepared for a long wait. But he was lucky and on the first night confronted the ghost. It turned out that the ghost was friendly and even agreed to pose for as many snapshots as the photographer desired. So the photographer took picture after picture until he had run out of film.

He immediately raced to his studio to develop the pictures. Yet, as he worked in the dim red glow of his darkroom, he noticed that the negatives were underexposed and completely blank. As he bemoaned his failure he realized he had unwittingly run into a common problem: The spirit was willing but the flash was weak.

LAST MINUTE REPRIEVE

An entomologist at the University of the Incarnate Word was about to lose his job. He was up for tenure and the promotion that came with it but he had been unable to produce the necessary unique research that was required for this honor. The University insisted that their tenure candidates produce a paper on an insect, in his case, heretofore never covered.

Try as he might, he had been unable to satisfy this requirement and in his growing despondency he retreated to his garden. It had been there that he found his best ideas in the past. But when he got there he noticed his roses were dying and that further drove him into a life threatening depression.

When he examined the cause of the roses' decline, he discovered small, wingless, sucking insects on the leaves. They were everywhere and, more importantly, new to him. With great excitement he rushed to his laboratory for further analysis.

The result of this happenchance discovery of a new species of lice was that he was granted his promotion and tenure. That single event breathed new life into his career and he became a widely respected entomologist thereafter.

Some would even say that he had discovered a new lice on leaf.

LIFT YOUR SPIRITS

Although Socrates left no writings, his disciples point out that he believed ignorance to be the cause of all wickedness and knowledge the creator of all virtue.

So it was that Socrates took onto himself the challenge to educate the town idiot, who, in today's slang, would be known as a "geek". The poor lad was not only dyslexic, tongue-tied, and prone to confusion, but also so short he had to wear lifts in his sandals to avoid constant ridicule from his peers.

Socrates paid special attention to this geek during the last years of his life and the positive changes that took place in the geek were astonishing. Soon, because of their superstitions, the community leaders began to believe Socrates must be associated with evil or he could never have achieved such great things. It was not long before they arrested him and sentenced him to death for corrupting the town's youth.

History says Socrates drank hemlock because of his failure to succeed. The truth is the geek was a rather intelligent spy for the town leaders and set Socrates up. This is further proof that you should always beware of geeks wearing lifts.

LIONS 4 - SEERS 0

Nero summoned his finance officer and complained about the profitability of the amphitheater in Rome. He ordered the finance officer to conduct a study into the reasons for the amphitheater's weakening financial strength and report back with the answer before a month had gone buy.

The first consultant failed to come up with an answer and left in shame. The second consultant fared no better. The third consultant was far superior and had the solution in very short order.

Exactly three weeks later, the finance officer returned to Nero with the explanation. It was simple, he said. The lions keep eating up all the prophets.

LOCATION. LOCATION. LOCATION.

Many years ago there was a horse that achieved fame because of its ability to solve problems. Its owner had discovered the horse's unusual talent when he mused a question into thin air and the horse led him to the answer. After a short period of training, the horse was able to demonstrate his unique capabilities in front of large crowds.

During these de-monstrations, the owner often invited questions from the audience. And one day a math professor from the local college posed a question that stumped the horse. The professor asked the horse to calculate a formula involving rectangular coordinates. Surprisingly, the horse was not even able to understand the question.

The owner closed the demonstration with great embarrassment and sought help from as many sources as he could think of. No one was able to provide a clue as to why the horse had become illiterate at that one question while still remaining intelligent with the others. Finally, a friend of a friend who happened to be an engineer thought he knew the answer.

"Seems fairly simple to me," he said. "From my brief analysis it is pretty obvious the horse can't do it. You see, you're putting Descartes before the horse."

LOCK AND LOAD

A Koala bear entered a restaurant and ordered a seven course meal. For more than three hours, he ate his food with great delight, savoring every morsel. Finally, he pushed back from the table and relaxed with pleasure.

He then stood suddenly and produced a pistol from under his thick fur and began shooting all the dinnerware on his table. When he had finished destroying everything, he turned and strode out of the restaurant.

The police arrived shortly after the Koala Bear had left and had no problem finding him as he walked leisurely down the sidewalk. Without delay, they arrested him and took him to the station for interrogation.

"Why, pray tell, did you do that?" they asked.

"It's what Koala Bears do," was the immediate reply. "Look it up in your encyclopedia."

The interrogator did so then turned to the Koala Bear. "There's nothing there about you acting as you did," he said.

"Yes there is," the Koala Bear insisted. "Right there at the bottom is says that a Koala Bear eats shoots and leaves."

LOOK BOTH WAYS

There once was a young lady of both Spanish and Jewish ancestry known as Carmen for her Spanish heritage and Cohen for her Jewish relatives. Her mother on the Spanish side of the family insisted on calling her Carmen, while her father would only call her Cohen. At first she responded to both of her parents equally, but, as the years went on, she became frequently confused. Eventually, the constantly changing references to her name left her absolutely convinced she didn't know if she was Carmen or Cohen.

LOOKING FOR THE PERFECT WAVE

The King stood in his ramparts overlooking the battle. He noticed that his men were no longer launching the catapult. He quickly called his commander to task over this lack of activity and demanded to know why.

"We have nothing more to hurl," the commander replied. "We have used up all of our ammunition."
The King thought for a moment and then ordered: "Round up some peasants. We have many of them. Fill the catapult with peasants."

The commander's men rushed into the countryside and soon returned with peasants to spare. They loaded the catapult with more than a dozen of the unlucky citizens. The catapult was tied to the winch with a rope and ready to be launched.

The commander turned to the king and said: "Your Excellency. These are your subjects. They will be giving their lives in your honor. Do you want to at least say something before sending them on their way?"

The King approached the catapult and removed his sword from its scabbard. He then cut the rope with a mighty swing sending the subjects in a grand arc over the battlefield. As he did this he shouted: "Serf's Up!"

LOST AND FOUND

A mechanic who worked out of his home had a dog named Mace. This dog had an undesirable habit of eating grass. His appetite for the green blades was voracious and, if left unattended, he would eat all the grass on the mechanic's lawn. Because of the extensive bare spots in his yard, the mechanic eventually had to confine Mace inside the house.

After a number of months, the lawn had recovered and the grass was tall and thick. So it was that one day the mechanic, while working on a car in his backyard, dropped his wrench. With the backyard so overgrown with grass and weeds he couldn't find the lost tool. He searched everywhere to no avail. He finally decided to call it a day.

That night Mace escaped from the house and, as was his past behavior, he ate all the grass in the backyard. By morning, when the mechanic went outside, the entire yard was as barren as a pool table. At first the mechanic was angry. He was about to chastise Mace when he saw his wrench glinting in the morning sunlight.

As the reality of what had happened sunk in, the mechanic looked toward the heavens and proclaimed: "A grazing Mace, how sweet the hound that saved a wrench for me!"

LOVE POTION

A young man was smitten by a very lovely lady. Try as he might he could never get her to return the passionate feelings he had for her. In desperate hopes of resolving this impasse he visited a group of witches. He told them he was in search of a love potion that would do the trick.

They informed him that, contrary to popular belief, they no longer produced such an item. They had gotten in trouble in the past for allowing the unethical use of a potion on someone without that person's permission.

They did have an alternate solution, however. They sold the young man a small quantity of white pellets and instructed him to bury one of these pellets in the young lady's garden every night at midnight for a month. He followed the instructions to the letter.

Six weeks later he returned to visit the witches. He was filled with excitement and good news. He and the young lady were engaged to be married within a month.

The witches joined in his joy while they bragged about their contribution to the solution. Together, they chanted: "Nothin' says lovin' like something from a coven. And pills buried says it best."

MAILMAN'S WIFE

After thirty years of labor on the U.S. Postal routes, the mailman decided to retire. For three years all went well. He and his wife lived in their small cottage on the east coast and enjoyed what they could of their remaining years.

One day, the mailman became ill and his wife rushed him to the hospital. After the examination, both he and she consented to an appendectomy. Six months later, it was a rush to the hospital for a hernia operation. Another six months and it was a gall stone operation. And still another six months it was a rush trip for a bowel blockage operation.

As he was recuperating from his last operation, he suffered a prostate problem and called the ambulance for the familiar ride to the hospital. But when the ambulance arrived, his wife stood in the door and prevented anyone from entering.

"Stay away," she hollered. "You can't come in. I'm sick and tired of you opening my male."

MAKE IT UP AS YOU GO

Andy Ashwood was sentenced to prison for making funny money. He had been successfully evading arrest for many years but a recent mistake on one of his jobs spelled his doom and he was sentenced to 10 years.

He was an amenable person and worked well with everyone. The guards and fellow inmates came to appreciate him as a valuable member of the prison society. As a token of reward, the warden assigned him to the carpenter shop so he could learn a trade that would be useful on the outside.

Because he had earned the trust of those managing the prison and had become a superb carpenter, the warden allowed him out of prison on weekends to complete projects for the local community. He always did an outstanding job and returned to prison as scheduled.

One day the warden considered changing the countertops in his own kitchen and immediately thought of Andy for the job. He called Andy into his office to discuss this proposition. The warden was perplexed when Andy refused.

"I don't understand," he said. "You would be the perfect person for this job."

"I'd love to help you, Warden," Andy replied. "But you certainly understand that counter fitting is what put me behind bars in the first place."

MAY THE BEST MAN WIN

A local jazz nightclub was widely known for its current and fresh jazz music. Over the years a number of concerts were held on its small stage around which a cluster of small tables and comfortable chairs were grouped. It became an honor to perform in this club so there was never a shortage of musicians to entertain the clientele.

One evening a famous saxophone player arrived on the scene. After listening to many of the local musicians play their sets, he stood and took the stage. Those who recognized him broke into a vigorous applause and he bowed deeply to these adoring fans. After all, he was the best there was – a master.

In the back of the room an unknown musician wandered to the front and challenged the master to a contest. Each would take a turn playing a favorite piece and let the audience decide who was best. The master accepted and for the next three hours they played their hearts out for the crowd.

It was not so easy to pick a winner as the unknown musician was as good as, if not better than, the master. So it was only when they both called it a draw that the contest ended without a winner. But the word spread throughout the city that on that night, everyone in attendance had seen the Battle of the Saxes.

MEMORIES ARE MADE OF THIS

A middle-aged man joined a health club with a goal of losing 100 pounds. Starting out at 290, his one-year goal was to reach 190 pounds prior to Christmas. He would come to the health club every morning and work out for at least one and a half hours. He lifted weights, used the treadmill, and completed prescribed exercises under the supervision of a personal trainer.

At the end of each session he would walk over to the scale and weigh himself. The other participants at the health club became accustomed to his habit of calling out his new weight once the scale settled on a number. Statements such as '276 already! Wow. It's really working' and 'Whatever happened to 250?' and 'Who can forget 225?!' were trademark declarations as he worked towards his goal.

One morning, as he stood on the scale repeating his daily mantra, a new customer joined the others in the regular audience. The man ended his morning dialogue with a smile and a melancholy voice. "Boy, those were the weights!"

"What's that all about?" the newcomer asked.

"Oh, not much," was the reply. "He's just one of those people who like to reminisce about the 'good old weights.' "

MIND OVER MATTER

After the successful battles against the evil forces in the Star Wars series, Luke Skywalker and Obi-Wan Kenobi went to a Chinese restaurant for a celebration meal. It was Luke's first experience with Chinese food and he was looking forward to an enjoyable time.

Obi-Wan did the ordering. He had the waiter serve up steamed rice, noodles, and an array of specialty foods fit for a king. After the food was laid out before them, Obi-Wan picked up his chopsticks and deftly maneuvered the food from his plate to his mouth. It seemed like second nature to him and he savored the tasty morsels with quiet satisfaction.

Luke, however, was having great difficulty. His attempts to use the chopsticks resulted in disaster. He just couldn't get the hang of it and ended up losing his food to gravity before he could even lift it off the plate. He was an embarrassment to all the other Jedi Masters. After a dozen or so attempts he looked at Obi-Wan, his inner frustrations showing clearly in his expression.

Obi-Wan set down his own chopsticks and folded his hands in front of him. He looked at Luke and after a period of silence said in a strong yet soft voice: "Use the forks, Luke."

MOONLIGHT ROMANCE

A young married couple proceeded into the world after their wedding ceremony with visions of grandeur. Life, however, can be a cruel taskmaster and had other plans for their future. The reality was that they would become itinerant farm workers instead of the wealthy landowners they dreamed they would become.

A woman rancher hired them one year to help harvest her hay crop. She impressed upon these two young people the need for speed and long hours so the hay could be gathered and put safely away before the rains arrived. And because the hay was to be displayed at the annual fair, she insisted that they exercise great care.

The couple worked far past sunset to cut the hay and arrange it in the lines needed for proper drying. In the darkness they both managed to cut themselves with their scythes. And since there was only one Band-Aid between them, the husband cut it in two and shared it with his wife.

As he was about to place the bandage on his wife's wound he felt a surge of romance course through his body. He looked into her eyes in the moonlight and said: "Honey. This is sort of romantic. You know. But I feel like I'm about to share an aid in the night by a fair lady's windrow."

MOTORCYCLE SICKNESS *(Risqué)*

A young man returned to his fancy motorcycle in a supermarket parking lot after shopping in the store. As he approached his motorcycle, a large van pulled in beside it and stopped. The driver opened the van door and hit the motorcycle, knocking it to the ground. The young man immediately confronted the careless van driver and an argument began about the van driver's heritage and the cycle driver's intelligence. This soon escalated to more serious accusations and the wild swings of anger.

The motorcycle rider seemed to be getting the worst of the affair so he broke the antennae from the van and began wielding it as a rapier. In this effort of defense, the van driver sustained several cuts and slashes over his face and body, finally calling it quits. Passers-by, noticing the fight in progress, summoned both the police and emergency medical assistance.

The injured van driver lay on the ground bleeding when the medics arrived. The paramedic made his way through the crowd that had gathered. He stood motionless, shocked at what he saw.

"What are you waiting for?" the policeman asked. "The man needs treatment. Help him."

"I was just taken back a bit," the paramedic said. "This is the worst case of van aerial disease I've ever seen."

MULLIGAN'S STEW

Father Mulligan's most destructive habit was his penchant for misplacing things. He could handle a recitation of the Easter Contata, recall the names of all his students when he taught at the seminary, and remember the financial specifics of his parish operations. But he could never seem to find his keys, his watch, his pen, or a score of other items he used day-to-day.

So it was when he was dressing to attend a national convention of church laymen, where he was to be the keynote speaker, he found himself in this all too familiar quandary. He searched through his quarters for his clerical collar, having set it aside only moments before he shaved. He and his assistant searched in every nook and cranny without success. As time dragged on, it became apparent that father Mulligan was going to be late.

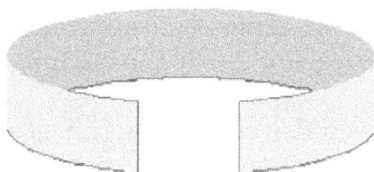

In a moment of extreme frustration he threw his shirt on the floor and sat forcefully in a chair. His assistant encouraged him to relax but he refused citing the importance of a successful search. "I am to speak to a room of laymen and I can't find my symbolic clothes. It's a horrible situation," he went on. "A lay date and a collar short."

MULTIPLE CUTS

When Giuseppe the baker lost his job, he tried to find similar employment for weeks. He was about to give up when he found an advertisement for bread cutters. He decided if he couldn't start as a baker, he'd at least start as a bread cutter and left immediately to apply for the job. He came home a few hours later quite dejected.

"I showed up on time," he told his wife. "And I knew I'd get the job because all the other applicants were young and inexperienced. The owner said whoever could slice the most bread in five minutes would get the job. Then they let us choose our cutting tools from a stack of bread knives, regular knives, scissors, meat cleavers, paper cutters and other instruments.

"I cut 200 loaves in five minutes. I was able to do so because I had spied a meat cleaver that would cut two entire loaves of bread with one swing. But a youngster cut 300 loaves in the same amount of time so I didn't get the job."

"Ah. Giuseppi," his wife said. " 'Tis a sad thing. But surely there must be an explanation."

"There is," Giuseppi replied. "And it is my own fault that I did not win. When I chose my tool to cut the bread, I overlooked a four loaf cleaver."

MUSIC TO MY EARS

A well-known movie director and producer, in planning his next film, thought the idea of a movie about famous composers and their interactions during the period when classical music was at its peak would be excellent entertainment.

To assist him he assembled four of the biggest movie stars in the industry. Robert DeNiro, Gene Hackman, Tom Hanks, and Arnold Schwarzenegger gathered in his office to discuss the idea and determine who would play what part. The actors were enthusiastic about the project and readily volunteered to be their favorite composer.

The first actor, DeNiro, admitted that he had always been a fan of Chopin's work. "If I could be him I think it would improve my reputation," he said.

Hackman, chimed in saying: "Mozart has been my favorite for years. I would be honored to be him."

"Strauss is the one for me," Hanks said. "I love to dance and I could fit in with his music easily."

Arnold Schwarzenegger had been silent the entire time. The others turned to him waiting for him to speak. He finally stood up, stepped in front of them and said with forceful determination: "I'll be Bach."

MY MIND'S MADE UP

During one of the many old Chinese dynasties it was decreed that time would be told by the striking of gongs at two-hour intervals. Therefore, from eight in the morning until ten at night, the gong striker would announce the current time every two hours. He would ring the gong once at eight o'clock, twice at ten o'clock, three times at noon, four times at two o'clock, and so forth throughout the day.

During this period, the practice of law was just getting under way. The lawyers were inexperienced and the process of prosecution and defense had not been completely ironed out. Also, many times these lawyers were paid by the hour and would frequently drag out these proceedings far beyond their natural length.

Eventually, the judges became frustrated with this practice. And to put an end to it they appealed to the Emperor for relief. His solution was simple: all trials must be concluded by the ringing of the gong at two PM.

This ruling was successful in shortening the length of the trials but it had one unfortunate side effect. It wasn't long until everyone realized that every trial conducted under this rule would end with a four gong conclusion.

NAME CALLING

Christmas was finally over and all of the presents were put away. The child's toys had, for the most part, become boring. The decorations were dismantled and the Christmas tree sat forlornly at the side of the road awaiting pickup.

As the mother was putting the finishing touches on the box of Christmas tree lights, her child approached her. "Mama," she said. "You know that song about Rudolph the red nosed reindeer?"

The mother stopped what she was doing and squatted so as to be on the same level as her daughter. "Yes, honey."

"Well, I was wondering. How come they never sing about the reindeer named Olive?"

"Honey," the mother replied. "I don't think there is a reindeer named Olive."

"Yes there is," the daughter insisted. "They sing about her when they sing about Rudolph."

"I'm afraid I don't understand," the mother said. "Where do they sing about it in the Rudolph song?"

The little girl looked into her mother's eyes and said: "Right there where they sing Olive, the other reindeer, used to laugh and call him names."

NAME THAT FACE

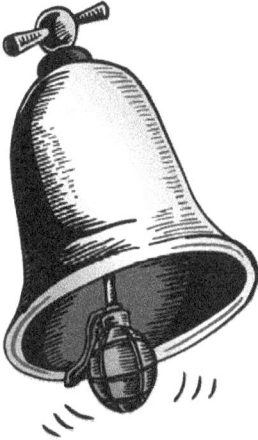

Quasimodo had rung the bells in the Notre Dame Cathedral for many years without relief. One day the priest suggested that he find a temporary replacement and take a vacation.

Quasimodo proceeded to show the first applicant how to ring the bell. He reached up, grabbed the large iron cone and pushed it far out. Quasimodo then ducked under the bell as is swung back allowing the clapper to strike the bell and send a ringing sound over the entire city. He then climbed down the ladder to face the applicant.

"Now. You try it," he said.

The applicant repeated what Quasimodo had done. But as the bell swung back it struck him in the face. He staggered and fell through the opening in the tower to the ground below. A crowd soon gathered as Quasimodo hurried to the pavement. He forced himself through the crowd and past the policemen who had come to the scene of the accident. And as he bent over the applicant the policeman said: "Do you know this man?"

Quasimodo looked up at the gendarme. "No, I don't", he said. "But his face sure rings a bell."

NET ASSETS *(Risqué)*

The world's oldest profession was certainly in full swing during the Old Testament times. Sodom and Gomorrah were famous for their loose and lascivious life styles. Other cities around the old world were rife with the prostitutes trying to make a living in times when staying alive was foremost in everyone's mind.

The leaders in the communities across the land wanted to put a stop to the philandering but had no laws or edicts they could use to enforce their wishes. All they had were the teachings of the religious scholars who themselves partook in the pleasures of the flesh. If the prostitutes did not violate those teachings, there was little the leaders could do.

Then one day someone came up with a brilliant solution. It was only a matter of definition, they claimed. So they lay in wait to test their assumption and before long a prostitute approached one of the religious figures and began her efforts to lure him into her lair.

At that time, the leaders emerged from their hiding place and arrested her on the spot.

"And under what pretense do you make this arrest?" she demanded.

"It's simple," was the reply. "You were trying to make a prophet."

NEVER TELL A LIE

Researchers have discovered that William Tell and his family were avid bowlers. They participated in the popular leagues that were prevalent during their time. In fact, they became good enough to win championships. Reportedly, they were ranked among the best bowlers world-wide. They had numerous perfect games to their credit.

Most of this information was gleaned from records kept by people not associated with the leagues. News reports and journals kept by fans were the major sources of the information. This was necessary because all the league's records were destroyed in a fire many years ago.

So, although we know of their successes, we'll never know for whom the Tells bowled.

NIP IT IN THE BUD

Three Friars, banished from the monastery for rules violations, opened a plant shop in a nearby village. Before long, their floral business was thriving.

One day, while a woman was strolling down the aisle with her toddler, a large plant reached out, grabbed the child, and ate it. The Friars refused to believe that one of their plants could have done such a thing in spite of the woman's protestations. So the townspeople rose up en masse and demanded they leave town. The Friars adamant refusal resulted in the townspeople giving up and going home.

A few weeks later the plant ate another child. The townspeople once again demanded the Friars leave. And again the Friars strong refusal intimidated the townspeople into another retreat. The village council convened and demanded that the mayor, known as Hugh, personally drive the Friars and their child eating plants from town.

When the mayor arrived at the flower shop, the three Friars gathered nervously behind their counter. He confronted them saying: "Get out of town. Now!"

They immediately packed up all their belongings and fled that very day, never to be heard from again. This was possible because, as we all know so well, only Hugh can prevent florist Friars.

NO DOUBT ABOUT IT

Atoms, like any other being, need a day of rest from time to time. After they have finished a full day's work keeping things together they exhibit signs of weariness. Without the requisite rejuvenation, they have a tendency to fall apart.

So it was that two atoms were strolling through town after a strenuous day at the office. As they turned a corner they ran into each other. And as fate would have it, they were two long-time friends who had not seen each other for quite some time.

They exchanged the normal niceties and asked about each other's families. After catching up on the important events, they became silent for a moment.

Finally, one atom said to the other: "You don't look so good. Are you all right?"

"Well, not really," the other atom replied. "I've lost an electron!"

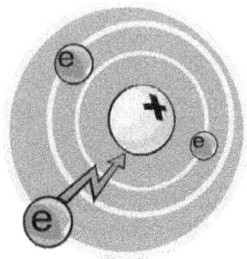

"That's horrible," his friend said. "Are you sure?"

"Yeah," was the muted reply. "I am positive!"

NO MATTER HOW YOU SLICE IT

The local butcher was known for his efficiency and the quality of his meat products. He could produce the finest tasting sausage in the area. He had the spiciest salami and the smoothest bologna for miles around. Additionally, he could respond to any custom order faster than any other butcher in the state.

One day as he was grinding the assortment of meats he used to make his famous sausage, he received a phone call from one of his loyal customers for a pound of his sliced bologna. He promised he would have it ready to be picked up by the customer within minutes as was his custom.

As he turned and picked up the log of bologna, his butt backed into the meat grinder. As a result, a generous section of his buttock became mixed in with the sausage ingredients.

The customer who ordered the bologna arrived as the butcher was being helped out of the shop by the emergency medical technician. The butcher looked at the customer and apologized.

"I'm sorry I couldn't fill your order in time. It seems I've gotten a little behind in my work."

NOT PLAYING WITH A FULL DECK

Terence Taylor established an operation he named Culture Farms and began marketing a powder that formed curds in milk. He sold the powdered cultures to investors and promised to double their money in 15 weeks when he would buy back the curds for use in women's make up products.

Unfortunately for the investors, Terence Taylor was a scam artist and was milking them of their investment funds. Within six months, he had skimmed the investors for more than $80 million.

When regulators got word of his operation, they began an immediate investigation. In the process they uncovered evidence of false advertising by mail, tax evasion, and fraud. Without delay they arrested him and hauled him into court.

He pled not guilty but the judge would have nothing to do with it. Bank records proved that he had hidden millions of dollars in an offshore account. His illegal activities had harmed many innocent investors.

In announcing his guilty verdict the judge said: "You're a smart man, Mr. Taylor. You should have known your house of curds would certainly fall down."

NOTHING TO CROW ABOUT

Harry Huntsman fancied himself one of the greatest hunters of all time. He was quite proud of his ability to outmaneuver such swift animals as the deer and the hare. But when it came to the crow, he was frustrated and confused. Try as he did, he could never seem to defeat the wily crow who managed to remain just outside his reach.

One cold autumn day, Harry was in pursuit of a crow and for the first time in his life got close enough to the bird to at least grab a handful of tail feathers. This small accomplishment was significant enough to create a rush of excitement like nothing he had known before, especially when he noticed that the crow was blushing from its sudden nakedness. In his amazement at the subtle hint of red that flushed over the crow's entire body, Harry tripped over his own feet thus losing his chance to grab the crow and finally defeat the only animal that had eluded him. His friends, who had witnessed this embarrassing failure, teased him mercilessly.

In the years to follow, Sammy never again got close enough to capture any feathered blackbird and it was rumored that even his self respect had suffered from the blushing crow.

OFF THE BEATEN TRACK

The authorities were transporting a train load of old napalm from California to Illinois. Someone had come up with the idea of converting it into heating oil and using it during the cold winters there. Unfortunately, the Illinois people believed that it might make bad publicity to recycle an old weapon into heating fuel and refused to allow the train to enter the state. The train had to return from whence it came.

The napalm then joined the other aging and degrading bits of arsenal stored in an army base on the west coast. Because of the dangerous attributes of the napalm, constant surveillance was required. Therefore, there are soldiers whose entire duty is to guard these old unusable weapons. It is considered undesirable duty by the soldiers because, as everyone knows, "A waste is a terrible thing to mind".

ON YOUR MARKS

Everyone knows that bears love honey and will rip into a beehive with impunity. So it is that bees are ever alert for a bear's approach. It is only with the concerted effort of the entire colony that they can drive the bear away.

Because they had been caught unaware in the past, this one particular colony devised a plan of protection. This plan assured them that the entire colony could gather at the first sign of attack. Even those far away could rush to the scene and join in the defense.

They devised an alarm system that involves stationing a single bee as a lookout. They positioned this bee by a lever he would pull if he saw a bear approaching the hive. Once the bee pulled the lever an alarm would sound summoning all bees home.

The alarm duties were rotated so that each bee pulled his share. And when the bee was on duty he was called the Lever Bee. It is understandable that this bee had to be constantly alert and ready to do his job with the slightest provocation.

Since the institution of the system, the hive never succumbed to a bear attack. This success was therefore responsible for the well-known phrase: "I am as ready as a Lever Bee."

ONE PAGE AT A TIME

The king's daughter was kidnapped by an evil lord of a neighboring kingdom so he ordered his mightiest knight to rescue her. As the knight charged the evil lord's castle, a large yellow hand rose from the moat and grasped the knight, squeezing him until his bones snapped. The hand then cast him from its yellow-fingered grasp onto the nearby hillside.

When the first knight failed to return, the king sent another to rescue the fair maiden. But, alas, he too became a victim of the yellow hand. The same fate met every knight the king sent until he was certain he would never see his daughter again.

A Page then convinced the king to let him try and he approached the castle as the knights had done before him. Yet, as he crossed it, no yellow hand came up to grab him and he entered the castle easily. Soon he emerged with the king's daughter astride his horse.

The king was elated and wished to reward the page. But first, he asked the page to share with him the secret of his success.

"I can't explain it," the page said. "But the lesson is clear: you should always let your Pages do the walking through the yellow fingers."

ONE SIZE FITS ALL *(Risqué)*

The young anthropologist was
studying the lifestyle of an
aborigine tribe in Australia.
One morning as he stepped
outside his tent, a bird flew
over and pooped on his head.
As he was walking to the river to wash it off, the local
medicine man stopped him.

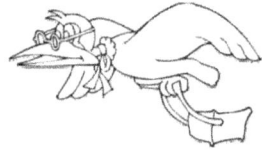

"Do not wash it off," the medicine man said. "It is the
dropping of the ancient Foo Bird and he has chosen
you. It is good luck to leave it alone. If you wash it off
you will suffer extremely bad luck."

The anthropologist therefore left the poop in place
thinking simply: 'I can live with good luck.'
Unfortunately, it began to rot and create a foul smell.
And after a week, when he visited the big city of
Sydney, people on the street avoided him and cast
disgusting looks his way. Soon no one would even
speak with him and he became a lonely man in the
big city.

Thinking he had been misled by the medicine man,
he decided to remove the crusty poop. When he was
done, he dressed in a fine suit and left the hotel to
have a meal in a fine restaurant - his first in a long,
long time.

As he crossed the street in front of the hotel he was
struck by a truck and killed. In his desire to be rid
of his smelly burden he had disregarded the
medicine man's admonition: "If the Foo shits wear
it!"

ONE, TWO, WHAT DO WE DO?

The police chief came to work at the local police station and found it to be in disarray. The desks were overturned, the filing cabinet contents had been strewn about the floor, and the chairs had all been broken.

The policemen who had already arrived at the station were milling about the room with some degree of anxiety. "It's thieves that did this." The sergeant said. "They came in here in the middle of the night and trashed the place."

The police chief, noting their agitation, tried to console them. "It's okay men," he said. "We can replace all of this furniture. In fact, we will end up with newer and better furniture as a result. And we'll catch the bastards who did this and string 'em up!"

"You don't understand," the sergeant said. "They also trashed the lavatory. So we have absolutely nothing to go on."

ONE WAY OR ANOTHER

The farmer had spent many years on his dairy farm milking cows and cleaning up after them. He was so focused on his job over the years that his wife accused him of feigning deafness to avoid admitting he heard what she said.

One day she followed him to the barn constantly talking and him constantly not listening. She followed him as he walked into the milking stalls still talking and him still not listening.

He sat on his stool to begin milking the first of his many cows. And as he began pulling on the cow's teats, shooting the milk into a galvanized bucket, his wife continued her diatribe. At that moment a bug flew into the barn and circled around the farmer's head. After two trips it flew into the cow's ear.

The farmer didn't think much about this and he continued milking as his wife continued talking. But as soon as the farmer got a good rhythm going the bug squirted out of the cow's teat into the bucket. This, of course, surprised the farmer. The wife, however, didn't skip a beat.

"Just like your response to everything I have to say," she said. "In one ear and out the udder."

ONLY TIME WILL TELL

There was a thief who had the most unusual penchant for his chosen occupation. He consistently targeted stationery stores. Once inside in the darkness of night, he would steal only calendars and every calendar he could find.

His success at his thievery soon earned him recognition as the Calendar Crook. He took great pride in owning that name and worked hard at evading arrest. It was not long before he became a household word and the number one fugitive in the region. In some respects he was even considered a hero.

As happens to nearly all criminals, however, he slipped up one evening. The proprietor of the stationery store he was looting caught him in the act. The police arrived quickly and took him into custody. The Calendar Crook was captured.

When the judge asked him why he stole only calendars he had no answer. "I just love the calendars," he said. "I couldn't help myself. Calendars are what it's all about. It's simply an obsession with me."

"Well then," the judge replied. "I will do my best to make you feel at home. You are hereby sentenced to 12 months."

ORGANIC COMMUNION *(Risqué)*

A Baptist minister, ordained by the Southern Baptist Convention, began to feel ill one Sunday morning during his sermon. When Monday morning came he was not feeling any better so he made an appointment with a local doctor.

After the doctor completed his examination, he ordered some blood tests. When those blood tests were available, he called the minister in for a consultation.

"This is the strangest case I've ever had to deal with," the doctor said. "I can't understand why or how you may have contracted the sickness I'm about to disclose to you."

"Not to worry," said the minister. "I can handle any bad news. My future is in heaven anyway if it is as serious as your countenance seems to reflect."

The doctor paused only a moment then said: "It's unexplainable to me, but you are infected with the AIDS virus. I don't know how that can be."

"Well, you are aware I am gay aren't you?" the minister asked.

"I wasn't," the doctor answered. "But that explains it all. You must have forgotten to wash your organ between hymns."

OUT OF BREATH

A young inflatable boy did not want to go to school but his parents knew he had great talent and insisted. After a few weeks of classes in the inflatable school, he had had enough and stormed out of his class. As he walked down the hallway, the inflatable principal approached and asked him where he was going. The young boy said he hated school and was leaving for good. Then he stuck a pin into the principal's thin skin and ran onto the playground.

He stood there for a moment contemplating his next move then walked up to the side of the inflatable school and stuck a pin in its thin skin before running home. After he arrived at his house, his shame began to grow and he locked himself in his bedroom.

A short time later the police arrived and the inflatable boy attempted suicide by jabbing himself with the pin he had used on the principal and the school. In short order he crumpled to the floor, unconscious.

He woke up in the hospital and noticed the principal was in the bed next to his. The principal looked at him with sad and mournful eyes.

"I am so sorry for you," he said to the young boy. "You let me down. You let the school down. But the tragedy of it all is that you let yourself down."

PECKING ORDER *(Risqué)*

In the eastern hardwood forest near the Blue Ridge Parkway, two trees were growing close by each other. As the years went by, a small tree began to grow between them. Eventually, one of the larger trees said to the other one: "You got any idea whether that youngun' there is a son of a beech or a son of a birch?"

The other tree studied the sapling for some time. He finally responded. "You know. I can't rightly tell."

At that moment a woodpecker landed in the sapling. The tall tree turned its branches to face the woodpecker and said: "Hey there woodpecker. You're a tree expert aren't you? Can you tell us if that tree you are sitting in is a son of a beech or a son of a birch?"

The woodpecker faced the trunk of the small sampling. He repeated tapped his beak against the bark until he had dislodged a small piece. He then tasted it and savored it. He seemed quite satisfied with the morsel.

"That, my friends, is neither a son of a beech nor a son of a birch," he finally said. "But it is the best piece of ash I have ever put my pecker in."

PENNIES FROM HEAVEN

A wealthy entrepreneur bought one of the first Nissan automobiles known as the Datsun. So devoted was he to his car that he would drive no other in spite of his wealth. Unfortunately, it broke down after 150,000 miles of hard driving. He needed only a single gear with seven cogs on it and the repair could be made, but the dealer said the owner would have to travel to Japan to purchase the gear with seven cogs.

The wealthy Datsun owner was not deterred. He flew directly to Japan where, much to his chagrin, he discovered he had to buy an entire box of one thousand gears with seven cogs to get only one since the factory could not economically produce only one .

Enroute home, the airplane began having engine trouble and the pilot ordered all baggage thrown overboard to lighten the load. As the owner of the airplane, the loyal Datsun driver saved his gears until it became evident he would have to part with them. So he threw all but one of them from the airplane just as they reached California.

At that time a farmer, who had been plowing his field, was pummeled by the falling objects. He looked around as the gears fell, then jumped from his tractor and ran toward his house calling his wife. "Honey! Honey!" he shouted. "Come quick. It's raining Datsun Cogs out here."

PERIPHERAL VISION

A man was dining in a fancy restaurant and noticed a gorgeous redhead sitting at the next table. He had been checking her out since he sat down, but lacked the nerve to start a conversation.

Suddenly she sneezed and her glass eye came flying out of its socket toward the man. He reflexively reached out, grabbed it out of the air, and, with some uncertainty, handed it back.

"Oh my! I am so sorry!" the woman said as she popped the eye back in place. "Let me buy your dinner to make it up to you."

They enjoyed a wonderful dinner together and afterwards they went to the theater followed by drinks. They talked, they laughed, and shared their deepest dreams. After paying for everything, she asked him if he would like to come to her place for a nightcap and stay for breakfast. He, of course accepted and they had a wonderful time.

The next morning, as she cooked a gourmet meal with all the trimmings, he said: "You know, you are the perfect woman. Are you this nice to every guy you meet?"

"No," she replied. "You just happened to catch my eye."

PETE AND REPETE

Henry and Helen Hopeful from London, England, had been trying to have a child for what seemed years. They had followed all of the guidance published in the hundreds of books they read and tried all of the quackery available in the seamier side of the business. Nothing seemed to work.

Finally, they decided to shell out the money and visit a fertility doctor. Their desire for a child was so great that they were more than happy to pay the considerable fee required for the doctor's assistance. And then they awaited good news.

They were not to be disappointed for the doctor soon told them that Helen was pregnant. In fact, she would be delivering twin boys instead of a single child. They were ecstatic and could barely wait for the twin's arrival.

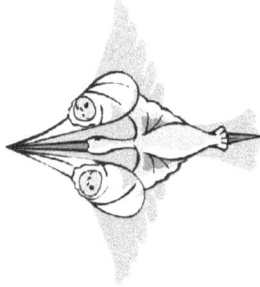

On the happy day of the twins' birth Harry and Helen were beside themselves with joy. And when the nurse asked them for the names of the twins for the birth certificate they replied that they had named each one 'Edward'.

"That's crazy," the nurse said. "Why would you want to do that?"

Harry replied: "It's pretty obvious. Isn't it? Don't you know that two Eds are better than one?"

PINS AND NEEDLES

For years Jimmy Germaine had followed his habit of visiting the local bar every day for a drink on his way home from work. On one particular evening a newcomer struck up a conversation and a drink turned to two then three then more. In short order, Jimmy was drinking so much he couldn't remember what happened each night. But he did know he was becoming more and more tired - almost to the point of exhaustion.

One evening when his strange new friend wasn't looking, Jimmy poured out his drinks so he could remain in control of his senses. He hated this as it was his friend's money that bought most of the drinks. But it paid off as, by staying sober, he discovered his friend was a vampire who was feeding on his blood when he became drunk.

He immediately stopped going to the bar and associating with the now not so strange friend. After some weeks, Jimmy ran across the bartender who asked him why he never came by anymore.

"It has nothing to do with you," Jimmy said. "It's just that I got tired of getting stuck for the drinks."

PLAINLY SPEAKING

The young cowboys had been rounding up cattle on the Great Plains for more than a month. They had been living off pinto beans and beef jerky for the past two weeks and decided to hunt for some wildlife to add to their menu.

Buster, the crew's youngest cowboy, was a practical jokester. However, he was also their most proficient hunter. They chose him to bag some meat for their evening meal.

Buster departed at first light and disappeared over a distant hill. The others continued their round up activities while dreaming of the delicious meal they anticipated for that evening. It was late in the afternoon when they saw Buster returning. He was galloping his horse toward them and shouting something into the wind.

He drew near enough for them to hear him clearly and he said: "Come with me and you can see an antelope."

And so they followed him to a shallow dell that contained a single small mound of dirt. "We don't see an antelope." they said.

"Right there," he answered, pointing to the small ant hill. "Look real close and you'll be able to see her coming down the ladder to her boyfriend's car!"

PLAY IT AGAIN, SAM

The drummer in a local band was in a bar on his night off and saw the saxophone player from the band performing on stage with a piccolo. It had always been the rule in the band that no player would take a job unless the entire band was hired for the gig. The drummer decided to wait until the next day to question the saxophone player about his infidelity.

At practice the next day, the drummer motioned the saxophone player to the side. He intended to ease into the subject rather than make immediate accusations so he said: "Who was that piccolo I saw you with last night?"

The saxophone player was unabashed. He replied smartly: "That was no piccolo. That was my fife."

POTATO CHIPS FOR THE SOUL

A traveler, lost on a rainy night, stumbled across a monastery and took shelter there. Fortunately, she was just in time for dinner, which turns out to be the best fish and chips she's ever had. After dinner, she goes into the kitchen.

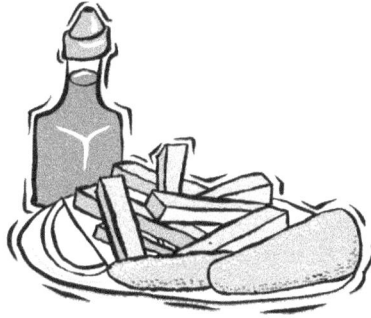

"Excuse me," she says. "But who cooked that meat?"

Two of the brothers stepped forward in response. "Hello, I'm Brother Michael and this is Brother Charles. We prepared your dinner. We hope it was to your liking."

"It was a wonderful dinner and I want to thank you."

Both brothers smiled and murmured: "It was our pleasure, to be sure."

"Out of curiosity, who cooked what?"

Brother Charles replied first saying: "Well, I'm the fish friar."

The lady winced and turned to the other brother. "Oh, no," she sighed. Then you must be ..."

"Yes," Brother Michael interjected. "I'm afraid I'm the chip monk."

POWERFUL ADVICE

On his way to the grocery store one Saturday morning George saw a line up of cars at his favorite gas station. He stopped to talk to the owner as his curiosity was strong. The owner told him there had been a big gas spill down the road and his station was the only one open in the neighborhood. And since he was the only remaining full service station in the area, he was having trouble keeping up with the number of customers.

George was a good friend and customer and offered to help the owner pump gas into the cars. He hoped to reduce the wait time and the frustration of those waiting in line. So he began pumping gas on a first come-first served basis. Things were going quite well until one customer, aggravated by the lengthy wait, stormed off in a punk.

"I'm sorry," George said to the owner. "I'm going as fast as I can. I just couldn't get to him as soon as he wanted me to."

"Don't worry about it," the owner replied. "You can fuel some of the people some of the time. And you can fuel some of the people all of the time. But you can't fuel all of the people all of the time."

RAINY WEATHER

An amateur weatherman and his wife watched the evening news every night. The high point of the evening was the weather forecast by Rudolph, a red-headed weatherman known by his nickname, "Red". His forecasts were so accurate that he had not missed a forecast of rain in the past three years.

Because the wife showed so much attention to the weatherman, the husband became a little jealous and began to deride Red's abilities. However, he was unable to change her mind.

"You wish you were as good as he is," she would say to him. "He knows how to forecast rain and you can't do any better than him."

Although the husband insisted that such was not true, he secretly wished he was better at forecasting rain. But, alas, Rudolph always seemed to be more accurate than he was.

In the midst of a particularly heavy rainstorm, his wife cajoled the amateur weatherman. In his typical manner, he told her that "Red" didn't know anything and she was just infatuated with the weatherman's good looks. "Not true," she insisted. "In fact, between the two of you, only Rudolph the Red knows rain, dear."

RECEDING GUMLINES

The big game hunter was invited to give a talk to the members of a local hunting group. He had completed successful hunts throughout the African continent and had become somewhat of a hunting war hero because of his exploits.

Following his talk, he opened the floor for questions. After the usual number of questions concerning the equipment he used, the status of hunting conditions in the Sub-Sahara, and the future for hunting in Africa, a member asked him what was the most difficult aspect of African hunting.

The speaker thought for a moment and then answered. "I'd have to say it comes after the hunt is over. All those things that happen after the kill are most difficult."

"Can you be a little more specific?" The member asked.

"Well, for instance, whenever I've shot an elephant in Africa I find that the tusk's are almost impossible to remove."

"And why does that rate as the most difficult aspect of hunting?"

Without as much as a hiccup the speaker replied: "Because where I come from in Alabama the Tuscaloosa."

RED SKY IN THE MORNING

An American Indian chief's son had reached college age so the chief set about the task of selecting an appropriate university for the son's education. After lengthy thought and deliberation, the chief announced that his choice was Yale University. The son, wondering why his father had not chosen an institution closer by, questioned his father's wisdom.

"I did not choose a closer university because none of them have a yacht club," the chief explained. And noting his son's continued puzzlement, he added: "You will join the Yale Yacht Club and help me realize a life long dream."

"And what dream might that be?" the son asked.

"Since your birth," the chief replied. "I have always wanted to see my red son in the sail set."

REPEAT AS NEEDED

The young high school graduate went off to college and settled in for a busy semester. Her mother called her regularly to keep up with activities and talked about every subject possible. The daughter shared all the nitty gritty about her classes and social life and bubbled over with her happiness on being on her own.

The one subject the daughter never discussed was her love life. Although her mother was insistent in her questioning, both direct and indirect, the young coed refused to disclose any information about who she was seeing, where she went, or what she did on her dates.

The mother's frustration bubbled to the surface one day during a discussion with her husband about the daughter's college life. She expressed her disappointment that she couldn't get the daughter to share even the smallest detail.

The husband looked at her and said: "Well. You know what they say about a mother's determination."

"No I don't," came her reply.

He continued: "If at first you don't succeed - pry, pry again."

RESORT TO THE RETORT

There are many unique and unusual animals that live on the African plains. Chief among them is the wildebeests who many people call the gnu. Because of the spelling many Americans pronounce this name with an emphasis on a hard G at the beginning.

There were two especially friendly families of gnus who often picnicked and traveled together. As the youngsters grew, it became apparent each family harbored a troublemaker. Of course, each mother was convinced that her own child was not a problem and that it was the other mother's child who was the mischievous one.

One thing led to another and during a moment of stress and anger one of the mothers said: "Your child has become a bothersome brat. He needs to be punished. An old-fashioned spanking would do him good."

The offended mother looked at her old friend with shock written across her face. "You think I should spank my son? You think he's a problem?" She shuffled her feet as if trying to gain control of her emotions. She started another reply. "Why don't you..." She seemed lost for words but recovered quickly. With obvious frustration she continued: "You just might want to go paddle your own gnu."

RIGHT TIME, RIGHT PLACE

Marco Polo was the first to open trade routes to China. However, the first thing he discovered was the Chinese fireworks expertise. He was quite impressed with what they had done and the tales of their talents intrigued him.

Their fireworks were not that much different from what we know today. They shot up into the air, explode, and create many beautiful displays. No matter where he went, he found Chinese people producing fireworks; yet, he was unable to find anyone to demonstrate them for him. Everyone told him they never use fireworks locally.

Marco was considerably confused until he came upon an ancient military fortification in a remote community called Chu'Lai. It was in this place that fireworks were launched every night. Marco remained in the area for some time enjoying the spectacle but his confusion remained.

He finally could stand it no longer and approached his guide for an answer. "Why do people come from great distances to ignite their fireworks only in this location?" he asked.

The guide, a little surprised, replied: "It has been our tradition for centuries. We always set off fireworks on the Forts of Chu'Lai."

RING A DING DING

The opening of China to the inspection of western newsmen some years back was a major breakthrough for modern politics. But the most significant finding by the journalists was the shortage of telephones. There were so few of the instruments that many times the newsmen had to share a phone to call in their stories.

One particularly curious journalist decided to find out why there were so few phones and began asking questions. Unfortunately, his task was difficult because the Chinese were shy and avoided any direct conversation with the Americans. Still, the journalist continued on his quest.

After much study, he finally discovered the reason and it was an even greater find than he had expected. What he found out was that the last name of nearly everyone in China was either Wong or Wing. He also discovered that the Chinese were exceptionally considerate of others. Therefore, the reason they had so few phones was because they were afraid they might Wing the Wong number.

RISING ABOVE IT ALL

A Buddhist monk awoke one morning with a terrible toothache. When he went to his morning prayers, it took all of his energy to concentrate on the task at hand. Later, he walked around the compound in his saffron robe in constant pain.

For the first few days he considered it his personal sacrifice for the common good of all mankind. He wore the pain as a badge of honor and a demonstration of his commitment to his religious beliefs. Although his fellow Buddhists encouraged him to see a dental professional, he'd demurred in his belief that he was chosen to suffer.

After a few weeks, the pain had become so intense that he finally acquiesced and made an appointment with the dentist. When the dentist saw the condition of his infected tooth, he took a deep breath and told the Buddhist it was one of the worst he had ever seen.

"I'll need to give you some pain killer before I start," the dentist said.

"No thank you," the Buddhist replied. "It has been my life commitment to live with pain or rise above it. And if you give me an anesthetic I will be unable to transcend dental medication."

RITE OF PASSAGE

The old man had lived on his property as long as anyone could remember. The lake on his land was situated exactly between the main road and the textile mill across the way. For years, the locals used his frozen lake in the winter to haul bales of cotton to the mill, thus avoiding the long, circuitous trek around its shores. And for many years, the arrangement worked well for everyone.

Then, a shepherd began to raise sheep on the slopes of the nearby mountains and convinced the mill to begin producing materials made of wool. So long as it was summer and the farmer carried his wool to the mill around the lake, there was no problem. But, as winter took hold on the land, the shepherd began to use the lake as the cotton growers had for many years.

It was not long until the old man set up camp on the edge of his lake to await the shepherd with his bundles of wool.

"You can't cross here," the old man said when the shepherd arrived.

"And, why not?" the shepherd asked. "You allow all the others to use your lake."

"It is simple," the old man said. "I vowed long ago to never let anyone pull the wool over my ice."

ROAD MAINTENANCE

It was a slow day at the Roadside Saloon and the bartender was washing glasses and generally cleaning up the bar. The music was playing his favorite song on the jukebox and three customers sat at separate tables scattered around the floor. An occasional automobile or truck drove past in the still summer air outside. The ceiling fans spun slowly producing little if any breeze.

The bartender heard steps at the doorway and looked up to see a dark shadow against the bright sunlight outside. The figure of a man with what looked like a large bundle under his arm strode into the saloon and up to the bar. As the man approached, the bartender noticed he was holding a large piece of sun heated asphalt..

"Afternoon," the bartender said. "Mighty hot out today."

"You can say that again," the man replied. "I wouldn't doubt that you could fry an egg on the sidewalk just outside your door."

"Well you've come to the right place to cool off," the bartender continued. He tried not to stare at the slab the man held. "What can I get you?"

The stranger pondered his thoughts and looked down at the piece of asphalt he was holding. When he looked back at the bartender he said: "How about a beer please. And one more for the road."

ROAD TRIP TRIPS ROGERS

Kenny Rogers often traveled to his concert venues by way of bus. He found it relaxing as well as helpful as he prepared for his stage performances. So it was that on one trip the bus suffered a flat tire and threatened to delay his arrival at the next concert.

The onboard mechanic assured Mr. Rogers that he could replace the tire and they would be able to still make their scheduled arrival time. And, in fact, he changed the tire in record time and they were soon under way. Unfortunately, the mechanic had failed to adequately tighten the lug nuts.

It wasn't long thereafter, as the bus worked its way through a narrow mountain pass, that the wheel worked its way loose. The large vehicle veered from the road and plunged over the edge. It tumbled end over end through the trees. At one point it passed near the campsite of a hiker before it disappeared into the ravine.

The rescue crews arrived to recover any survivors that may have been trapped in the bus. As they passed the hiker's campsite they stopped to ask him what he had witnessed.

"Was anyone in the bus alive when it came through here?" they asked the hiker.

"I believe so," the hiker responded. "At least Kenny was. I could clearly hear him singing 'You picked a fine time to leave me, loose wheel!'"

ROME IS WHERE THE HEART IS

The power of Rome is well known. It has been the seat of worldwide influence throughout a major portion of this globe's history. Some of the greatest advances in human endeavor occurred there. Some of the most important discoveries about the earth we inhabit happened when Rome was dominant. And many of the world's greatest writers and thinkers walked the streets of Rome as common citizens in a thriving metropolis.

The fall of the Roman Empire is often attributed to its loss of focus on the individual, the debauchery of its leaders, and the failure of the ruling elite to provide for the masses. Greed, disrespect, and the growth of the class society also led to the collapse of the greatest civilization of all time.

Unfortunately, these explanations omit a major facet of the fall of Rome. It seems that the various armies of Rome brought any number of diseases home with them when returning from their conquests. They brought back Bubonic Plague, Measles, Smallpox, Malaria, and Typhus among others. And these debilitating and often fatal diseases had a major impact on the population.

In fact, it was the prevalence of these major diseases that gave rise to the oft quoted phrase: "There's No Plagues Like Rome."

SAD SONGS MAKE ME CRY

Many years ago in a small European country, a single family made all the bells for all the churches in the surrounding communities. After many centuries of fine bell making, only one member of this unique family was left.

The one remaining bell maker was also the mayor of the small town. Because he felt threatened that competition may ruin his monopoly on the bell building industry, he decreed that no wedding bells could be used in the village unless they were made by him. His ruthless enforcement of this decree resulted in him being known as the wedding Bell Czar.

It came to pass that a young couple decided to marry without using the Czar's bells. A friend of theirs owned an ancient Chinese gong and they borrowed it for their wedding.

During the reception everyone heard a terrible noise coming from the gong owner's house. It echoed throughout the small town with a frightening reverberation. The bride and groom rushed from their reception to investigate.

"What is happening?" they cried.

And their friend, wringing his hands, said: "That wedding bell Czar's breaking up that old gong of mine."

SANTA'S FINAL HO

After a particularly trying Christmas season, Santa Claus was not especially enthuse-iastic about par-ticipating in the annual Rose Bowl Parade. But he was, of course, a caring person and not wanting to dis-appoint the young folks he agreed to fill the seat of honor at the front of the parade.

Down road after road, Santa moved slowly, calling out "Ho, Ho, Ho" to all the people lined up on the sides of the roads. As the hours slowly dragged on, his mounting weariness began to take its toll.

He turned to his host and whispered his mild complaint and spoke of his tiredness. He confessed that he wasn't certain he could Ho Ho his way to the end of the long parade. He had very few Hos left in him.

"Oh, please don't give up now," the host said. "It's really not that much farther. In fact there is only one more road to Ho."

SAVED BY THE BELL *(Risqué)*

Fred Fowler's unique business consisted solely of fertilizing chicken eggs for the area's poultry farmers. He used a stable of ten roosters and several hundred young layers, called pullets, to fulfill his orders. He kept records of each rooster's success and culled the laggards for the stew pot. This manual effort was, of course, time consuming.

To save him the effort of always watching the flock to keep records, he affixed bells that emitted a different tone for each rooster. He then recorded the rooster's activity by the sound of the bell as he sat on his porch drinking mint juleps. This worked wonderfully for some time and Fred was pleased.

One day Fred noticed that Brewster, his favorite and most productive rooster, was not ringing his bell. When Fred went to investigate, he discovered that Brewster had his bell in his beak so it could not ring. In this fashion, Brewster was able to sneak up on a pullet, do his job and move on to the next unsuspecting hen.

Fred was so proud of this ingenuity that he entered Brewster in the county fair. When all the judging was finished, Brewster was a winner twice over. He won not only the No Bell Prize but also the Pullet Surprise.

SECRET FORMULA *(Risqué)*

Few people are aware that there was another adventure seeker in Africa besides Dr. Livingston. This man is unknown to most because he fell prey to a band of cannibals in the jungle.

It seems he was captured as he approached their village on an errand of conciliation. They misunderstood his intent and, because of his rotund shape, decided to make a meal out of him. Therefore, they immediately killed him and threw him into a pot of boiling water.

Considering his size, it was necessary to boil him for a lengthy period of time. And, although they kept the fires fanned, it took many hours before he was ready to eat. While they waited for his flesh to become tender, they sent the youngest of the tribe to the nearest corner store to pick up a case of soda pop which they would use to top off their meal.

They were finally able to devour their supper and readily ate everything except the unfortunate man's 'thing'. The youngest cannibal, who had brought back the soda, was unfamiliar with this practice and questioned the chief.

"Not to worry," the chief said as he popped open a can of the carbonated beverage. "The 'thing' is next. For, as you know, 'things go better with Coke®'."

SEEING IS BELIEVING

Sally, the salmon fisher woman, worked long hours during fishing season to capture enough salmon to support her family for the entire year. Because of her long hours at sea, Sally was exhausted nearly every waking hour for the three-month period of fishing season.

The extreme physical labor of capturing ocean going salmon, combined with the unforgiving elements of the weather, often resulted in misjudgments and miscalculations. These errors could often lead to dire consequences. As a result, all actions taken had to be carefully analyzed and executed.

One day Sally, looking off toward the distant horizon, was convinced she saw an eye doctor standing on the shores of an Alaskan isle. Since there was a break in the fishing activity, she headed her boat in that direction to confirm what she saw.

Unfortunately, she could not reach the source of her vision because the faster she pursued her target the more it drew away from her. She finally had to abandon her chase and admit to herself that the doctor was merely an optical Aleutian.

SEEK AND YOU SHALL FIND

Syngman Rhee of Korean fame had a cousin, Kimchee Rhee, who was a renowned photographer. Although he was a freelance photographer, he did his most popular work for Life Magazine. Eventually, the magazine offered him a permanent position which he quickly accepted.

One day he did not show up for work and after a week went by with him still missing, his editor began to worry. He called Kimchee's hotel to no avail. He contacted Kimchee's family and they had not heard from him either. Kimchee seemed to have vanished.

The editor then formed a posse and began combing the city block by block. They checked all the places he was known to frequent. They went to all the sites he had photographed thinking he may have returned for more photos. They tried to find him everywhere, including the morgue.

Then one desperate searcher, who feared the worst, entered a bar in a sleazy part of town to drown his own sorrow in whisky. And there standing by the counter was the object of his search. Overcome with joy and relief, the searcher rushed to Kimchee and exclaimed: "Ah sweet Mr. Rhee of Life, at last I've found you."

SEMI-SKILLED LABOR

Sven and Ole worked together and both were laid off so they went together to the unemployment office. When asked about his occupation, Ole said, "I am a Panty Stitcher. I sew da elastic onto da cotton panties."

The clerk looked up the occupation "Panty Stitcher." Finding it classified as unskilled labor, she put him down for $300 a week unemployment pay.

Sven was then asked about his occupation he simply said: "Diesel Fitter."

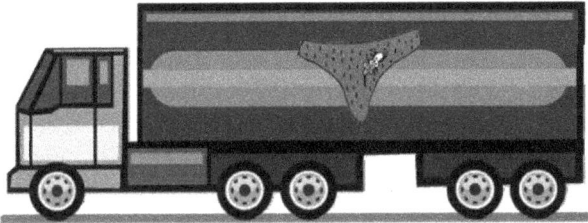

Since "Diesel Fitter" was listed as a skilled job, the clerk gave Sven $600 week.

When Ole found out that Sven was earning twice his own pay, he was furious. He stormed back into the unemployment office and asked why his friend and co-worker was collecting double his pay.

The clerk explained that Panty Stitchers were unskilled labor and Diesel Fitters were skilled labor. Thus the difference.

"Skill? Vat skill?" demanded Ole. "I sew on da elastic, den Sven pulls on it and says, 'Yep, diesel fitter.'"

SET 'EM UP JOE *(Risqué)*

The local bar was known throughout the city for its unusual drink concoctions. Each week, hundreds of patrons came to the bar to sample the delicious and unique drinks. Fridays were the busiest days because that's when the drink of the week was announced.

One of the most enjoyable aspects of the tradition was requiring the patrons to guess what the new drink was called. Its name remained a secret until someone got it right. The person who named it properly received free drinks all that evening.

Wanda Wannawin frequented the bar every Friday, but she had never won the prize. And on this particular Friday, she went to the bar in a dejected state of mind. Her week had been horrible and her consistent losses made her believe she would never win.

When Joe, the bartender, served her the special of the week, she asked him the ingredients as she had done for weeks on end. He replied quickly that it was a simple drink made from a mixture of Smirnoff Vodka and Pabst Blue Ribbon Beer.

Her eyes lit up like they were on fire and her attitude immediately improved. She suddenly knew that this time she had the name that surely would win. "Got the name?" Joe asked. "I do I do." Wanda shouted. She could hardly contain herself in her excitement. "It's called a Pabst Smear."

SHEEPY HOLLOW

For over twenty-five years the sleepy ranch community of Baxter's Hollow held a sheep shearing competition. Local shepherds from miles around would gather for a week of beer drinking and sheep shearing. They would come for the chance to gather socially and to pit their skills against each other in hopes of winning the grand prize of a valuable breeding ewe.

For the past eight years, Bud won the championship. He was an old timer who not only won the shearing contest but could also drink all the contestants under the table. It had become a challenge to all the entrants to defeat Bud, either in the bar with beer or in the shearing shed with shears. Each year they came close, but never close enough to win.

So it was when the finals approached and Bud was behind in total points that a large crowd gathered. Bud and his opponent took their tools and began the last day of shearing and when it was over they were both buried in separate mounds of wool. The crowd looked on with great anticipation as the judge walked into the arena with the prize ewe and assessed the results of the shearing match. Then with great theatrics he said: "Ladies and gentlemen. For the ninth straight year in a row, this ewe's for Bud."

SHERTH'S WORTH

Edward Sherth, the owner of the world's most famous circus, was a devoutly religious man. So it was when his star attraction, the gorilla called Boy George, came down with the flu and passed away that he searched for the message the Almighty certainly was sending. Edward Sherth spent many nights trying to find the message, crying: "Woe is me. Woe is me."

Two weeks later, the pride of lions broke loose from their cages and all of them had to be hunted down. This ruined his schedule for the summer and Mr. Sherth spent the time crying: "Woe is me. Woe is me. Will this be the end?"

At the opening show the next spring, his main tent burned to the ground and he still hadn't found the message he was certain was being sent from above. He began to feel like Job and he cried into the night: "Woe is me. Woe is me. This surely must be the worst you can do to me."

Finally, the greatest of tragedies befell him when his elephants stampeded through town and he was hauled into court. His sentence was two weeks in jail. And he cried throughout the night: "Woe is me, Lord. Of all these tragedies this truly is the greatest woe on Sherth!"

SHIPWRECK TREASURE

A young man, searching for an easy and quick channel to wealth, was walking on the beach after a storm when he spied an old galleon stuck on the coral reef. He was soon swimming throughout the wreck in search of the booty that surely was hidden there. For three days he continued his search for the long wanted booty, burrowing into every nook and cranny he could reach.

He finally gave up the search, convinced that this ship either had been stripped already of its booty or that it had never carried any in the first place. His dreams of wealth and fame faded as he left the ship and swam to shore. He struggled through the surf, a broken man, his chance of a life time gone. He felt the sand beneath his feet and stood, walking slowly toward the shore.

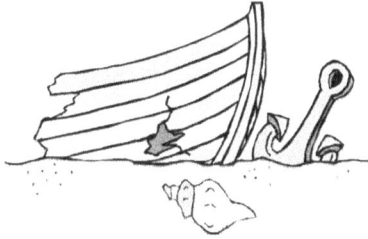

Then, as a wave came in behind him and threw him into the ocean surf, he tripped over an old discarded and rusty metal box, leaving his shins scraped and bleeding. He cursed the old box believing that it held no treasure. He stood back on his feet and continued on his way, an unhappy man at his lack of fortune.

Although he continued his search for riches many more years, he never found his instant wealth because he never came to understand that booty is only shin deep.

SHORT END OF THE STICK

David Dangerfield struggled throughout the Great Depression to provide a home, clothes, and adequate food for his family. He took any job that was available and pinched his pennies so he could buy frankfurters for his family at least once every two weeks. Because the price of meat was so high, he could only afford enough frankfurters to place one piece on each end of the skewer, complemented by a large number of vegetables, and cook them over a wood fire.

One week he was not able to buy as many frankfurters as usual and the skewers were loaded with all vegetables and only one piece of the meat placed in the center. His hungry children had come to anticipate the nights they had meat on both ends and were disappointed when they discovered this shortage. All but the youngest understood and kept quiet. But the youngest voiced his disappointment and complained tearfully.

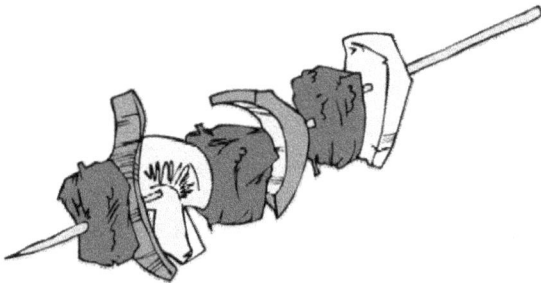

David's heart pained for his children but there was no way he could make it any different. In the desperate times in which they lived, it was sometimes impossible to make ends meat.

SIBLING RIVALRY

Rodney Rockfan and his sister Sally were the closest of siblings and cared for each other throughout their lives to the exclusion of all else. But Sally often dreamed of having a sister to help her out of her many predicaments. Rodney did his best to fill this void. Unfortunately, he could never do enough.

One day he came into possession of two front row tickets to a Rolling Stones concert. This group was his very favorite group and he was able to get a date for this concert with the most sought after girl in high school. It was a perfect situation and Rodney was ecstatic.

As he was about to leave on his date, his mother called to report that Sally was stranded at the side of the highway. Her car had broken down and she needed her brother to pick her up and take her to work.

This was the final straw in an unending series of sisterly sacrifices he was called on to make. If he did this, he would miss both the concert and his date. So, it didn't take him long to make a decision. All his life he had been doing his sister's bidding. It was time for him to put his foot down. He told his mother he couldn't help.

"But you have to," his mother insisted.

"But I can't," he replied. "When are you going to understand? I just can't be a brother and assist her."

SIGNED, SEALED, AND DELIVERED

Shelley Smith was a talent scout for a well-known recording studio. One day as he was walking past a convent he heard beautiful music wafting out the window. Someone with a voice beyond compare was singing a hymn and the sound was the most profound Shelley had ever heard.

He approached the convent and hammered the iron knocker three times against the thick wooden door. After a short wait, a young nun opened the door.

"Sister," Shelley said. "I am a talent scout for Up And Coming, Inc., a music publishing and recording company. I'd like to record the hymns that the nun with the beautiful voice I hear is singing. You can donate the profits from the sale of the recording to charity."

The nun's eyes opened wide. "That would be wonderful," she said. "But Mother Superior must first provide written permission before we could proceed."

"Great!" Shelley said. "Call me as soon as you get it."

Shelly rushed to his office and immediately found his boss. He told his boss what had happened and asked for a raise based on this superior find.

The boss had only one thing to say: "Wait 'til the nun signs Shelley."

SMOKING OUT THE BAD GUYS

A trio of bank robbers fled to San Francisco after a very successful round of robberies. To celebrate their successes, they rented rooms in the Chinese District in one of the most expensive hotels in the area. In fact, each of the rooms had its own fireplace.

They gathered early the first night in one of the rooms to count all the money they had garnered over the past few weeks. As they counted the cash, smoke began to back up from the fireplace into the room and, before long, it was so thick none of the robbers could see each other. Soon, the smoke began to drift out the window and a passerby called the fire station. The sheriff and other local officials joined the firemen at the scene and it was only a matter of time before each of the bank robbers was hauled off to jail.

The following morning the newspaper gave a detailed account of how the famous bank robbers had been captured under headlines that read: "Robbers Laid Up Because Of Asian Flue.

SOMEONE'S GONNA PAY

A farmer frequently used the road in front of his farm to move his goats and the protector donkey he kept with them from pasture to pasture. One day he noticed a crack in the pavement where his driveway met the road and called the county road department to alert them that it needed repair.

After two months without any response from the county, the crack had expanded into a pothole. The farmer called the county road department again complaining that the situation had worsened because of the poor quality of their work and the lack of response.

The next day, a crew of workmen arrived to examine the problem. The supervisor noticed the farmer herding his sheep and donkey over the road when he arrived. He approached the farmer while shaking his head slightly.

"The problem with this road has nothing to do with the quality of our workmanship," he said. "We pride ourselves in delivering superb well-built roads. In this case, that pothole is, un-fortunately, your liability."

"How so?" the farmer asked.

The supervisor pointed to the donkey. "He walks over that section of pavement every day doesn't he?" And without waiting for the farmer's reply he continued: "It ain't the quality of our work, it's the asphalt."

SOMEONE'S GOTTA DO IT

A skunk had twins and, strangely, named them In and Out. Her husband thought the names were odd, but because he lost his last argument with her, chose to remain silent.

One day, as the mother was preparing supper, she noticed that her son, In, was nowhere to be found. She summoned Out and told him to go find his brother. He went in search of In but because of his laziness did not try too hard. Some time later, Out returned without his sibling.

"You go back out, Out," she said. "And do a much more serious look around. It's supper time and I want him home. If you don't bring him home you will go to bed without supper."

Now Out was a voracious eater and could not stand the thought of going to bed hungry. So within minutes he had his brother in tow and dragged him into the house.

"Very good," his mother said. "That was very quick. You mind telling me how you managed it?"

Out looked at his mother and shrugged his shoulders. "Pretty simple, Mom. In stinked."

SOMETHING FISHY GOING ON

Once upon a time there was a brilliant sea bass who developed a tool that allowed fish who were caught in gill nets to escape. His tool was so successful that he became one of the richest sea bass in the ocean.

One day his tool failed to free a fish who was then hauled to the surface and taken to the cannery. The fish's family immediately retained a lawyer and sued the sea bass for everything he had.

The case dragged on for years while the sea bass presented a mighty defense. Witness after witness testified about the gill net tool and how it had never failed them. Engineers were called to the stand and they provided scientific evidence that the gill net tool was incapable of failure. The unfortunate fish had failed to use the tool properly.

All of this effort to defend his name cost the sea bass all of his wealth. He soon had to close his factories. And when the jury was prepared to announce their verdict, the sea bass was nowhere to be found.

"Not guilty," the jury foreman said.

And everyone ran out to inform the sea bass of his success. But, alas, it was too late. He had already ended up on Squid Row.

SOUTH SEAS SHIFT

A young New York fashion designer needed a new look for the upcoming spring season. Because of the fierce competition in his chosen career field, he knew he must produce a winner or he would be relegated to the graveyard of the unsuccessful.

He tried everything he could think of but nothing he designed made him feel confident he had a winner. And just when he was about to give up, he received a phone call from a solicitor who had hired Indians to make sales calls from a bank of phones in Polynesia.

When the designer realized who his caller was and where the call was coming from, he had a flash of insight that nearly knocked him out of his chair. He rushed to his design table and sketched out what he knew would be a wonderful success in that year's line of clothing.

He kept his design a secret until displaying it on the runway at the New Designer's Convention in New York City. The audience 'ooohed' and 'aaahed' then stood and applauded as the models displayed the new line of clothing. He then took the stage and bowed in appreciation and announced this new line would be called his "Sari, Sarong" number.

SPEAK NOW OR FOREVER HOLD YOUR PEACE

A ruthless king issued an edict that all his noblemen must swear allegiance to him and pay a tribute each year. Because they were threatened with death, all the King's men, save one, complied. One Count, though happy to swear allegiance, refused to pay the tribute.

The King was fond of this rebellious count so he threw him into jail to think about his decision. After a week with no change in the Count's position, the King reluctantly issued an order to behead him at sunrise. When dawn arrived, the executioner awaited the count at the chopping block.

"I'm giving you one more chance," the King said. "Will you pay your tribute?"

"Never," the Count replied.

The King nodded to the executioner who positioned the Count's neck on the block and raised his ax high into the air. As the executioner started his swing, the Count finally cried out: "Okay! I'll pay! I'll pay!"

Unfortunately and much to the King's dismay, the executioner was unable to arrest his swing. The ax fell with a mighty 'thunk' and the Count's head fell to the ground.

Of course there is a moral to the story which is: You should never hatchet your Counts before they've chickened.

SPEED READER GETS IN TROUBLE

A middle aged man of the cloth had read no book but the bible for more than thirty years. On his fiftieth birthday, he approached the father superior of the monastery and appealed to him for the opportunity to procure and devour some other material. Because he was such a faithful and uncomplaining resident, the father superior believed no harm could come and agreed to let this fellow devotee read one other book during the following year. On his next birthday, he again petitioned the father superior for yet another book. Again, his request was honored. Soon, others began to request and receive books and it became an annual event. All the men of the cloth read many books, their appetites never fully sated.

On his eightieth birthday, the monk left the monastery to experience all he had read about. He could no longer follow in the way of the Lord. There were just too many pleasures to be enjoyed.

The father superior was devastated by this action and immediately banned all books but the bible. When the remaining monks questioned his decision he said: "I do it with great pain for I know what the books mean to you. However, it is unfortunately also true that too many books spoil the cloth."

SPEEDY PRINCE

A prince was fond of fast cars and drove them recklessly throughout the kingdom. His habit of running his cars off the twisting roads caused his father to take drastic action.

The king, concerned for his son's safety, charged his chief road engineer to erect a stone warning sign before each turn to inform the prince that a curve was ahead.

It seemed to work. The prince didn't wreck a single car during the next four months. He drove as recklessly as ever and with the same disregard for his safety but without incident.

Then one day the prince was pulled from a badly damaged car, still alive but battered severely. The king immediately ordered his engineer to the scene and asked him to point out the stone tablet that warned of this curve. When the engineer made excuses that the prince never used this road and the stone was therefore not really needed, the king sentenced him to death.

"I don't understand such a drastic penalty as death," the engineer said. "Certainly you will show me mercy."

"I see no reason why," the king replied as he walked away. "I specifically ordered you to leave no turn unstoned."

START WITH THE PROPER INGREDIENTS

Two cannibals met for their usual weekly coffee and conversation. The first cannibal complained about a recent recipe she had tried.

"I am having trouble cooking missionaries. No matter what I do they don't come out tender. I have baked, roasted, stewed, and barbecued them. All to no avail. I've tried marinade, tenderizer, and everything I can think of. Nothing works."

"What brand of missionary do you use?" her companion cannibal asked.

The other replied: "The ones down by the bend in the river. You know. They wear those brownish cloaks tied with a rope around their waist. They are the ones that are bald on top and a ring of hair wrapped in around their heads."

"Ah. That's your problem. Those will never get tender the way you're cooking them."

"And why not?" the other cannibal asked.

"Because those missionaries are friars!"

STATE YOUR PORPOISE

The keeper at the new Minnesota State Zoo had experienced great difficulty in getting the resident porpoises to propagate. You can imagine his excitement when he ran across a solution to his problem. It appeared his porpoises didn't mate because they lacked a special hormone found only in the flesh of seagulls.

Upon completing his feeding chores in the lion house the next morning, the zookeeper set off to collect some seagulls. The idea of feeding seagulls to porpoises was distasteful to him, but he was willing to try anything. In his haste, however, he failed to secure the door to the lion's cage.

When he returned with a burlap bag filled with seagulls, the zookeeper found a lion stretched lazily in the sun, blocking the entrance to the porpoise tank. The zookeeper hopped over the drowsy lion and was busy emptying the seagulls from the sack when the local policemen arrested him and carted him off to jail.

The zookeeper had, in fact, violated a law that made it illegal to transport gulls across a state lion for immoral porpoises.

STICK OUT YOUR TONGUE AND SAY AHH

Freddy Frogman, a green leopard frog, loved to frolic around the pond all day. But when the sun began to fall late in the afternoon, he would hurry home to his mud house near the pond's bank. In this house he had built a warm and cozy den where he would spend his evenings reading.

Freddy liked many different kinds of reading subjects. But his favorite was Time Magazine. He was able to catch up on the news and enjoy the many and varied activities happening throughout the world.

His most favorite of all evenings was when he could settle into his easy chair with a new issue of the magazine and a bowl of fried flies on the table beside the chair. He would sit there late into the night learning about the world and enjoying his snack.

It was an addiction to him and he came to depend on these quiet evenings. Because, to a frog, time's fun when you're having flies.

STORMY WEATHER

Warren Weatherby had been predicting the weather on the local television news program for three years. He was qualified in his field as a meteorologist but his record for accuracy was abysmal. As likely as not he would be far off the mark on both forecasted temperature and precipitation.

His employer had to respond to the complaints the television audience was submitting. So he kept a record of Weatherby's predictions. The result was that Warren Weatherby was wrong 80% of the time. The employer had no choice but to fire him.

Warren then moved to another section of the country and settled in a small house on the outskirts of town. When his unemployment insurance payments stopped, he decided he would have to seek another job and approached the local television station about weather forecasting.

His interview went quite well and he was able to answer all the questions satisfactorily. Then the question he feared most presented itself.

"Can you share with us the reason you left your last job?" the interviewer asked.

Warren thought for a moment, convinced the truthful answer would ruin his chances. Then he had a stroke of genius and replied: "The climate didn't agree with me."

STRAIGHTEN UP AND DRY RIGHT

One of the most significant problems in Julius Caesar's Rome was the sheer volume of white togas and the need to keep them clean. In one of the first attempts at mass production he directed his servants to place the togas in a tidal pool and add enough detergent for their cleansing. He figured the ebb and flow of the tide would clean the togas and his problem would be solved. As an afterthought, he had his servants add starch to the tidal pool so the togas would retain their fresh, crisp appearance in the muggy summer heat.

Unfortunately, just as the servants were preparing to remove the starched togas from the water, Neptune caused a tidal wave to form and wash over all of the workers. Immediately thereafter, a strong breeze blew in from the city quickly drying the workers into stiff statues by the shore.

Caesar arrived a short while later to observe the progress of his idea. What he saw puzzled him. The servants were immobile and the togas were scattered about on the beach. He turned to his most trusted advisor. "What say you to the meaning of this?"

"'Tis as I suspected," the adviser responded. "We talked about this yesterday. And I warned you then to beware the tides of starch."

STRANGE COLLATERAL

Ms. Patty Sue Wack was a loyal and trusted loan officer with the Anytime Savings and Loan Association. So it was a challenge for her when a frog came to the office in search of a loan.

"I can approve the loan if you can provide collateral," Patty told the frog.

"All I have of any value is this little ceramic statue of my grandfather. It is old and it is irreplaceable. But it is certainly worth more than what I need to borrow."

When Patty indicated that it wasn't enough, the frog pleaded with her to reconsider her decision. When that failed, he insisted she talk to her supervisor.

"And why are you against giving the frog what he wants?" the supervisor asked.

"All he has for collateral is this silly little ceramic statue," Patty said. "It isn't in our policy to honor these valueless things for collateral."

"Ah," the supervisor exclaimed. "After all these years you have finally overlooked something. Can't you see? It's a knick knack Patty Wack. Give the frog a loan."

STRETCHING THE TRUTH

Young Johnny had been playing cops and robbers in his neighborhood over the weekend. His weapon of choice in this childhood activity was a rubber band pistol. It was a fine, home made pistol his father had fashioned from some scrap lumber in the garage. And it was extremely accurate and intimidating during his pursuits of the bad guys.

Come Monday, Johnny carried the rubber band pistol with him to school. He kept it in his rear pocket hoping that he may be able to use it during recess.

However, when he was in the midst of the daily test in his algebra class, he began to play with his pistol to the dismay of students surrounding him. The teacher noticed the commotion that the toy weapon was causing and confiscated the gun.

Johnny's immediate reaction was to challenge the confiscation. "You can't do that," he said.

"I most certainly can," the teacher responded. "This is obviously a weapon of math disruption."

SUBMARINE SANDWICH

After the sinking of the Titanic many stories related to the tragedy surfaced and made the rounds. Some of these tales involved heroism and love. Some involved lost opportunity. And some have only recently come to light due to the success of the movie based on that sinking.

One of the most intriguing of these new stories is one most people don't know about. Back in 1912 Hellmann's mayonnaise was manufactured in England and the Titanic was carrying 12,000 jars of the condiment. This entire shipment was scheduled for delivery in Vera Cruz, Mexico, which was to be the next port of call for the great ship after New York City.

The Mexican people were eagerly awaiting delivery of this shipment and were disconsolate at the loss. Their sadness was so great that they declared a national day of mourning that they still observe today.

It is known, of course, as Sinko de Mayo.

TACO SALAD

The Taco Bell Chihuahua, a Doberman, and a Bulldog were in a fancy doggie bar having a gin and tonic when a good-looking and well-groomed female Collie came up to them and looked them over.

Each of the three male dogs were at first nervous then curious.

Finally, the Collie said: "Whoever can say liver and cheese in a sentence to my satisfaction can be my friend."

So the Doberman pumped himself up and said: "I love liver and cheese."

"That's not good enough," the Collie said in return.

The Bulldog flexed his shoulders and said: "I hate liver and cheese."

The Collie replied: "That's not creative."

Finally, the Chihuahua jumped up on the table and shouted: "Liver alone, cheese mine."

TAKE YOUR PICK

It was time to take the national census and the government hired Charlie McCounter to collect the information in a small community in Iowa. Charlie wanted to do his job better than any census taker had in the past so he prepared diligently to ensure his counting was accurate.

At each home he visited, he asked the same questions: number of people in the family, their sexes, their ages, and other pertinent information that would help him complete his job to the standards he set for himself. At one home he noticed a number of toys scattered throughout the yard and assumed children lived there. When the woman answered the door he asked her how many children she had.

"Four," she said.

"May I have their names, please?" Charlie asked.

The mother recited their names in rapid fashion. "Eenie, Meenie, Minie, and George."

Charlie was startled at this response and said: "Very interesting. I am curious. Why did you name your fourth child George?"

The woman looked him straight in the eyes and said: "Because we didn't want any Mo."

TAKING CARE OF BIRDS 'N NESTS

A compassionate woman had taken care of unfortunate birds all her life. She would nurse sick and injured birds back to health often having scores of them in her house at one time. Although she was happily married, her husband complained occasionally about how her compassion caused her to neglect basic housekeeping duties.

One November evening as he returned from work, he discovered her working on a crow who had broken its beak, an eagle who had a fever, and a little wren she had found abandoned in the snow. What bothered him most about this was that the crow was in his easy chair, the eagle was in his kitchen chair, and, because of the effort she was devoting to the wren, supper had not even been started.

"I've had it!" he shouted. "I can't take it anymore. I know how you feel but you have to understand. This is our home. And it's not the zoo. It's time you got rid of all these dam..."

His wife held up her hand halting his curse in midstream. "Now now, dear," she said. "You know as well as I do. We don't speak that way in front of the chilled wren."

TEXAS TWO-STEP

During a Texas rodeo, the usual horse races were underway and two good buddies were illegally betting all their cash on the trotters. As the evening wore on, they had lost nearly all they had and with only one race remaining they bet their last dollar.

As the horses warmed up for the race in front of the stands, the cowboys assured themselves they would win all their money back. Suddenly, one of them turned to the other. "Who'd we bet on?" he said.

"That one," the other answered. "That one there warming up in front of us."

"What's his name?"

"I don't rightly know," came the reply. "I can't remember his name, but his pace sure is familiar."

THE BEAR AND THE BAR FLY

A foul tempered grizzly bear strode into the cow town tavern.

"I want beer," he shouted as he approached the bar.

The cowboys moved out of his way, but a lady on a bar stool, her back to him, showed no sign of making way. The bear tapped her on the shoulder.

"Out of my way, lady," he growled. "I need a beer." The lady turned to face him with eyes of fire. She hissed in his face. "Get lost, punk," she said coldly. "Your breath is bad, you need a shave, and your hair is ugly. In fact, you're pitiful. Why don't you get lost?"

Without delay, the bear grabbed her between his front paws and swallowed her with one bite. When he turned back to the bar he felt dizzy. And as he leaned against the brass rail he could hardly hold himself up.

"What's the matter with me?" he shouted. "Why am I so dizzy?"

The bartender leaned over toward the bear and whispered to him. "You dummy. That was the bar bitch you ate."

THE CHOICE BREED

Pete, a pet pit bull terrier, lived in a small apartment with his owners. Because he was, from time to time, a nuisance, the neighbors complained regularly about Pete's presence in the apartment complex. Reluctantly, the owners decided they had to resolve this pesky issue.

On a Sunday afternoon, the owners took Pete to the town park in hopes of finding someone who would want him. The park was filled with pedestrians enjoying the warm sunshine. There were families, couples, walkers, and bicyclists. There were also many amateur entertainers such as mimes, clowns, jugglers, orators, and painters plying their crafts.

Pete's owners strolled throughout the park for many hours trying to convince someone to give the dog a good home. Finally, they found two people, a mime and a juggler, who each wanted the dog. They were both well qualified to be Pete's new owner, but Pete's current masters couldn't decide which of them should get the dog.

To solve this problem, the owners decided they would let Pete choose his own future owner. So they unleashed him and waited to see which of the two he would approach. There might have been a slight hesitation as Pete deliberated who he would go to, but it was not at all noticeable to anyone watching. For, as it is often, though erroneously, said: pit bulls always go for the juggler.

THE DIRECT PITCH

A young man had been fascinated with baseball since he was just a toddler. All his life into his twenties he had dreamed of facing a major league pitcher. Unfortunately, he did not have the physical abilities to compete in the sport and rise into the major leagues for this opportunity. On the other hand, he did win a contest that allowed him to receive three pitches from the most successful major league pitcher of all time.

In preparation for his time at bat and to calm his nerves he had a couple of drinks. The couple became more than a couple and he went to his place at home plate a little under the effects of his drinking.

As he warmed up his swing, he noticed that the pitcher seem to be wavering. Thinking this was a facet of major league competition and not the result of his preparation, he was not concerned. He stood at the plate ready to live his life long dream.

The pitcher wound up and released the ball toward the plate. And the young man in his inebriated state saw it in its rush toward him. As the ball hurtled toward him, he wondered to himself: "Why is that ball getting bigger and bigger?"

Then, suddenly, it hit him.

THE GORY TRUTH

It is well known that Al Gore once claimed to have invented the Internet. What led him to that assertion has never been determined but a couple of young techie types believe they have unraveled the mystery.

Using high-tech instruments and unmatched patience, they monitored the data packets that flow throughout the Internet. In the process of this research they thought they detected a pattern to the data packets in both the send mode and the receive mode.

They collected a sizable number of these packets and converted them to an audio format. When they sent this audio to an amplifier, they were astonished at what they heard.

Simultaneously, they looked at each other and exclaimed: "It's an Al Gore rhythm!"

THE HARDER THEY FALL

During the Spanish Civil War, Russia sent many airplanes and pilots to help the beleaguered Spanish Nationalists. They fought side-by-side with the Spanish Air Force against an inferior rebel force.

Soon after they arrived, the rebels discovered a weakness in the Russian aircraft and began to take advantage of it at every opportunity. It seemed that whenever the Russians were lured into a fight during rainy weather, they would lose control of their aircraft and plummet to the ground.

Although the Russian aircraft was far superior to those of the rebels in terms of maneuverability and range, there were no all-weather instruments and the pilots soon became disoriented within the cloudy and rainy sky.

Within a year, the Russians had lost hundreds of aircraft to this weakness. They worked diligently to correct the deficiency and did so before the second year of the war was well underway. However, the new aircraft arrived too late to prevent the widespread belief that the planes in Spain fall mainly in the rain.

THE HIGH COST OF TRAVEL

During a short period of time in the 1800s the stagecoach was the preferred mode of travel as the pioneers expanded their presence in the West. Although it was an uncomfortable way to travel, it was the fastest and most convenient method.

The stagecoach operators were constantly thinking of ways to increase their profits. They had tried to do this by shipping goods and by charging for the passenger's luggage. Neither of these additional income streams helped them achieve their goals. It seemed the only way to increase profits was to increase the number of passengers per trip.

As a result, the stagecoach companies instituted a policy that would allow them to fit three people per seat instead of the customary two. To achieve this they required their customers to comply with certain weight restrictions whose goal was to reduce the passenger's hip size.

This approach worked. Passenger volume increased and profits exploded. And the stagecoach owner's felt proud that they had influenced the health of the nation's travelers. This pride was misplaced, however, for no one had lost weight. The fact was that many people traveled by other means; for they knew that if they traveled by stagecoach there would be no West for the reary.

THE MAIN EVENT

The lion, although held in fear by all the other jungle beasts, found himself faced with a disturbing dilemma. It seems some small birds had absolutely no fear of him. In fact, they chose his mighty mane as their preferred place of residence.

The lion tried everything he could to evict them. But no amount of scratching, shaking, stamping, or even loud roaring seemed to faze them. They consequently chirped, sang, rustled about and generally drove him crazy.

He finally dressed in his finest and went to the local village where he sought the help of a witch doctor who promised to correct the problem. The doctor then began a dance with no particular pattern. When the dance was finished he unbuttoned the lion's vest, threw in a handful of yeast, and ordered the lion back to his domain.

"By morning you will be rid of the birds," the witch doctor chanted. And so it was. As the sun rose, the birds were gone!

The lion returned to the village immediately and asked the witch doctor: "How did you do it?"

"It is really quite simple when you know the right formula and incantation," the witch doctor replied. "You see, I know that yeast is yeast and vest is vest and never the mane shall tweet."

THE MILLION DOLLAR QUESTION

The game show contestant had reached that point in the show where there was one last question between him and the million dollars. So, when he was unable to answer that question, he saw his winnings fleeting before his eyes. However, he had a plan for just this situation.

Placing two fingers into his mouth he produced a loud whistle that summoned four knights who charged from backstage astride beautiful white horses. They carried lances and bore down on the show's host threateningly.

The host didn't skip a beat. He faced the knights and relieved the first one of his spear. He then deftly dismounted and dispatched that knight without delay. Spinning rapidly, he caught the second knight by surprise and dealt with that one as quickly as he had done the first. The score was now two up two down. The third knight charged even more deliberately. But he was no match for the game show host and in the blink of an eye he too became a casualty.

The contestant sat on his stool in awe of this display of heroics. The host readied himself for the fourth knight. He grasped his spear firmly and prepared for the attack. And just before charging, he pointed the spear at the knight. Then he called out over his shoulder to the contestant: "Is that your final lancer?"

THE NAME SAYS IT ALL

The San Antonio zoo had the rare privilege of hosting two distinct species of camels. One was a Dromedary, which was known for the large single hump on its back. The other was a Bactrian, which was known for the double hump on its back.

The two camels displayed their dominant humps for years. Eventually someone thought it would be a good idea to mate the different camels. After some discussions, the zoo staff and board of directors agreed and the pairing was authorized.

The lovemaking was deemed successful and several months later a young and healthy camel was born. The zoo employees were all excited beyond measurement. It was an event without equal in the zoo industry.

Once they cleaned the new camel and could determine its status, they saw it had no hump. There was neither a single nor a double hump prominently affixed to its back.

As a result, they were stumped as to what to call it until a lowly street sweeper told them it was obvious. He said: "You should name it Humphrey."

THE NIGHT BEFORE CHRISTMAS *(Risqué)*

Three men die in a car accident on Christmas Eve.
They all find themselves at the pearly gates waiting
to enter Heaven. Before they are allowed in, however,
they each must present something that represents
Christmas.

The first man searches his pockets, and finds some
mistletoe, so he is allowed in.

The second man presents a Christmas card, so he is
also allowed in.

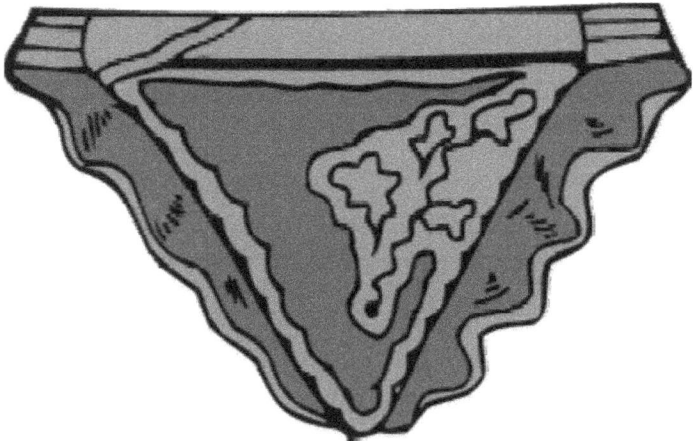

The third man pulls out a pair of panties and waves
them in front of him..

Confused at this last gesture, St. Peter asks, "How do
these represent Christmas?"

The man answered: "They're Carol's."

THE ODDS WERE FAVORABLE

There was this guy who enjoyed hearing others tell punny stories so much that he decided to write a few of his own. There was a contest in the local area in search of the most imaginative puns to be included in a collection for publication and he was intent on entering.

This rookie punster worked diligently to produce ten pun stories that he believed were exceptionally brilliant. He entered all of them in the contest convinced that with ten outstanding entries he would win with at least one of them.

After the judges had completed their deliberations and began to read the list of winners, the rookie stood transfixed with anticipation of the announcement of him as the winner.

Unfortunately, in spite of the quality of his ten puns and his conviction that one of them would win, no pun in ten did.

THE PAUSE THAT REFRESHES

The polar bear had been hunting on the ice flows in the Hudson Bay territory for many months. Although it had been a successful hunting season, the bear had not been able to enjoy his favorite drink - a tall gin and tonic.

So it was that as soon as the season was over he made his way to Churchill, an outpost community on the bay. He was confident he would find a tavern there that could satisfy his libation craving.

After rejecting the first two saloons as not up to his standards, he settled on a quiet out-of-the-way bar that advertised the best martinis in town. Surely, they could whip up a gin and tonic of merit.

Once inside, the bear got the bartender's attention and said: "I'll have a gin.n.n..." he paused for some time as he relished the thought of sipping his drink. And then he finally completed his request: "... and tonic."

The bartender began to pour. "Why the long pause?" he asked.

"Don't know," the polar bear said, looking down. "I've always had them."

THE RECEIVING LINE

There once was a large ham radio antenna that lived atop an enterprising amateur radio operator's home. It was a handsome antenna with arms spread wide and a stature that made it stand out from all the lonely television antennas in the neighborhood.

One day the amateur radio operator brought home a satellite dish antenna and installed it near the ham radio antenna on his roof. At first, the two antennas ignored each other. But eventually they came to appreciate the other's presence. The ham radio antenna came to understand how lonely he had been. And the satellite dish antenna, newly born to this world, reveled in the newfound relationship.

It wasn't long until these two antennas fell in love. They gazed upon each other across the roofline and dreamed of a future together. Each day, as the sun rose and spread its warmth on their anchoring brackets, they discussed their growing happiness together. And as life events of this nature usually go, they decided to get married.

They planned a simple wedding that would contain little fanfare. It was their desire to celebrate lavishly following the wedding rather than during their exchange of vows. Therefore, when the wedding day arrived, the ceremony wasn't much, but the reception was excellent.

THE ROAD LESS RIDDEN

The patrons in the saloon were peacefully sipping their drinks when a piece of County Roadway walked through the swinging doors and announced that he was the hardest pavement in the area.

Before he could walk two steps toward the bar, a piece of State Highway rose from its chair and challenged the roadway to prove that it was harder than him.

And before that challenge could be accepted, a chunk of Interstate Highway spun around at the bar and faced them both. He asserted that the County Roadway and the State Highway may think themselves hard but there was no chance that they could ever match his hardness.

The bartender thought he was soon to have a fight on his hands and was reaching for the phone to call the police when the saloon doors swung open again. A piece of pavement with a blue stripe down the middle sauntered in and scoped out the saloon.

The three pieces of pavement, who were in mid-argument, gathered at the bar, became silent, and huddled over their drinks.

"What's the problem?" the bartender asked.

"Shhhh!" the Interstate Highway cautioned. "Be careful! That one's a cycle path."

THE SAGA OF WOUNDED KNEE

An unlucky young man limped into the emergency room in obvious need of help. Blood ran down his legs from multiple cuts and abrasions on both knees. As he approached the reception desk he cradled his left wrist in the cup of his right hand. His sole purpose for the visit was to seek help for his broken wrist.

The nurses, on seeing his bloody condition, hurried him onto a gurney and in the process strapped his arms to his side. Because he began to struggle they also strapped his entire torso to the cart.

The doctors began to repair the damage to his knees and the young man struggled in his attempt to tell them it was his wrist he wanted attended to. They misunderstood his protestations and sedated him. Once they had completed the work to their satisfaction they patted themselves on their backs for such a fine job.

Unfortunately, the young man's real problem - a broken wrist - remained untreated. Doctors are, above all else, still people. They had gotten too wrapped up in their work and couldn't see the sore wrist for the knees.

THE SAME OLD SONG

An Indian chief ordered the medicine man to cure the persistent stomach pains he had been experiencing. To achieve the desired results, the medicine man examined the chief thoroughly and then meditated for two days. When he returned to the chief's tent, the only thing he brought with him was a thong of elk hide.

"Each day for thirty days you are to bite off and chew a piece of this thong," the medicine man said. "I will return then to see how you are doing."

Thirty days passed and the chief followed the medicine man's instruction to the letter. On the thirtieth day the medicine man returned.

"How are you feeling today?" the medicine man asked.

The chief's reply was short and sweet. He said: "The thong is ended but the malady lingers on."

THE STAGES OF LIFE

A young cowboy went to the psychiatrist to discuss the meaning of a recurring dream he had. He settled into the comfort of the couch and spoke slowly.

"I keep having the same dream night after night," he said. "I dream I am in the old West and I am riding my horse when a stage coach comes over the hill. I work my way over to the stagecoach and ride beside it for awhile. That's all I do for the longest time."

"Then what happens?" the doctor asked.

"The strangest thing," the cowboy answered. "All of a sudden I notice a horse with no rider keeping pace with me on the other side of the stage. Then I pull the door open and jump off my horse into the stage. From there I move to the other side and jump on the other horse and ride away into the distance."

"Very interesting," the doctor said. "But I don't think you have anything to worry about. It's a simple matter."

"And what, pray tell, would that be?" asked the cowboy.

The psychiatrist looked at him, shrugged and said: "It's just a stage you're going through."

THE WRONG STYLE

A rather sadistic king kidnapped a young damsel as she was going to market and when she refused his amorous advances, threw her into the cell at the top of the tower. There she languished for days, alone, with only a small window to look out onto the landscape.

Soon, she began to call to passers by for help, but none would come to her aid, not even the passing knights in their shining armor. On the verge of a deep depression, she was convinced she would never be rescued and would rot away in the tower.

Some time later, the door to her cell opened and another young damsel was thrown into the room. The first damsel began to pour out her soul about the lack of compassion of all those who failed to give her freedom. The new arrival listened intently, absorbing every word. "It's na'wonder no one wants ta help ya escape," she said, grasping the loose folds of the other damsel's skirt and holding it to the light of the small window. "Who'd want ta rescue a damsel in 'dis' dress?"

THERE ARE TWO SIDES TO EVERY STORY

The professor proposed a riddle to his Logics Class. "Consider a box with an opening at each end," he said. "Now imagine a rabbit inside the box."

He drew a diagram of the box on the chalkboard and drew a circular hole in each end. "Now visualize the rabbit sticking his head out of the hole on one end of the box and one minute later doing the same at the other end of the box. Half a minute later visualize his head appearing at the opposite end. Again visualize his head popping out of the hole on the other end of the box at 15 seconds. Once again see his head pop out of the opposite end 7 1/2 seconds later."

He motioned with his hand back and forth between the two ends of the boxes then asked: "If the rabbit continues to do this, how long will it be before the rabbit sticks his head through the hole at each end of the box simultaneously?"

A few students began to scribble formulas in their notebooks but soon joined the silence the rest of the class had assumed at the end of the question. None of them had the answer.

The professor was excited at having stumped his students. He said: "If you applied theory it would be two minutes. But the theory won't work here. There is no answer possible, you see, unless you split hares."

THERE OUGHTTA BE A LAW

Senators William Spong of Texas and Hiram Fong of Hawaii were both avid table tennis fans. They followed the victories of the United States table tennis team as the team traveled throughout the world. The team's final tournaments took place in the Republic of China. Although both Senators Spong and Fong would like to have accompanied the team on its tour, the press of business in Washington prohibited it.

The team did well against the highly rated Chinese players. And when the tour came to an end, the US table tennis team emerged victorious. After accepting the accolades of the Chinese government, the team planned to stop over in Hong Kong en route home.

The two senators put their heads together and authored a bill that would require the ringing of church bells throughout the country at the time the team arrived in Hong Kong. They presented the bill to an assembled Congress and pleaded for its passage.

Unfortunately, in the absence of like-minded table tennis fans the bill failed to pass. As a result, no one outside Congress has ever heard of the Spong-Fong Hong Kong Ping Pong Ding Dong Bell Bill.

THERE'S GOLD IN THEM THAR HILLS

In the forgotten days of old, Genghis Khan and his men, known simply as Khans, conquered all of Asia. Their appetite for treasure was unabated, so they launched boats in search of other lands to subdue. At each stop on their journey, they would load their boats with loot and proceed again on the sea.

One of the islands they conquered was populated by lepers and most of the crew became infected. They immediately departed and set sail for Ireland, but by the time they arrived they had been physically changed. All that was left of them were stubby limbs and they scurried away to hide in the hills.

Because of the treasure they kept in pots, the locals constantly attempted to steal their wealth. They would try to sneak into the camps of the Leper Kahn's (as they were now called). And once there they would try to exchange the full pots with ones that were empty.

The Leper Kahns, however, were not fooled by those trying to trick them out of their gold. They defeated the thieves on every occasion. And from this successful defense came the phrase: "You can't change a leper's pots."

THIS CRAZY THING THEY CALL SHOWBIZ

Visitors Day at the insane asylum was an occasion of great significance to the inmates. It was their opportunity to rub elbows, if only for a short time, with the outside world and achieve some feeling of sanity in an otherwise crazy atmosphere.

Some of the inmates liked to sing, so they formed a choir and would perform for the visitors throughout the day. They had been doing this for some time and had become quite good at it. They had mastered the techniques of harmony and their voices were steady and professional. The only oddity to their performance was that each of the inmates held a red apple in one hand and tapped it in rhythm with the music they were singing.

During one of these special days, a visitor approached the conductor after the choir had finished its performance. "I am amazed," he said. "This is one of the best choirs I've ever heard."

"They've worked hard to achieve this. Thank you," the conductor said.

"You should take them on tour," the visitor said. "Do they have a name?"

"Sure do," the conductor replied. "They are the Moron Tap An Apple Choir."

THOSE EVIL COWBOYS

The cattle rustler was converted at a local revival meeting and pledged to go straight. That night, he sent his two sons out onto the range to tend the herd and contemplate the changes to the previously wicked life he had deemed necessary. Each son was to watch a portion of the herd and think hard about how they would live a respectable life away from crime.

Later in the night, the father wrapped himself in a warm coat and walked out to where the sons were watching the herd. The first son was awake but shivering and greeted his father. "How are things going?" the father said. And the son told him of how his candle had gone out and how cold it was. The father gave him a new candle and lit it for him.

A few yards hence, the father approached the second son who was wrapped in blankets and sound asleep. This bothered him and, after some effort, he finally awoke the boy and asked how things were going. "They go well," the boy said. "But my candle is out and I need a replacement."

"Unfortunately," the father said. "You must suffer in cold the rest of the night. For 'tis truly said that there is no wick for the rested."

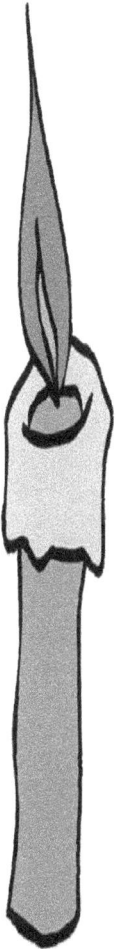

THROAT LOZENGES

As the pall bearers carried the casket down the church steps, one of them was unable to hold back the cough building in his throat. No matter how hard he tried, the tickle began to develop toward a violent spasm. Soon, much to his chagrin, he produced a vibrant cough that shook the entire assemblage and weakened their very foundation.

Before the pall bearers could reach the bottom of the stairs, they had lost their grip on the casket and it fell to the ground at such an angle that it began to slide toward the street and finally, through heavy traffic, across the street and through the front window of a drug store.

The young man, whose cough had caused the entire debacle, quickly ran after the casket. As he rushed into the drug store, the casket was crashing into the counter in the back where the pharmacist was at work. Rushing to the counter beside the casket, the young man, still coughing, tried to tell the pharmacist of his embarrassment but couldn't speak because of the still present tickle in his throat.

The pharmacist, expressing pity on the young man's plight, took charge of the situation and said: "I see you have a problem, sir, and could use something to stop your coffin."

THROUGH AND THROUGH *(Risqué)*

On a bright, sunny day a man walks into a psychiatrist's office. He stands in front of the doctor clad only in underpants made entirely of clear Saran plastic wrap.

"How can I help you," the doctor asks.

The man looks at him with a puzzled expression on his face. "Isn't it obvious?" He asks. "I need you to tell me what's wrong with me. Why do I dress up like this?"

The doctor strokes his goatee carefully before responding.

"Well. For one thing," he says. "I can clearly see you're nuts."

TIED UP TIGHT

Four strings went into a bar for an evening drink. As the other three found a place to sit, the fourth walked to the bar to order the drinks. "I'd like a drink for my friends and myself," he said to the bartender.

"I'm sorry, but we don't serve strings here," the bartender answered.

The string told his friends what had happened and another string said he would take care of it. He soon returned just as unsuccessful as his buddy. The third string then approached the bar. "What is this?" he asked. "My friends and I would like a drink."

"Like I told your pals, we don't serve strings here. So why don't you all just leave?"

The remaining string was visibly upset and began twisting so much in his seat he frazzled his ends. Finally, he went to the bar.

"I don't serve strings here," the bartender said again. "And that describes you doesn't it?"

The string looked the bartender square in the eyes and said: "No. I'm a frayed knot."

TIME TO CHILL OUT

The lady and her husband had been on a week long vacation and the arduous trip home by aircraft had been without a meal. The layovers in the airport were too short for them to grab a bite. Therefore, as soon as they had unpacked their suitcases she went to the refrigerator to see what might be available for supper.

When she opened the door, she saw a rabbit lounging on one of the shelves. She immediately called her husband to come and look at the strange occurrence. When he saw what she pointed out he was extremely puzzled. "What are you doing in the refrigerator?" he asked.

The rabbit sat up and moved to the edge of the shelf. He then spoke in a clear and distinct voice. "This is a Westinghouse, isn't it?"

The lady responded while the man tried to understand how a rabbit could talk. "Why yes it is," she said. "But what does that have to do with you being in my refrigerator?"

"Well," the rabbit replied with some exasperation. "Can't you see? I'm westing."

TO TELL THE TRUTH

The young punster traveled the kingdom over telling his shaggy dog stories and relating other puns to anyone who would listen. He had become so adept at speaking puns that it became second nature to him.

One day, while in the palace courtyard, he devised a pun that turned out to be a personal embarrassment to the king. Because of this act, the punster was sentenced to the gallows the next day.

All night long the punster pleaded with the warden to intercede with the king inasmuch as no harm was meant by the pun. It was merely what he did. And by morning, as the noose was placed around the punster's neck, the warden came out of the palace and halted the execution.

"The king said your life would be spared if you never again utter another pun," the warden said. "If you agree to the terms, the king has authorized me to remove the noose. If you fail to keep your word, I am ordered to hang you at first opportunity."

"I agree to the terms," the punster quickly shouted. "And I am truly grateful to the king. As you must understand, no noose is good noose."

TOMMY KNOCKER

The summer band class was just getting under way. As the students opened their instrument cases a large insect of unknown species flew into the room. The sixth-graders, eager to play their shiny new instruments, tried to ignore the buzzing intruder, but it flew constantly among them harassing each student in one way or another.

Finally, one student, Tommy, could stand it no more. He rolled up his music book and swatted the insect, knocking it against the wall. It bounced from the wall and fell to the ground where Tommy quickly stomped on it to ensure its fate.

"Was that a bee?" another student asked.

"Nope," Tommy replied. "Bee flat."

TRIANGULAR RELATIONSHIP *(Risqué)*

An aging Indian chief had been childless for his entire life and was losing face with his warriors. In a desperate attempt to regain his authority, he took three squaws as his wives and gave each a special blanket for a bed. He reasoned that one of his wives would provide him what he wanted. The one who slept on a deerskin blanket was the most promising, being the youngest, but the one who slept on a bearskin blanket was also in the running. The squaw who slept on a hippopotamus blanket was the least likely to succeed, but she was also the most confident.

It was therefore a surprise to the entire tribe when all three squaws announced that they were pregnant. The celebration lasted for weeks. When the time approached for the babies to be born, all three squaws began labor simultaneously. They retired to their communal tent and their individual blankets. Soon the sounds of newborn babies filled the air inside the tent and the chief discovered he had four sons: one from the squaw of the deerskin blanket, one from the squaw of the bearskin blanket, and two from the squaw of the hippopotamus blanket. He could hardly believe his eyes.

"It is true," he shouted. "What the medicine man says is true and here is proof that he was right. The sons of the squaw of the hippopotamus are equal to the sons of the squaws of the other two hides."

TROUBLE IN GRAPETOWN

France is well known for the quality of its vineyards and there was no exception for the small vineyard run by a family of witches. The main difference with this vineyard was that the grapes were used only for producing raisins.

The witches believed the quality of the raisins was solely dependent on the timing of the harvest. They would only remove the grapes from the vine under a full moon, thus, so they believed, retaining the grape's magic properties.

This method of harvesting worked well except for one full moon out of seven. That one full moon was considered to be a bad omen. Therefore, grapes harvested then were not of the quality of the grapes harvested under the other six full moons. The witches saved only the largest and strongest grapes of that harvest letting all the others rot.

The grapes that survived this one harvest practice eventually became known throughout the territory as the Bad Moon Raisin.

TRY IT ON FOR SIZE

A young man by the name of Lewis Trek had the unfortunate habit of constantly tripping over his own feet. Throughout his pre-teens his tripping episodes had resulted in numerous bumps and bruises. But because of his youth he was able to put this clumsiness behind him.

Lew, as he had come to be known, grew into his teens and the same clumsiness became an element of embarrassment. He spent many years attempting to overcome this impediment - to no avail. No matter how he practiced or what effort he exerted, he continued to trip over his feet.

Having finally had enough, he decided to seek the assistance of the family doctor. He arrived at the doctor's office and stumbled into the waiting room. When he was called for his appointment he tripped into the examination room.

The doctor looked him over and with just a glance was able to tell what the problem was. There was no need for any further evaluation.

"The solution to your embarrassment is simple," he said. "Tie your shoelaces - they are too loose, Lew Trek."

TWO MAN TENT

A desperate, stress-ridden patient attended his weekly session with his psychiatrist and collapsed in the plush recliner.

"Doc," he said. "You gotta help me. I can't figure it out. It's the strangest thing. On Mondays, Wednesdays and Fridays I have this dream that I'm an Iroquois Wig Wam. It happens every Monday, Wednesday and Friday and I wake up shaking. It's so bad I can't get back to sleep."

"I see," said the psychiatrist, nodding.

"And on Tuesdays, Thursdays and Saturdays I have another dream. This time I dream I'm an Apache Tee Pee. Every Tuesday, Thursday and Saturday the same thing. I wake up shaking and remain awake until morning."

"I see," said the psychiatrist, stroking his beard.

"What's wrong, Doc? Do you know what's wrong? You gotta help me out."

"Well, for starters," the doctor said. "I think you're too tents."

TWO PINTS A QUART DON'T MAKE

Paul Painter awoke on a fine Saturday morning feeling somewhat the worse for wear after having painted the town the night before. "It's no wonder," his alert wife chided. "For all the carousing and sinning you have done. Just don't forget you promised to paint the garage door this morning."

Paul then dragged his weary body to the garage and rummaged through his assortment of paint cans finding only one pint of paint suitable for the task. He decided to thin it with paint thinner and, therefore, have a sufficient quantity for the job. If he was also lucky, his wife would not notice.

As he was completing the job and applying the last stroke, a thunderstorm that had taken shape nearby spattered the first of its drops of rain on the driveway. To his horror, Paul watched as the torrent gained momentum and washed his thin paint mixture from the garage door and into the street.

"What am I to do?" he wailed.
"My wife will chastise me severely." He pulled at his hair praying for an answer.

Suddenly, the clouds parted with a loud and frightening thunderclap, and a deep voice boomed out in response: "Repaint, you thinner, and thin no more."

UNLIMITED VISIBILITY

Larry Loyalty was a man whose fierce devotion to his friends and family had often worked to his detriment. But with the help of his girlfriend, Lorraine, he had been able to leverage that loyalty for positive gain.

One day he found that a new girl had started working in his office. Her name was Claire Lee and she was the most beautiful woman he had ever seen. In short order he had fallen head over heels for Claire Lee and it was quite obvious that she had fallen for him too.

His loyalty came into play again and he knew he would do nothing to advance his relationship with Claire Lee while he was still dating Lorraine. It wasn't long before he determined there was nothing left to do but breakup with Lorraine.

He planned to tell her and many times tried but failed. He just couldn't bring himself to do it. But one day as they walked along the river, Lorraine slipped and fell. The current carried her off where she soon drowned.

Larry stood for a moment, shocked, frightened. Then with a flash of insight he realized his problem was solved. He turned and ran off singing: "I can see Claire Lee now Lorraine is gone."

328 - Gary Younglove

WHAT AN AWFUL MESS WE'VE MADE

The young, female bloodhound was heavy in her pregnancy with puppies. Because of her inexperience, she was unaware that she was due to give birth when the labor pains began. Therefore, those pains only caused her to move across the road in search of a more comfortable place to doze.

The final and excruciating labor pain hit her as she approached the shoulder of the road. She was forced to lie down in a makeshift gravel bed and give birth to the ten puppies that clamored for an escape. When the final puppy was born she circled her body around all ten to comfort them.

As she lay there, the local sheriff drove by in his patrol car. After traveling some distance beyond the mother and her pups, he turned around and parked across the road from her. This sheriff was known throughout the county as one of the strictest interpreters of the laws in the state.

The sheriff wrote something in his ticket book before opening the door to his patrol car. He then crossed the road and laid a ticket on the bloodhound's body. After shaking a finger in the bloodhound's face, he returned to his car.

It seems the bloodhound was cited for littering.

WHAT GOES UP MUST COME DOWN

The Swinging Smiths were famous for their acrobatic feats on the high wire and when cloning was perfected they considered cloning themselves in order to perpetuate the perfection they had developed. As a test case, they decided to clone only one of themselves. If that worked out well, they would do the same with the rest of the family. They chose the youngest, a sixteen year old, as their test.

The clone was an exact duplicate in physical appearance and high wire abilities. However, he suffered from a desire to insert four letter profanities in every sentence he uttered. No matter how hard they tried, the Smiths could not break him of the habit and their popularity began to plummet.

The family decided they must do away with the clone and settled on a plan wherein one of them would miss a critical catch. The clone, with no protecting safety net, would fall to his certain death as if by accident.

The time came and after the clone had succumbed to his preplanned fate, the family retired to their dressing room to quietly celebrate. However, a knock at the door interrupted them. On opening the door, they discovered the hallway was filled with policemen who took them under arrest and carted every one of them off to jail. You see, they had all been involved in making an obscene clone fall.

WHEN THINGS WERE ROTTEN

In the olden days, about the time of the Middle Ages, there lived a knight of great prowess, though of very small stature. Instead of a steed, this daring do chap rode a St. Bernard, a big dog who was more suited to the knight's proportions and quite capable of carrying him on long journeys.

One stormy evening, the knight sought lodging in a small village. Unfortunately, innkeeper after innkeeper refused his pleas for lodging, saying there was no room available. It appeared he would have to spend the night out in the cold rain.

At the last inn, he pleaded desperately and eloquently for lodging and the sympathetic proprietor grandly offered the knight his own bed.

"After all," he said, pointing to the knight's shaggy mount. "I couldn't put a knight out on a dog like this."

WHERE'S THERE SMOKE, THERE'S FIRE

Two Catholic boys, Timothy Murphy from Ireland and Antonio Secola from Italy, attended parochial school from kindergarten through their senior year in High School. They took their vows to enter the priesthood early in college, and upon graduation both became priests.

Both their careers were meteoric but it was generally acknowledged that Antonio was more than just a cut above Timothy in all respects. Their rapid rise to Cardinal convinced the Catholic world that either Timothy or Antonio would become the next Pope.

When the Pope eventually died, the College of Cardinals went into seclusion. They wasted little time and sent the white smoke upwards sooner than anyone expected; in fact, sooner than ever before. The announcement that Timothy Murphy had been elected Pope was, of course, a surprise to all.

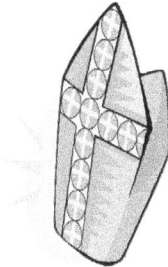

However, Antonio was beyond surprise because he knew he was the better qualified. So, with an unprecedented gall that shocked the Cardinals, Antonio insisted on a private session with them in which he candidly asked: "Why Timothy?"

After a long silence, one old Cardinal took pity on the bewildered Antonio and said: "We know you are the better of the two; but we just can't bear the thought of the leader of the Roman Catholic Church being called Pope Secola."

WHY DID THE CHICKEN CROSS THE ROAD?

Everyone knows about the chicken crossing the road. In fact, it is plausible that there has been no new answer to that right question in years. There have been numerous puns, there have been untold double entendres. There have been a slew of plain nonsensical answers.

In the wake of the often expressed disgust over this question and the ensuing possible answers, the true meaning behind this question has been lost. The origin was not a question at all but a statement of fact that somehow got turned into the ridiculousness it has become.

Research has shown that the reference to the chicken crossing the road began in the 1700s when a Vermont farmer observed one of his Plymouth Rock chickens strutting across the dirt road by his home. As he watched the fowl fly from one side to the other, he had an epiphany.

"By cracky!" He exclaimed. "A chicken crossing the road is poultry in motion."

WHY IS IT?

A swarm of honey bees was migrating to Florida to escape the oncoming winter in Minnesota. These unusual bees were powered by gasoline and not by the nectar rich flowers growing along their path. As they flew, they would fly down to gas stations along the way, fill up on spilled fuel, and rejoin the swarm on its journey.

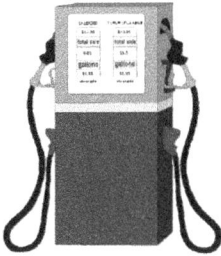

One bee seemed rather choosy about where he refueled. In fact, he passed up a perfectly good gas station when he was low on fuel and another when he began to sputter. It was not until he ran out of gas and coasted into a station that he took on enough fuel to continue his migration.

A companion in the swarm challenged him when he returned. "Why did you pass up those two stations and wait until you had run out of fuel before you decided to land?" he asked.

The peculiar bee answered matter-of-factly. "It's pretty simple really. The first station was a Gulf station and I really don't like Gulf at all. The second was a Texaco station and I consider that even worse. But lucky for me when I ran out of gas, the station below me was an Esso - my kind of gasoline. "

"Strange," the other bee stated.

"Not really," the peculiar one answered. "You surely know there's an Esso Bee in every crowd!"

WINDEX® WONDERMENT

SC Johnson, the makers of Windex®, announced a contest in which participants vied to become the fastest and most streak free window cleaner in the world. The winner would receive an all expenses paid trip to see the Seven Wonders of the World and a lifetime supply of the famous window cleaner.

The response to this announcement was greater than the officials ever imagined. Entrants came from the far corners of the world eager to prove their capabilities and win the prize. For two weeks they battled until only two were left. The Pro Bowl of window cleaning began on a warm and sunny day and the two contestants approached the contest with unmatched enthusiasm.

Each of them cleaned their windowpanes with uninterruptible concentration until they both threw their cleaning materials into the air simultaneously thus signaling they had finished the job.

Because they had both completed their work at the same time, the choice of who would be the winner had to depend on the quality of the work. The judges studied the windowpanes with great interest and eventually anointed the winner as King of the Cleaners and awarded him the prize.

The loser's challenge was quickly defeated. "Look at the winner's windowpane compared to yours," the judges said. "It's obvious. The glass is cleaner on the other side."

WITH THANKFUL REVERENCE

The Anaheim professional hockey team known as the Mighty Ducks had a superstar goalie who was unmatched throughout the league. The Mighty Ducks superstar's father had never seen him play which was a source of disappointment throughout the goalie's career. Therefore, he was thrilled when his father announced that he was coming to see his son play in the championships.

In honor of this occasion the superstar goalie organized a special banquet at a renowned local Scandinavian restaurant. He brought in the most sought after chef who prepared a gourmet dinner of his father's most favorite dishes.

In addition to the entire Mighty Ducks team and staff, the superstar goalie also hosted Disney and Orange County dignitaries at the dinner. It was considered the social event of the year and received considerable coverage by the press in anticipation of its occurrence.

As testament to its resounding success, the Orange County Register reported the following day that it was certainly a dinner worthy of the father, the son, and the goalie host.

WORDS TO GO BY

A common conundrum for every motorcyclist involved in buying a new bike is the decision concerning the bike's drive train. There are hundreds of different models of motorcycles on the market and each of these models has its own unique benefits. Depending on how the manufacturer designs the engine and then connects it through a series of gears pulleys and belts to the rear wheel, the motorcycle will perform differently under different circumstances.

So it was that a famous stuntman was faced with the dilemma of which bike to buy for an event in which he was scheduled to participate. He had narrowed his choice down to one of two motorcycles on display in the dealership. Although either one of the motorcycles was of the highest quality, he was uncertain which would give him the greatest advantage in his upcoming performance.

One of the bikes had an excellent top speed and handled extremely well at that speed. However, it lacked rapid acceleration to that speed. The other bike had an almost unbelievable acceleration because of the torque produced in the drive train. However, it lacked a high top speed.

The stuntman spent a long time making up his mind. Eventually, he chose the second bike with the greatest acceleration. When asked why he chose the second bike his answer was simply: "Torque is cheap."

WORKING LATE AT NIGHT

Lee Iacocca is well known for his efforts to rescue the Ford Motor Company in the 1960s with the revolutionary Ford Mustang. He further cemented his place in the automotive industry with the well-publicized reversal of Chrysler's demise and the ever popular minivan.

He then wrote a book or two on managing large companies and gained a following devoted to his guru like guidance for top-level executives.

What most people don't know is that Mr. Iacocca became a vampire in his retirement and now lives a life in constant darkness. Anyone who is interested in following his current exploits can do so by accessing his website at Autoexec.Bat.

YOU CAN RUN BUT YOU CAN'T HIDE

The nudist camp at the edge of the medium-sized city had been there for years. In compliance with local law, a tall privacy fence had been constructed surrounding the entire camp. The nudists had lived peacefully on the outskirts of the city and the camp had become a model for other nudist camps throughout the country.

One summer at the height of the nudist season, the police station received a call that someone had bored a hole in the privacy fence. The nudists complained about this violation of their privacy and wanted the Police Department to do something about it.

After a week had passed with no apparent action taken, the nudists called the police station again to complain. They advised the desk sergeant of their previous call and demanded that the department take immediate action.

"Relax," the grizzled old desk sergeant replied. "We heard you the first time you complained. And I assure you we are looking into it."

YOU HAD TO BE THERE

Two cannibals were wandering through the jungle when they came upon a circus troupe who had become lost. They felt very fortunate at this fortuitous find and schemed to trap the members of this troupe for their evening meal. As the troupe stumbled through the undergrowth in the search of a way out, the cannibals lay in wait.

Eventually, the cannibals determined it was time to attack and sprung from the cover of a patch of holly ferns. The startled troupe scattered every which way. In the confusion, the cannibals lost their advantage and had to settle on capturing the slowest of the party.

The clown's escape attempt was hindered by the large shoes he wore and he became an easy target for the cannibals. In no time flat they had captured him and began boiling him in their large cast-iron pot.

They sprinkled on the appropriate seasonings and monitored the preparation of their meal with great interest. This would be the first time they had ever eaten a clown and they anticipated the experience with glee.

As soon as the meal was finished cooking, they dished out a generous portion for each cannibal. And after a few ravenous bites, one cannibal said to the other: "Does this taste funny to you?"

YOU MAKE THE CALL

The young botanist had decided to focus his research on ferns. He spent many months in the field classifying his findings and recording them in his journal. One day, he came across a species of fern, Ptridium aquilinum, known commonly as Bracken Fern.

Because he needed more information to properly record details in his journal, he sent a fax to all of his colleagues requesting input. He knew they could help him as they had discussed his specialty many times in the past.

His fax machine almost immediately began receiving calls. Scores of responses poured in but none of them dealt with this species he had found. He realized then that the wording on his request had not been specific enough to ensure the responses were related only to the fern he had found.

He then sat down immediately and penned up another request and sent it out to everyone.

"Thank you all for your assistance. I appreciate your responses. But to clarify my request, if it ain't Bracken, don't fax it."

YOU WANNA WHAT!?

Near the end of a lengthy operation the surgeon turns to his assistant.

"I've completed the procedure" he said. "The rest is up to you."

The entire operating arena is surprised when the patient wakes, sits up, and demands to know what's going on.

"I'm about to close," says the surgeon's assistant.

"Why not the surgeon?" the patient demands.

"I am also a surgeon. I usually close after the primary surgeon has finished the procedure."

The patient grabs the assistant surgeon's hand and says, "If the primary surgeon won't close, I won't let you either. I'll close my own incision."

After a few moments of confusion and uncertainty, the assistant surgeon hands him the needle and thread and says: "Well then - suture self."

I Think - Therefore Is A Conjunction

ONE LINERS FOR YOUR DEVELOPMENT

As mentioned in the introduction, there is an infinite number of puns circulating within the culture of the English language and an infinite number yet to be developed or stumbled upon. Those presented here are just a few of the ones that merit retelling.

Any of these can be expanded into a true 'groaner' with the appropriate addition of useless and irrelevant sentences that at first seem germane and important to the telling. Enjoy the reading and the expanding as desired.

DAFFYNITIONS

Abitrator: A cook who leaves Arby's to work at McDonald's.

Accupuncture: A jab well done.

Avoidable: what a bull fighter tries to do.

Baloney: Where some hemlines fall.

Burnadette: The act of torching a mortgage.

Burglarize: What a crook sees with.

Control: A short, ugly inmate.

Crick: The sound a Japanese camera makes.

Eclipse: What a Cockney barber does for a living.

Eyedropper: A clumsy ophthalmologist.

Gossip: Someone with a great sense of rumor.

Heroes: What's a guy in a boat does.

Incongruous: Where bills are passed.

Khakis: What you need to start the car in Boston.

Left Bank: What the robber did when his bag was full of loot.

Misty: How golfers create divots.

Oboe: An English tramp.

Paradox: Two doctors.

Pasteurize: Too far to see.

Polarize: What penguins see with.

Primate: Removing your spouse from in front of the TV.

Propaganda: A gentlemanly goose.

Relief: What trees do in the spring.

Selfish: What the owner of a seafood store does.

Subdued: Like, a guy who, like, works on one of those, like, submarines, man.

Sudafed™: Brought litigation against a government official.

Toboggan: Why we go to an auction.

Qs AND As

Q: Why are acorns considered mathematicians?
A: Because when they grow up they say Geometry.

Q: Why was the Energizer™ Bunny arrested?
A: Because he was charged with a battery.

Q: What blood type does a pessimist have?
A: It's always b-negative.

Q: Why did the man fire his masseuse?
A: Because she rubbed him the wrong way.

Q: Why can't a bicycle stand on its own?
A: Because it's two tired.

Q: What's the definition of a will?
A: A dead giveaway.

Q: How do you catch a unique rabbit?
A: Unique up on it.

Q: How to you catch a tame rabbit?
A: Tame way.

Q: How do crazy people go through the forest?
A: They take the psyco path

Q: How do you get holy water?
A: You boil the hell out of it.

Q: What do fish say when they hit a concrete wall?
A: Dam.

Q: What do you call a boomerang that doesn't return?
A: A stick.

Q: What do you call cheese that isn't yours?
A: Nacho cheese.

Q: What do you call Santa's helpers?
A: Subordinate clauses.

Q: What's the difference between roast beef and pea soup?
A: Anyone can roast beef.

Q: Where do you find a dog with no legs?
A: Right where you left him.

Q: What kind of coffee was served on the Titanic?
A: Sanka™.

Q: What's the difference between a bad golfer and a bad sky diver?
A: A bad golfer goes Whack. Damn! A bad sky diver goes Damn! Whack.

SIMPLE STATEMENTS

A shotgun wedding is a case of wife or death.

A successful diet is the triumph of mind over platter.

Bakers trade bread recipes on a knead-to-know basis.

Banning the bras was a big flop.

Does the name Pavlov ring a bell?

Marriage is the mourning after the knot before.

Math teachers are never in short supply because they multiply.

Reading while sunbathing makes one well red.

Sea captains don't like crew cuts.

Those who get too big for their britches will be exposed in the end.

Those who jump off bridge in Paris are in Seine.

To write with a broken pencil is pointless.

When a clock is hungry, it goes back four seconds.

When fish are in schools they sometimes take debate.

When two egotists meet, it's an I for an I.

With her marriage, she got a new name and a dress.

UNEMPLOYMENT CO-MISERY

The lumberjack was let go because he just couldn't hack it.

The orange juice factory worker got canned because he couldn't concentrate.

The tailor wasn't suited for his job because all he could do was just sew-sew.

The math teacher was fired because he did a number on the blackboard.

The dentist and the manicurist were fired because they always fought tooth and nail.

The mechanic in the muffler shop had to quit because the work was too exhausting.

The chef quit because he didn't have the thyme.

The deli worker lost his job because no matter how he sliced it, he couldn't cut the mustard.

The musician had to leave the orchestra because he wasn't noteworthy.

The doctor changed professions because he didn't have any patience.

The cobbler was laid off because he didn't fit in.

The fisherman had to find a new job because he couldn't live off his net income.

The pool maintenance man had to change professions because his job was too draining.

The fitness trainer was fired because he was fit for the job.

The historian quit when he determined there was no future in the job.

The Starbucks clerk quit because the job was always the same old grind.

The thief turned cement worker was fired because he was a hardened criminal.

INTERNET LINKS OF VALUE TO THE PUNSTER

http://www.pungents.com
http://go.to/puns
http://shaggy-dogs.briancombs.net
http://www.punpunpun.com
http://toomanypuns.blogspot.com
http://www.punoftheday.com

For a free subscription to Stan Kegel's "Puns" list, send a blank e-mail to: puns-subscribe@yahoogroups.com and return the confirmation request.

For a free subscription to Stan Kegel's "Jest For Kids" list, send a blank email to: jest4kids-subscribe@yahoogroups.com and return the confirmation request.

For information on the O. Henry museum go to: http://www.cityofaustin.org/ohenry/default.htm

NOTES:

NOTES:

NOTES:

NOTES:

NOTES:

.

9 780982 938317